The Dominators

The Dominators
One of the greatest Test teams

HODDER

Allan Border, Justin Langer, Shane Warne, Steve Waugh

Contents

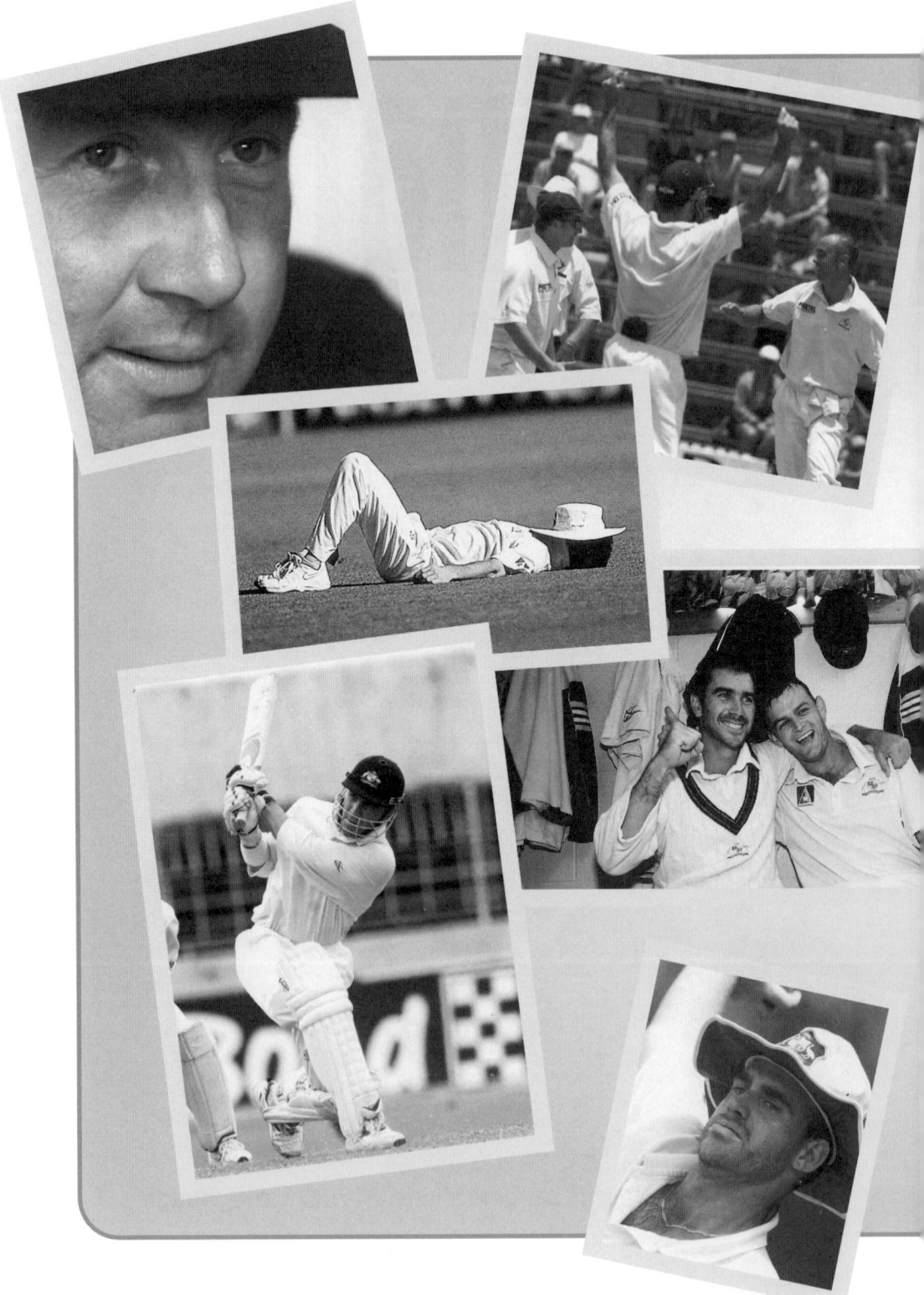

Contents

Foreword from
the Prime Minister vi

Introduction ix

The Baggy Green xii

What's in a Name xv

Allan Border's Big Picture
with *Justin's View* by Justin Langer 1

The Dominators by Steve Bernard 119

The Team
by Allan Border 129

Shane Warne's Story 185

Steve Waugh's Story 201

Poems from the Pitch
by Steve Bernard 233

Statistics 245

Index 273

Photographic Credits 279

Foreword

Foreword from the Prime Minister

The group of men who played for the Australian cricket team over the long 1999–2000 season demonstrated their tremendous capacity on the field in every facet of the game. Under the leadership of captain Steve Waugh this group of players accomplished what no other Australian team had managed to do: they won ten consecutive Test matches.

The achievements of the Australian team were not restricted to Test matches, with the players carrying their World Cup form into the 1999–2000 season and winning the one-day series at home and in New Zealand.

The 1999–2000 season saw the Australian team play exciting and positive cricket and Australian cricket fans responded, turning out in large numbers to watch both the Tests and one-day fixtures against Pakistan and India.

The talent, excitement and success of the team have brought immense pleasure, delight and a sense of national pride to all Australians. They have become known as 'The Dominators'. It says much about the character of the current Australian team that in ten Tests against four different nations no competitor was able to force a draw, let alone defeat it. The Australian team plays with great spirit and plays to win.

Steve Waugh in particular deserves the recognition that has been given to him. He has, in a short amount of time, lived up to a tradition of very fine Australian captains. In that time he has faced remarkably difficult circumstances yet he, as always, has shown tremendous grit and leadership when it has been most needed. He has also led from the front, continuing to accumulate outstanding performances with the bat.

Under Steve Waugh's leadership the team has shown that it has a tremendous fighting spirit. The team members take pride in the tradition of playing for their country and in their loyalty to one other. The captain has imbued in his team a strong sense of self belief so that, no matter how desperate the situation, its members do not doubt their ability to prevail.

Allan Border was asked to take on the job of coach as the team was preparing to go to Sri Lanka and Zimbabwe. He was with the team when it commenced its record-breaking run of Test victories in Zimbabwe and his guidance reinforced the self belief instilled by the captain.

Foreword

The Dominators is an instructive record of the trip to Zimbabwe and the games that followed in Australia and New Zealand. It is instructive because much of the account is provided by Steve Waugh and Allan Border themselves. The book provides readers with the story of how the captain and coach prepared and led the team and how they saw the season unfold.

Shane Warne and Justin Langer are also co-authors of this book, providing a different perspective from that of the captain and coach. Both players made significant contributions to the success of the Australian team over this period. Shane Warne's season was made all the more memorable when, in the Auckland Test, he broke Dennis Lillee's record to become Australia's greatest wicket taker in Test cricket.

For his part, Justin Langer played some outstanding cricket. His partnership with Adam Gilchrist to guide Australia to victory in the Hobart Test against Pakistan exemplified the 'never say die' attitude of the Australian team.

Justin Langer and Shane Warne have, in their writing, demonstrated the spirit and camaraderie that exists among the players, as well as the dedication and sense of responsibility they feel for the sake of the team.

One of the central reasons the Australian team was so successful throughout 1999–2000 was that every member of the team made a major contribution. It was a remarkably even team performance.

The commitment, great cricketing skills and achievements of the Australian team have generated fresh enthusiasm, pride and respect for the game among cricket followers of all ages, particularly young people. This is important because cricket's future depends on the interest and support of young Australians.

The Dominators allows cricket fans to appreciate why the Australian team has been so successful and to re-live the record-breaking run that began in Zimbabwe. Given the many strengths of the current team, followers of cricket have a lot to look forward to on the cricket field for many years to come.

John Howard

At the first Test against India at the
Adelaide Oval, Adam Gilchrist in flight
as he catches Ganguly.

Introduction

At the end of the 20th century the Australian cricket team achieved a feat which set it apart from all other Australian cricket teams in history: it won 10 Tests in a row. Long before the Australians completed this great winning streak, however, they had established themselves beyond doubt as the most powerful Test side in the world. Nobody doubted they were a combination fit to compare with the greatest Australian teams of the past, most notably Don Bradman's famous 1948 side and the immensely powerful team which the Chappell brothers, Ian and Greg, led in the mid-1970s.

What was the secret of their success? In the first place, they were an immensely talented and skilled group of cricketers, but that's only part of the story. In a team sport like cricket, talent and skill alone can't sustain success over such a long period. To win and keep winning a team must also have spirit, and Steve Waugh's team clearly had spirit of a very special kind—a spirit based on the loyalty that the players felt, first, to their country and, second, to each other. This spirit of loyalty produced a remarkable sense of confidence within the team. No matter how hopeless the situation looked at any moment, the team always believed it could come out on top because of the faith the players had in each other.

Patriotism, nationalism, love of country—call it what you will—certainly isn't fashionable nowadays. Nor is the idea that team players should always play for the team first, not for themselves. Fashionable or not, it is obvious that both values counted heavily with Waugh's men. It's what motivated them to win match after match, sometimes from unwinnable positions. Witness the reverence the players have for the baggy green cap, a national symbol. Or witness their willingness to burst into the team song *Under The Southern Cross I Stand*, sung with an excess of volume and enthusiasm, whenever they triumphed again.

This book tells the inside story of Waugh's band of players and how they came to do what no other Australian team had done before. The story is told by members of the Australian party themselves: it springs straight from their laptops. They emerge as an ordinary bunch of blokes who happen to be extraordinary cricketers and competitors. The almost spiritual bonds between them that are revealed in this book will surprise people cynical enough to believe that Australian cricketers are no more than a band of hard-headed pros making a good living from their sport.

Another surprise is the players' determination to lift their playing standards to greater and greater heights, to keep striving for more excellence. This must surely have been a vital factor in their ability to maintain their focus and keep winning. They may have been regarded as the best team in the world, but they still had a passion for improvement. One explanation for this is that the culture of the team allows for constructive criticism to be levelled at players where necessary, even if it does get meted out in the guise of good fun. The team's fines committee, an informal and generally self-appointed group, takes delight in ordering team members who have performed less than brilliantly to find and wear the worst possible outfit, which largely accounts for the dress-up photos in the book.

There's a bit of everything in The Dominators team. There are hardened veterans in their mid-thirties and young tyros still fresh to the Test scene; there are sex symbols and family men; there are larrikins and models of good behaviour. What they all have in common, apart, of course, from their cricketing ability, is an amazing dedication to the task of performing at their best. Only one other team anywhere in the world, the West Indians, has had a longer winning run than them. Whether this team surpasses them or not, their accomplishments from mid-October 1999 in Zimbabwe to early April 2000 in New Zealand, will provide a measure of excellence against which future Australian teams are sure to compare themselves.

CLOCKWISE FROM TOP: Fast bowling Glenn McGrath in party mode, Heals and Tugga, Shane the record breaker, Justin and his proud mum, passing time on tour, the skipper relaxes.
CENTRE: Fitness manager, Dave Misson and Michael Slater, entrants in the beard growing competition in Zimbabwe.

The Baggy Green

*A passionate team member,
he loves the baggy green.
He's won his right to wear it, and
does with pride extreme.* — Steve Bernard

To a stranger to cricket, 'baggy green' could mean 'garden clippings bag', or it could be a method of composting in small spaces, or a variation on the long-gone fashion of the sack dress. But in the cricketing world, it's an icon—the rather full-bodied woollen peaked cap that is the official headwear of the Australian Test team. Nowadays it is also the title of the popular website which brings comprehensive cricketing information to the world. The baggy green cap is the site's logo.

Of course there are replica baggy greens sold at cricketing museums and memorabilia stores around Australia. Although these replicas have the same characteristic fullness of the real ones and are made from woollen cloth of the correct colour and cut, there is a big difference. Just like the genuine baggy greens they are stitched in eight segments, the meeting points of which are covered by a cloth-covered button, but they are not emblazoned with the official crest of kangaroo and emu attending the four part shield with its central starred cross topped by a sunrise emblem, and finished beneath with an articulated ribbon with 'Australia' embroidered in capital letters. These real, dinky-di baggy greens have to be earned, not purchased. And very few of the real thing are produced—just enough to present to new Test team members each season and to replenish the supply when an existing baggy green falls apart and goes to the big cricket bag in the sky.

The Baggy Green

In an era when there is little that cannot be bought, it is somewhat consoling to reflect on the fact that a baggy green is not for sale. The head-hugging, long-peaked New York Yankees cap with its distinctive intertwined white embroidered initials is a prime example of saturation marketing. Anyone can have one and practically everyone does. They are everywhere, from Canton to Christmas Island. Not so with the shorter-brimmed baggy green. It is one of a select few and when found abroad it will be an exclusive visitor only in the UK, the West Indies, the sub continent, those southern parts of Africa, Australia and New Zealand. Steve Waugh, Test team captain, is a big baggy green enthusiast. At the beginning of the first fielding session of each Test, his team carries on the tradition of wearing their baggy greens as a matter of course. And before play, in a special ceremony, a Test debutant is presented with his baggy green..
For the first Test of the year 2000, caps which are faithful replicas of those worn by the Test team a hundred years ago and in paticular by the cricket hero, Victor Trumper, were presented to each member of the team by prime minister, John Howard who also got to keep one. They are made from bottle green velvet instead of wool worsted, are more tailored and fitting in style than the regular baggy green and also incorporate metallic thread in the embroidered emblem. As much as this historic change of headwear was enjoyed and appreciated by the team, after this special one-off occasion the velvet skull caps were put away in a safe place and the baggy greens brought back into play. The baggy green will always be one of the nation's most venerated sporting symbols and the undisputed crown of the Australian cricketing greats.

Mark Waugh signs cricket bats
during the Pre Season Training Camp in Brisbane.

What's in a Name?

It has long been Australian practice to shorten a person's name as a sign of friendship or familiarity and to give others nicknames such as Dusty, Swampy, Lofty and so on. With a little thought these can usually be worked out, but sometimes a nickname has been awarded (such as Pigeon or Hooter) which can leave the reader non-plussed. While it's not always appropriate to explain just how some people came by their names, the following list may help readers of this book to identify who's who as the momentum of the winning run of Test matches mounts.

Michael Slater — SLATS
Damien Fleming — FLEM
Mark Waugh — JUNIOR
Shane Warne — WARNEY
Steve Waugh — TUGGA (sometimes The Iceman)
Errol Alcott — HOOTER (physio)
Colin Miller — FUNKY
Adam Gilchrist — GILLY
Dave Misson — MISSO (fitness co-ordinator)
Greg Blewett — BLEWEY
Ricky Ponting — PUNTER
Glenn McGrath — PIGEON
Justin Langer — LANG
Ian Healy — HEALS
Brett Lee — BING or BINGERS
Damien Martyn — MARTO
Allan Border — AB
Michael Kasprowicz — KASPER
Geoff Marsh — SWAMP or SWAMPY

Nerds & Julios

There was a time in cricket long ago when off the field, Australian cricketers wore a sort of formal uniform of cricket blazer and grey trousers. They still have blazers, and smart travelling suits as well but the options for unofficial clothing have increased dramatically. In the 70s, flared trousers, long hair, and sometimes even bared midriffs appeared. While this was happening travelling cricketers soon found themselves falling into two groups. These were the snappy dressers and the others who were more concerned with comfort and convenience. The former soon became called Julios (after the Spanish singer in a suit, Julio Iglesias) and the Nerds (whose core oufit is track suit pants and thongs). Like most categories of anything, the boundaries can be crossed and there is often a bit of the Nerd in a Julio and vice versa. When on tour, as part of the off-pitch activities, competitions and team games are frequently held between these two factions, often with hilarious results.

Typical of the enthusiasm of the Australian team, Ian Healy, Justin Langer and Colin Miller celebrate as Langer catches Marvan Attapatu during day two of the first Test against Sri Lanka.

Allan Border's Big Picture

1

The Prelude – Sri Lanka

Australia's great run in Test cricket in 1999–2000 began with something of a whimper. The tour to Sri Lanka in August and September 1999 was a typical tour of that country at that time of the year. It was frustrating and high on hard work. There was the monsoon, which returned half-way through and ruined the second and third Tests and the slow, low pitches proved as difficult as ever. We were 7 for 61 at lunch on the first day of the first Test and that set a trend from which we never really recovered, especially once the rains came.

Justin's View... *Zimbabwe*

With the pretty, purple jacaranda trees in blossom and the sun shining from the magical blue skies, it felt like a perfect spring day in Perth, when we climbed out of the Cathay Pacific jumbo. Never having been to Zimbabwe before, but having heard many positive stories about the climate, the people, and the safari parks, I am looking forward to this new experience. After five weeks of frustratingly grey thunderclouds in Colombo and Galle, the Bulawayo sunshine feels as refreshing as a dive into the ocean on a hot summer's day.

Michael Slater keeps to the high ground, negotiating puddles of water on the wet Galle ground, Sri Lanka.

The Dominators

Guided by the driver, Glenn McGrath takes his first ride on an elephant during a rest day on the Sri Lankan tour.

Traditionally we have struggled on the sub-continent and that particular tour was no different. Steve Waugh and Jason Gillespie were badly hurt in a now-famous fielding collision in Kandy, which put Jason out for the rest of the season with a broken leg. It seems that if something terrible is going to happen it will always happen on the sub-continent. Some of the team fell ill and most found it difficult to come to terms with the conditions. In that way, this was another typically tough tour of the sub-continent for Australia.

Michael Slater, Greg Blewett and Ricky Ponting all batted well, with Ricky's performance being outstanding. He showed a lot of class and maturity, especially when facing Mutthiah Muralitharan on spinning pitches. The two openers put on century stands in the second and third Tests as they began to read Muralitharan better the more they saw of him. Blewett used his feet to drive him down the ground while Slater worked really hard in that busy way of his to counter the flight and turn. The more the series went on the better our batsmen played Murali. Coach Geoff Marsh and captain Steve Waugh said they could have won the second Test if the rain had not ended it early, but the odds were that with a likely target of 160 or more in the fourth innings we would have struggled to win. We would have won the third Test had the rain held off so there was obvious improvement from our guys as the series developed. But no one could beat the monsoon.

Farewell Swampy

Apart from the Waugh–Gillespie accident in the first Test, the main news from that tour was the retirement of Geoff Marsh as team coach. I would have to say I was both surprised and not surprised by his decision. Geoff had been negotiating a new contract with the Australian Cricket Board so it looked as though he was going to continue for a couple of years at least. But the conversations I had had with him over the previous six months suggested that he was doing it tough because of the time spent away from home, the constant travelling and the same old day-in, day-out routine of the job. For a former player who is used to being directly involved, coaching can be awkward. Often the day finishes as early as 10.30 am after overseeing the warm-up. Once the side takes the field, you put your feet up, get out the notepad and watch play. You might talk to a few players during the lunch or tea breaks but for most of the day you are in the dressing room just watching. And players and former players rarely enjoy watching. It sounds fantastic but the sameness and the living out of a suitcase can wear you down. So when Geoff made the announcement I wasn't totally surprised. Then there were the extenuating circumstances surrounding the tragic death in a car accident of his closest mate, former Western Australian batsman Mark McPhee. Swampy told me that that was a wake-up call for him. It confirmed in his mind that he wanted to spend more time with his family. He realised the time was right to bite the bullet and do something else.

Swampy did a fine job as coach. Obviously he had a very good side to work with, but he had a role in introducing a range of initiatives—especially the appointment of Dave Misson as the fitness adviser to help the guys cope with the amount

Geoff Marsh, coach of the Australian team, announces his resignation during a press conference at Taj Samundra Hotel in Colombo, Sri Lanka.

of cricket the team plays nowadays. With such a heavy schedule you have to go beyond traditional cricket thinking on fitness. Dave Misson has done well in that area and Swampy deserves credit for bringing him into the team set-up. Swampy also started using video analysis, although it was not until John Buchanan took over that that area expanded to what it is now. Swampy really pushed the expansion of the team structure to include not just a coach and a physiotherapist but also a fitness adviser, expert coaches, a full-time professional manager and regular video analysis. They were big changes and they all helped to keep Australia ahead of the pack. In Swampy's time Australia established itself as the best in the world at both forms of the game. With that behind him and then the sudden death of his best friend, Swampy decided that the time had come.

Border the Caretaker Coach

After Swampy told the ACB he wanted to withdraw, the Board asked me if I could do an interim job and go to Zimbabwe with the team while they started advertising for applicants. I really enjoyed the three weeks with the team in Zimbabwe, not only because it was good to be back among them but also because I knew it was only a temporary appointment. I did not want the job full-time because I would be away from home nine to 10 months a year and also because I wasn't sure whether I was the right person for the position. Looking back now, I feel that someone like John Buchanan is perfectly suited to it. I think these days it is acceptable to have a fresh head involved, someone who has not necessarily played at that level and who can see things from a different perspective. After all, with an experienced team like ours, with senior men like Steve Waugh, Shane Warne and Glenn McGrath, there is a large store of knowledge. It is that 'different' view that can really add to the set-up. As well, John is prepared to take things like the use of video and computer technology further than they've been taken so far.

John tests the guys' minds more, setting them little mental and physical tasks to stretch them. They do different things in preparation. A lot of them have to give talks to the team—not necessarily on cricket—

Allan Border, the new but temporary Australian coach, joined the team in Zimbabwe.

maybe about Australian history or their own personal lives and ambitions. Warney might have to get up and do something on Australian football. Justin Langer might have to talk about martial arts. You might ask what that has to do with playing international cricket, but these are the sort of things John does to get them thinking and staying fresh. It makes them sit down and prepare something, then get up in front of the boys and deliver it. Whether that is psychobabble or not, I don't know, but you can't knock the way it is going. The players are happy and the team is winning.

In Zimbabwe the one area where I could help was in practical cricket matters. The players had just come from Sri Lanka so they were all in playing mode. They just needed me to be the practice manager and an adviser if they needed to chat about something specific. I found it easy to slip into the team set-up for a brief stretch. I had not been out of the game that long and knew all the players well. One of the strengths in most Australian teams is team spirit. The blokes get on well and have a good work ethic. This team understands, maybe more than previous Australian

All in together—Darren Lehmann of the one-day team collects a rugby ball watched by coach Allan Border during Australian training at Bulawayo Athletics Club.

teams, the need to maintain fitness levels. There is not so much grumbling about the work they do these days. Despite the frustrations in Sri Lanka the mood was positive. Their attitude was that they were disappointed about what happened there but they were determined to get on with the next assignment. Because of that positive attitude, I had a really good time during those weeks in Zimbabwe.

The main thing I did when away from the nets was to chat with particular guys who asked for advice. Justin Langer is one who loves those sorts of conversations and will always come forward and ask my opinion on various things. We talked about previous tours to Sri Lanka and how we encountered similar problems to those this team had just met. It is like an informal cricket history lesson. 'What was Merv like? Boonie? How did you play Murali on the 1992 tour?' This is just a matter of fine-tuning players who are already the best in the country. Once you get into the nets and to specific drills it is merely a matter of keeping an eye on them. Each player has a different routine and knows what he wants and needs. For Steve Waugh it might be just a throw-down session where he wants to hit some drives. Another guy might ask the coach to check where his feet are going, or what his back lift is doing.

I did not offer too much at the team meetings, mainly because the players knew more about the Zimbabweans than I did. Australia's preparation is pretty specific these days. They go through each opposing player and assess strengths and weaknesses. Swampy, and now John, would show videos of various opponents and come up with plans of attack. That process has been going on for a long time. Stephen tends to run team meetings. My role resumed at the games when I could offer ideas during breaks in play, things like field settings or an idea on a new tactic for a bowler to try against a certain batsman.

Another factor which made it pretty easy for me was that the players were able to relax in Zimbabwe after the tight security in Sri Lanka. Zimbabwe is, or was before the recent trouble, a relatively comfortable place to tour. The team was happy to be there and confident of beating Zimbabwe in the one-off Test at Harare.

The Dominators

Justin's View... *Zimbabwe*

After a marathon journey from Colombo we arrived this afternoon in Bulawayo, Zimbabwe. With an evident revival in enthusiasm, the team looks and feels ready to enjoy this short tour in the clean African air. The transit period between countries has seemed to re-ignite the team's desire to become the most dominant Test-playing nation in the world.

Sri Lanka was tough, it was always likely to be, but now we have a chance to put the last five weeks behind us and reunite in our bid to play exciting and competitive Test match cricket. The squad views this one-off Test match as an opportunity to kick start what will be a long, exhilarating and challenging summer of cricket in this country, at home in Australia and in New Zealand. Although it was a long, tiring trip around the globe, it wasn't that big a deal considering most of the boys, including yours truly, were happy to leave the beautiful but intensely foreign shores of Sri Lanka.

There is no denying the tour of Sri Lanka taught us many valuable lessons about playing in arduous, sub-continent conditions. Saying this, I would be surprised if everyone in the team hasn't become a better player as a result of the experience. After a slow start to the series, particularly in the first session of the first Test match in Kandy, we improved with every session of cricket to a point where we played more consistently with every outing. Although we lost the series one nil, the experience, especially the way the team pulled together after the first Test, was very encouraging with regard to what we can expect from each other in the next six months.

Arriving today in Zimbabwe almost feels like the start of a new adventure and a new beginning for this Australian team. Now that we have left the heavy air, heavy security, and busy streets of Sri Lanka, we feel eager to start afresh and play great cricket. With Geoff Marsh's coaching stint ending in Sri Lanka and Allan Border taking over as the stand-in coach for this short tour, there is a sense of expectancy within the team. AB is an admired and respected icon all around the cricket world and just having his presence within the team adds an indescribable spirit to this talented and closely-knit team.

With one practice match and a Test match in the next 10 days, this visit will be short and hectic but, I am sure, important to the moulding of this unit. Only a few of the guys have been to this part of Africa before so there is sure to be mountains of interest in the first Test match between our two countries. The next two weeks promise to be a fantastic climax to what has been a long, taxing time away from home.

While one day is not a long time to get over our jet lag and prepare for these new conditions, we are all professional enough to know the clock is ticking before we get back onto the cricket field. In an environment much more conducive to what we are used to at home, the jet lag is the only thing holding us back from our best cricket. The blue sky and clear air are very attractive natural commodities, favourable to start playing competitive cricket again, even though our last series finished only a couple of days ago. The atmosphere is quietly exciting, almost like the changing of the guard; a new era seems to be dawning.

Justin's View...   *Zimbabwe*

8.10.99   There is no doubting the extra energy accompanying the team at training this morning. I'm not sure if it was because the guys were happy to be out of Sri Lanka or if it was a result of the new guy looking after the team for the next 10 days. Having AB around is a buzz as he is probably the most respected Australian player of the modern era. His influence and words of wisdom are sure to help in our preparation for this inaugural Test match against Zimbabwe and in our lead up for the upcoming summer. In terms of batting knowledge and advice, who could be better than the man who has scored more Test runs than any other? During the second Test in Galle, Sri Lanka, I telephoned AB in Brisbane for a few ideas on facing the Sri Lankan spinners. Firstly, he was only too happy to give me his thoughts on how he thought would be the best way to combat the freakish off spin of 'Murali' in particular. Secondly, picking his brain can only be beneficial for any batsmen, including yours truly. During our net session today the little master chatted to me about the importance of having a positive attitude when you walk out to bat. After a disappointing tour of Sri Lanka I have been less confident than usual and my feet haven't been dancing like I need them to when I am on top of my game. His advice to back myself and go out to score runs, rather than just survive, has given me a new lease of life and I am hanging out to play in our practice game tomorrow.

I am sure one of the reasons why Australian cricket is so strong is that we have incredible human resources like AB to help and guide the younger players coming through. Often the best sport psychologists come from within the team, from the guys who have experienced the cricket battlefield themselves. In the current team the Waugh brothers, Ian Healy, Shane Warne, Glenn McGrath and Michael Slater have rich Test cricket experience and they all pass on their experience and wisdom freely to their teammates. Allan Border has taken over in the short term from Geoff Marsh who replaced the great coach Bob Simpson. Our history is so plentiful with great players that it is not surprising that cricket is booming Down Under. Knowing how much of the game is a mental process played between the ears, it is very helpful having the best advice and resources in our changing room rather than in the opposition's.

After training this afternoon, we visited the Chipangali wildlife sanctuary here in Bulawayo. What a fantastic experience being up close and personal with rhinos, lions, cheetahs, leopards, snakes, baboons and hyenas. In Australia, it is rare to have such an opportunity to see these magnificent species of animals in relatively natural surroundings. The awesome power and presence of the rhinos was mind-blowing as they paraded around their dusty caged stable while looking over the baby rhino, which weighed more than all of us put together.

The Dominators

This is how it all begins—children play cricket in the streets of Crowbrough north, a suburb of Harare in Zimbabwe.

The lions and lionesses with their fierce eyes and razor sharp teeth roared their disapproval at being show-pieces for visitors from around the world. From behind bars they seem safe enough, yet when they roar or leap and bound around their territories the feeling of vulnerability if the barriers were terminated is frightening. Almost as a sign of his dominance and frustration one of the lions turned his back upon a group of us and without warning shot a torrent of urine like a powerful garden hose. While we all fell to the ground in fits of laughter, Steve Waugh wasn't as impressed as he left the park drenched in lion's urine. As is his way though Tugga just shrugged it off as a good luck omen for this trip to Zimbabwe. 'It's not every day you get leaked upon by one of the Big Five animals of the world' he laughed. 'That might just be a sign of good things to come I reckon.'

It was a little ironic watching the king of the jungle showing off his superiority over the king of the batting field. So often opposition bowlers walk away from our captain feeling as though they have had the mickey taken out of them by our decorated skipper. Maybe our new lion friend was showing us who really is the boss around here.

Without enough time to enjoy the traditional safaris or game parks while we are here in Africa, an afternoon like today is a good break from the cricket grounds or hotel rooms. With another game starting tomorrow, this short tour is sure to be over before it even starts. Ten days in this interesting country will hardly be enough to fill our memory scrapbooks with everything Zimbabwe can offer. It will leave me though with enough desire to come back in the future with my family to enjoy all the treats that this short experience threatens to tease me with.

Justin's View...

Practice: Aust v. Zimbabwe XI

9–11.10.99 As crazy as it may sound the last three days have been like heaven in terms of player comfort and enjoyment on the cricket field. After five weeks of playing cricket in hot, humid conditions where you are dripping wet with perspiration for every playing minute, it has been a relief being back to what we would consider normality. One pair of batting gloves per session, rather than having to change them due to saturation every 30 minutes, is a nice reminder that cricket doesn't have to be as rugged as it has been in Sri Lanka. Playing in a dry shirt where your sunglasses aren't fogging up every time you raise your heart beat above your sleeping rate has been a sweet comfort for everyone.

Any influence AB has already had on this team must have been positive because we have played the perfect preparation game. All of the batsmen spent valuable time at the crease with Tugga and Junior playing themselves into great Test match form, while I was lucky to hit a few balls in the middle in the first innings. On a flat Bulawayo pitch our captain was in ruthless form, smashing the ball with the same ferocity that he displayed during the World Cup. At the other end, his brother put aside his Sri Lankan misfortunes with an innings of typical ease and elegance.

On the bowling front Glenn McGrath is easing into his best rhythm and Damien Fleming simply continued his excellent form from the last Test in Colombo. We could not have asked to play a better three days of cricket. With the Test match starting on Friday we will go into the game feeling fresh and expectant after this confidence boosting practice match. 'Winning is a habit' is a motto we all believe in and after a barren few weeks in the victory department the last three days could be just the tonic the team needs.

Glenn McGrath and Justin Langer are clearly pleased after Mark Vermeulen of the President's XI was caught by Ian Healy off McGrath for 15 during Day 2 of the match.

The Dominators

Justin's View...   Monday night

11.10.99 Australian pop star Natalie Imbruglia's smash hit Torn has been running through my brain for the last few days, not so much for the words in the song but rather because I have been torn in my thinking. The question bothering me has been whether to take a trip to the Victoria Falls with a few of my teammates or travel straight to Harare to prepare for the Test match.

Weighing up the pros and cons has been difficult because I know how important this Test match is to me personally and to the team. When it came down to the final decision I figured that life is too short to miss such an opportunity. A visit to the Victoria Falls, one of the natural wonders of the world, could be as good a preparation for our team spirit as another session in the nets. It has been cricket day in, day out since we left Sydney for Colombo, so a break before the Test match may be as productive as more cricket training. Being in a good frame of mind is a crucial factor in success. My gut feeling therefore tells me that this adventure to the awesome Falls could prove to be a telling ingredient to the overall result of this short tour.

As it turned out, catching the slow, night train to the Victoria Falls was a long, relatively uncomfortable trek through Africa that took us 13 hours. Funnily enough, it was also one of the great experiences of my life. With nine of my teammates, we boarded the 7 p.m. train at Bulawayo station for what promised to be the adventure of a lifetime. We weren't disappointed!

Steve Waugh in a hat parade with two up-and-coming Dominators, Simon Katich and Matt Nicholson, on the train trip to Victoria Falls.

Armed with refreshments of the liquid and solid variety, a small music box, a classic compact disc collection and one change of clothes, we chugged along through the pitch black African night, having the time of our lives. This was a chance to talk, sing, laugh and just hang out with a couple of mates in a happy and relaxed environment. With the gold at the end of the rainbow being a visit to one of the seven natural wonders of the world, the journey along the rainbow was equally as rewarding.

Early in the trip a huge African man walked passed our cabin, wearing a black and white checked gangster's hat. Never one to pass up an opportunity I rushed out and asked him if he would be prepared to sell his hat to me. After some steady negotiation, we finally settled on 400 Zimbabwe dollars (approx A$20). Both pleased with the transaction, the stage was then set for a 'best hat competition' for the evening. Three hours into the journey seven of the guys had performed similar deals with strangers from the train who were willing to exchange their hats for a few local notes. While they were not exactly our beloved baggy green caps they were worn with a similar amount of pride for the journey.

In 13 hours and 27 station stops there was plenty of time to pop my newly capped head out of the cabin window and admire the heavens. I have never seen such a clear and beautiful sky. So many stars were sprinkled above us that it was almost like there was a natural light guiding the train driver to our Victoria Falls destination.
The light of the stars was almost symbolic of the light that was opening up within the team. With new boys Simon Katich and Matt Nicholson having the time of their lives, this was the perfect opportunity for everyone to be themselves away from the pressures of the game.

As silly as it may sound, I have been playing cricket with or against Stuey MacGill for the last decade, and it wasn't until tonight that I feel I have really met him. It was all about talking about old times, childhood experiences and listening to your mate's views away from the working environment. What a classic way to forge

The train trip to Victoria Falls was an opportunity to forge friendships with Stuey MacGill and other team members.

friendships and really get to know your team mates, who invariably turn out to be a lot more than just good cricket players. Magilla is a fantastic bloke who will become a better teammate and friend, simply because of this unusual but highly enjoyable journey that we have shared and will talk about for years to come. Like reminiscing about our Test victories together, there is no doubt this team bonding excursion to the middle of nowhere will take up many story-telling hours in the future.

The tension of being away from home slowly diminished as the sounds of The Eagles, John Williamson and the 'Best of the Seventies and Eighties' made their way from the team jukebox to everyone's auditory canals. When we finally arrived at the Vic Falls at 7.45 this morning, everyone was feeling, admittedly, a little worse for wear but in great spirits nonetheless. We may have missed a net session before the Test match starts on Thursday, but I would have to say the way everyone is now feeling we will enter the arena ready to take on the world. In fact, it might be time for the Australian cricket team to really take on the world and become the best around... Time will tell.

The Dominators

Test No.1 v Zimbabwe
HARARE 14–17 OCTOBER 1999

The pitch at the Harare Sports Ground had some bounce, some seam movement on most mornings and reasonable pace throughout this match. It was a good Test pitch and one that suited Australia's game. Zimbabwe won the toss and batted first, mainly because they were worried by the Warne factor, facing Shane in the fourth innings. However, that decision exposed their top order to McGrath and Fleming on a helpful first-day pitch. Sometimes against good teams you can't win either way. Our pace bowlers used the conditions well enough to have Zimbabwe all out just before stumps on the first day for 194.

Former school boy champion sprinter, Henry Olonga, whose swift return ran out Justin Langer.

With the pitch again seaming and bouncing early on the second day, we lost both openers before we had reached double figures. But Justin Langer steadied things with a very good 44 before risking a second run to Henry Olonga. Before this Olonga had had a bad day, bowling poorly and dropping an easy catch, but he produced a brilliant running pick-up and throw to easily beat Justin who berated himself for ruining what was shaping up as a very good innings. Later on we found out that Olonga had been a champion sprinter at school. A slight lapse in our preparations there. With that wicket, the Waughs came together at 3 for 96 and turned the game with a stand of 157. As the pitch settled and the Zimbabweans lost a little of their early fight, the Waugh boys cashed in—something they are very good at. Mark batted very well to reach 90 before chipping a return catch to part-time spinner Grant Flower. Mark was furious with himself but it was only that night that he learned that he had just missed a chance to be the first player from any nation to register a century against all eight Test-playing countries.

Allan Border's Big Picture

Colin Miller (centre) of Australia is congratulated
after trapping Trevor Gripper of Zimbabwe lbw, during day four
of the one off Test match against Zimbabwe.

And guess who was close behind him, with hundreds against Zimbabwe and India to go? Stephen, of course. Sure enough Steve ground Zimbabwe into the dirt, making 151 not out and leaving himself only India to go to get the eight. With India visiting Australia soon after this tour, a hundred against them seemed a formality.

Damien Fleming added some cream to the cake with an unorthodox and very effective 65 off 94 balls to take the total to 422 and the lead to 228. Colin Miller came to the fore in Zimbabwe's second innings, bowling better than his 3 for 66 suggested. Zimbabwe could only manage 232 in the second innings, leaving Australia five to win. The locals had done well in patches but, like most emerging teams, let themselves down with lapses in concentration, especially in the field where they dropped too many catches. Against a strong side like Australia, you will always be punished heavily if you do that. So a 10-wicket win was pretty much what Australia expected to achieve in this first ever Test between the two countries.

Matthew Hayden and Stuart MacGill were given permission to leave mid-way through this match so they would be home in time for a Sheffield Shield game and so gain the match practice they were missing out on in Zimbabwe. Just before they were about to leave the ground for the airport, the players took drinks and our guys waved Matty and Stuey on to the ground in a spontaneous gesture. There they were in suits and ties shaking hands and hugging their teammates while the Zimbabweans looked on, no doubt impressed by the obvious and genuine camaraderie between the Australians. Team spirit was not going to be a problem for this Australian team.

After the game, Zimbabwe captain Alistair Campbell talked about Australia's 'total cricket', comparing their relentless pressure and commitment to the famous total rugby played by the great All Black teams. It was quite a compliment and one that the Australian team would deserve more and more as the juggernaut rolled through the next few months. The frustrations of Sri Lanka were fading fast and all minds were turning towards the coming series against the talented Pakistanis.

During drinks in the Test match, Stuart MacGill and Matthew Hayden farewell the team before returning home from Zimbabwe for a Sheffield Shield game.

Justin's View...

Day 1 First Test v. Zimbabwe

14.10.99 Tugga may have lost the toss but I think we have certainly won the first day of this historic Test match in Harare. Never before have our two countries met in this form of the game. Although we never need any motivation to play in the baggy green cap, this factor alone acted as an extra incentive for us to fire on all cylinders. Before we took the field this morning, the spirit in the changing room was very upbeat. The arrival of Allan Border as the stand-in coach has helped pick up the overall enthusiasm of the guys, as his new ideas, thoughts and fresh style on the game have spurred the team.

Since losing the first Test in Sri Lanka we have all worked hard on getting back to our best cricket. Today our fast bowlers stuck to the team's game plan of Patience, Partnerships and Pressure as they put us into a position of strength at stumps. Led by Pigeon, Flemo and Colin Miller, the boys bowled immaculately all day on a pitch resembling a good WACA surface, in that it was quick and bouncy. Their combined efforts, with Warney, have laid a solid foundation for this Test match. Any hope Zimbabwe had of causing the good guys an early scare were quickly sent tumbling. An excellent exhibition of bowling from our quickies, who relished being back on a pitch that doesn't resemble a dust pit like in Sri Lanka, has us on top.

Gavin Rennie of Zimbabwe rears up after being struck by a delivery from Glenn McGrath.

Sadly, Matty Hayden and Stuey MacGill flew home this afternoon to play in the upcoming Shield game for their respective States. It was disappointing to see them leave the touring party although we can understand that it is important they play some cricket before the Aussie summer gets under way. In a positive move by the ACB, and the selectors, both guys will now play Shield cricket rather than sit on the bench watching like they've been doing for the majority of this tour. I know how frustrating it can be to be on tour without playing a game. Although they haven't seen much action on the field they have both done themselves proud by contributing to this team. One of the many reasons Australian cricket is so strong is that there is extraordinary depth of talent and character below the first eleven. The fringe players, of which I have been one for a long time, are all hard-working and exceptionally good team men who play an enormous role behind the scenes of this improving brigade of baggy green-capped cricketers.

The Dominators

Justin's View... *Day 2 First Test v. Zimbabwe*

15.10.99 Barring an unfortunate run out to yours truly and a couple of early wickets, the good guys took the honours for the second day running. Mark and Stephen batted beautifully, setting up a handy first innings lead. With five wickets still in hand at stumps, we will be looking to extend our score as far from Zimbabwe's reach as we can. When play resumes in the morning, we will have an opportunity to put intense pressure on our opponents who will now be feeling the dream of defeating Australia in our first Test slipping away.

Losing Slats and Blewey early sent a few shivers through our changing room leaving Junior and I with the task of batting through the first session. Like batting at the WACA, it is generally difficult getting settled on such a bouncy strip of turf, but when you 'get in' there is no better place to bat. With the ball coming onto the bat evenly and at a good pace it is as much fun as you can have with a bat in your hand.

Unfortunately, I didn't take full advantage of the conditions thanks to a crazy run out. The twins helped make up for my misfortune however, punishing any loose bowling by the Zimbabweans. It is an entertaining and heartening sight from our changing room seeing the twins batting together as if they were in their back garden in Bankstown. When the younger of the twins departed in the 90s it was as surprising as seeing him in deep conversation with his older brother.

It would be fair to say that our opposition attack is steady with a number of medium pacers making up the bowling attack. Heath Streak and Henry Olonga add some pace to this outfit but otherwise they rely heavily upon a patient line and length from Strang, Whittall and Johnson. On such a good batting surface this was always going to work in our favour if were able to remain equally as patient with the bat.

Mark Waugh goes on the attack, during day two.

At stumps our captain, and master of Test cricket batting, remains undefeated on 90. His consistency in this arena is simply outstanding. Once again he was as solid as oak, playing with the same ruthless intent in both attack and defence. He is as tough a competitor as there is playing the game and he is determined to continue his onslaught in the morning. With Heals also looking for a big score, and our tail due to wag, we are all hopeful of a big day tomorrow to put Zimbabwe out of this contest.

Justin's View...   Day 3 First Test v. Zimbabwe

16.10.99 The more I think about it I might have to re-name my daily diary articles on Test cricket days *The Test Cricket Exploits of Stephen Rodger Waugh*. Since I began writing my daily thoughts during the 1997 Ashes tour of England, there has hardly been a day when our captain hasn't featured in one way or the other because of his incredible batting prowess. Sure there are a thousand ways to tell a story, but even now I am still finding it increasingly difficult to find a new method of praising the mastery of Tugga's batting. Consistent, brutal, ruthless, controlled, single-minded, mentally tough are all adjectives that I have used to describe his genius with a cricket bat in his hand.

Today has been no exception with the second-highest Australian Test match run scorer, taking his overnight score of 90 to over the 150 mark. Again he was all of the above as he destroyed the soul of the Zimbabwe bowling with an aggression usually reserved for an army general in command. As per usual he copped an array of bruises to his hands, ribs and arms and, as usual, he just shrugged these off as part of the job. His leadership is inspiring and with Allan Border sitting in our viewing room during this Test match the feeling of accomplishment and toughness is changing the demeanour of the Australian cricket team.

Just being around the Waughs, Allan Border, Ian Healy, Shane Warne and increasingly Glenn McGrath is enough to motivate any soul into a higher standard of accomplishment. This is where Australian cricket is so lucky. We have people to aspire to, people who have given our cricket a rich history of achievement that has formed a pride in the baggy green cap that is incomparable. Our fortune in this regard will hold us in good spirit for years and hopefully generations to come. How can the youngsters of today lack inspiration from the achievements of greatness which Steve Waugh and his mates in this team consistently offer?

Damien Fleming congratulates Steve Waugh (left) after Waugh reached his century, on day three.

Damien Fleming gave the skipper unbelievable support by smashing 60-odd in very quick time. His confidence is growing with every journey to the batting crease. He laughs at the suggestion that he is starting to assume all-rounder status but, after his recent successes with the bat, he is offering more to the team than just destructive out swingers. We now need him to bowl with the same reliance tomorrow so that we can return to Australia with a Test victory to our name.

After the Barbados Test match earlier this year, we are not taking anything for granted, but there is an obvious air of expectation going into day four. Zimbabwe has a number of determined and talented batsmen to come so we will have to work very hard tomorrow to ensure a victory.

Justin's View...

Day 4 First Test v. Zimbabwe

17.10.99 Today is what you could describe as real 'hard yakka' at the office with the reward for our perseverance coming at 4 p.m., when this historic first Test against Zimbabwe was secured. Three balls before lunch the Zimbabweans, led by debutant Trevor Gripper and my ex-Western Australian teammate Murray Goodwin, were making us fight hard for their wickets. They were as stubborn as a deeply embedded splinter as they set about forming a platform for their teammates to set us a target some time tomorrow. To our relief Funky Miller was able to spin one past Gripper's defence just before the first break.

His dismissal gave us a boost at lunch, as we all realised the new ball was due to be taken in a couple of overs. When we returned to the field our opposition continued to fight us hard, scrambling and scraping for every run. The pressure out on the ground from our side was equally intense though we all felt that if we continued to build the pressure something was going to give.

And it did!

As so often happens in a game of cricket, rewards are won by putting enough pressure on your opposition. With all of our bowlers bowling superbly, the Zimbabweans were never able to break the shackles and dominate our attack. Having bowled for over 80 overs at less than two runs per over we had been in the field for a long time but knew that one more wicket could easily initiate a collapse. Fortunately, we weren't disappointed as the wicket of Goodwin started a dramatic disintegration in which the last eight wickets fell for just over 30 runs. At no stage during the day did anyone feel that this game was getting away from us even though the Zimbabwean players fought the first few rounds of the bout with admirable tenacity. Our senior players were so confident that a run of wickets was imminent if we maintained the pressure that their self-assurance became infectious. You cannot buy experience on the shelf and there is certainly plenty of that in this team.

With five runs needed to win this Test match, Blewey and Slats finished it off in the first over. Deservedly Steve Waugh was the man of the match but I think it would be fair to say that this Test match was won by a fantastic team effort. It has been a long time since Heals has stood on the changing room table singing *Under The Southern Cross...*

The sweet tune of our team song is still ringing in my ears. It has to be one of the main reasons we love playing for Australia.

Ian Healy Retires

During that Test in Harare, I don't remember seeing anything wrong with Ian Healy's wicketkeeping but his batting did look out of sorts. His footwork at the crease seemed sluggish and indecisive. Although the selectors had no definite plans regarding Heals and his future he had said himself that his batting in the West Indies earlier that year had been

Heals, with his beloved baggy green in hand, was a major contributor to the code of ethics for Australian Test players which is always taped to the dressing room wall.

disappointing and that he needed to maintain his high standards on this tour. He had not made any runs in Sri Lanka and so probably felt some pressure on his batting in Zimbabwe. Perhaps by that stage Heals had resigned himself to the fact that this tour was his last. I hadn't been witness to too many victory celebrations for a quite a few years and I was struck by how hard the guys **celebrated** the win in Harare, Heals as hard as any of them. After singing *Under The Southern Cross* they put on some music, linked arms around the room and carried on for quite a while. Some people might think they had only beaten Zimbabwe but they gave the impression that every win is important to them. Perhaps they also had an inkling that this was Heals's last Test match.

Heals has been absolutely fantastic for Australian cricket. History will remember him as right up there in the top echelon of our keepers. The fact that he made the Team of the Century means that the judges decided he was the best of our keepers in the twentieth century. I agree. In my time the two best keepers were Rodney Marsh and Heals. I lean towards Healy on a couple of points. Firstly, his batting. There was not much in it between the two. Rod was a bit more explosive with the bat, Heals a bit more settled. I think Heals probably got runs at the right time more often than Rodney. Secondly his keeping up to the stumps, especially to Warney. Rod didn't have to do a lot of that because quicks like Dennis Lillee and Jeff Thomson dominated, but I can't imagine anyone being better than Heals with the way Warney bowled early in his career. Warney would go around the wicket into the rough outside leg stump and Heals's work was unbelievably good to the toughest sort of spin bowling a keeper faces.

Heals made himself into a great wicketkeeper. When he got the call he had only played about half a dozen first class games and his keeping was still raw for Test cricket. But once he had a taste of it, he went away and did what he had to do to make himself into a very good keeper. His work ethic was second to none. We've all heard those stories about him going off to the depths of a hotel car park and going through his routines catching a golf ball with his inners. Throughout his career Heals suffered a lot of hand injuries, but he never complained. Off the field he was probably even more important to the side and its success than he was on the field. He was a very solid, reliable cricketer who taught the guys all the right lessons as far as working hard and doing everything you have to do to be at your best within the team framework. He did a lot to ensure the team was going the right way and getting the right results. He knew that when you have the opportunity to enjoy the fruits of your labour, you do it to the max. Then you're back on deck the next day or the day after. I reckon that is what sport is all about and Heals handled those situations very well. Sometimes some blokes might go too far one way or the other. Some get too serious about the sport and the money they are making while others go the other way. Things happen so fast that they start to enjoy the limelight too much and lose their direction. In that regard, I think Heals was the perfect model for younger players coming into the side.

Heals also had the knack of bridging the gap between the senior players, the heavies in the team, and the new guys coming into the side. He had that ability to be able to mix in the various circles. He was a very good lieutenant or senior player from that point of view and was always able to keep things on an even keel. When things needed to be serious he was serious. When it was party time he could be the centre of the party with that joker personality. His contribution was critical to the success the side enjoyed over most of his career. He is a very rounded character; an ideal support player for a captain. I have a great deal of respect for Ian Healy.

An example of Heals's contribution to the team culture: For a few years now, the side has put down on a piece of paper a set of ethics or rules they adhere to. If a player is struggling he can refer to it to check if he is doing all the things that go to make an Australian Test player. At an annual meeting, maybe in Brisbane where they get together again for the first Test of the home summer, they sit down and look at it again, see whether it still fits, whether they are maintaining these ethical standards. They might make a few adjustments. Typically, Heals was very proactive in all that, in setting a standard for Australian cricketers— things like wearing the baggy green, looking the part on and off the field. He was also a central figure in the players' dispute with the Australian Cricket Board in 1997–98. He has been a very proactive force for the players and for cricket in

Heals at the ready.

general, more than just a great wicketkeeper.

Heals was certainly tempted to play in the first Test against Pakistan in Brisbane. That way he would play his final game at his home ground and would have a good chance of being the first keeper in history to make 400 Test dismissals. It would have been a great end to a great career. But the other side of the issue was that at the start of a new season the selectors had an exciting player, Adam Gilchrist, ready to come into Heals's spot. Could we have one bloke playing the first Test match, retiring and another playing the second? Looking back, would Heals have played the innings that Gilly played in Brisbane? If Heals had played, would Gilly have been in the right state of mind to make that great, match-winning 149* in Hobart in what would have been his first Test match? This was a tricky situation for the selectors and for me as a friend and former teammate of Heals. In the end the selectors had to do the right thing by the team. We felt that the timing was right to bring in Adam for Brisbane rather than Hobart and with the benefit of hindsight it was the right decision. In the future, with the much greater financial rewards they receive, more and more players are going to extend their careers into their mid to late thirties. That is inevitable and fair enough as they are fully professional cricketers. But that means that selectors are going to face these sorts of decisions more often and it will be even harder for a selector who has played with the guy in question as there will be that emotional link. But selectors also have to be fair to a younger player coming through, one like Gilly who was obviously ready for the step up.

* signifies not out

SELECTION DILEMMAS:
Mark Waugh and Justin Langer

The Healy issue was not the only dilemma for the selectors going into the first Test of the home summer. There was speculation in some sections of the media that Mark Waugh and Justin Langer were both under pressure to retain their positions in the side.

Allan Border's Big Picture

The ever-stylish Mark Waugh prepares to cut a ball.

Justin Langer lifts one over the fielders for four runs.

Mark had not made a run in Sri Lanka and, although he made a good 90 in Harare, people were happy to dismiss that as runs against lesser opposition. Mark is an enigma. Because he makes his runs so easily people expect more of him. They think he should be making as many hundreds and as many runs as the other great talents in the game like Steve, Sachin Tendulkar and Brian Lara. But Mark is not as ruthless as those players. He does not worry about records or statistics. He just goes out and plays a certain way. Although he is not a ruthless run accumulator he still averages more than 40 and that is outstanding. As well, he is one of the best catchers in world cricket. Mark wins you games, but he also does a lot of other things that go unnoticed. He often makes a fighting 30 or 40 in difficult circumstances, then takes a crucial catch or a handy wicket. During this Australian season he took some great catches, including one in Hobart that I thought changed the game. He is a tremendous cricketer, a match-winner, and you do not drop such players lightly.

We probably give him more leeway than other players but we do that for the right reasons.

Justin also had a poor tour of Sri Lanka before making a good 40 in Zimbabwe, but we had got to the point with him where we just had to find out, to give him a bit of a run at the number three spot to see if he had it. We always rated his talent and were prepared to be patient. Justin was not the only one to struggle in Sri Lanka and often batsmen have to go through that process on a tour before they learn how to handle certain conditions. It can take a whole tour for that to happen. As well, we thought Justin could offer a lot to the team: a good left-hander to fill that role of number three and a player with a Healy-like work ethic.

Justin is a really solid style of kid who just loves that baggy green cap. He is good company in the lighter moments. He celebrates as hard as anyone, then he is back into the hard work the next day. Justin was the perfect man to fill the role Heals played in the side. In selecting teams we place a fair bit of importance on a player's contribution to team spirit. Justin feels the high and lows with the other players. He cares about their form and that builds team spirit.

Justin is also a fast learner, as he showed by the way he worked out a plan to play the spinners as this season progressed. He asked me about this in Zimbabwe after he had really struggled against Murali in Sri Lanka. All I said was that he had to have a plan. If he just stayed in the crease and poked and prodded he would get out. I used the sweep at times to break up the play and Justin began to try that. He also tried using the drive down the ground to break the spinners' rhythm. By the time he got to New Zealand in February he was the only batsman to really take to Daniel Vettori who is a very good bowler. Justin repaid our faith in him, but, although it is tempting to say we planned all of it, I cannot claim that. Basically we just thought he deserved a decent run at the job and in the end it worked very well.

Test No.2 First Test v. Pakistan
BRISBANE 5–9 NOVEMBER 1999

This was a terrific Test match on an excellent Gabba pitch. Pakistan did well to make 367 after Steve Waugh sent them in, but Damien Fleming was really the only Australian bowler who performed at his best. It was a decent score, but needed to be supported by good bowling and fielding and that was where the Pakistanis let themselves down.

Openers Michael Slater and Greg Blewett set up Australia's first innings of 575 with a 269-run stand. Blewett's 89 was his best innings of the summer while Slater's 169 off only 271 balls was another example of his ability to score heavily and quickly and put his side into a strong position. Pakistan dismissed Blewett and then Langer quickly but Mark Waugh halted any chance they had of getting back into the game with one of his most graceful hundreds. Adam Gilchrist came in at 5 for 342 and played shots from the start as if this was his 100th Test innings rather than his first. It was brilliant batting. With a good first innings lead likely, Shane Warne had a day out, hitting 86 off only 90 balls with nine fours and four sixes. At times I worry when Warney belts boundaries because he starts to think he is Viv Richards. But this day he chose the right balls to hit and hit them with real power. It was another example of Warney's genuine ability with the bat and an innings that would have pleased his skipper as Steve is always having digs at Warney about the gap between his ability with the bat and his results.

Facing a first innings deficit of 208, Pakistan made 281 in their second innings, with Fleming taking 5 for 59 to go with his 4 for 65 in the first. This was excellent bowling on a very good batting pitch. Slater and Blewett made the 74 required and Australia won by 10 wickets; a large margin given that the game was fairly even for most of the five days. One–nil to Australia and one-from-one for the new boys, coach John Buchanan and wicketkeeper–batsman Adam Gilchrist.

Justin's View...   *Victory 2 Day 1 First Test v. Pakistan*

5.11.99 There has been plenty happening in the Aussie cricket team since we left Zimbabwe a couple of weeks ago. John Buchanan has been appointed the new coach, and this is a brilliant appointment. The drummer in the band, Ian Healy, has retired, which was a tough decision. Now to top this all off, today Adam Gilchrist and Scotty Muller made their Test debuts for Australia.

The times are changing, and although Heals will be sorely missed for his incredible work ethic, talent and dedication to the team, it is an exciting time leading into this series against the highly talented and quite unpredictable Pakistanis. Never in my wildest dreams would I have thought that the triumphant celebrations in the Harare changing rooms would be the last time I would see Heals in his baggy green cap and immaculate whites singing *Under The Southern Cross...* It must be my semi-naïve mind because I would never have predicted the final Ashes Test match in Sydney last summer would be Mark Taylor's last in his baggy green. In a way it would have been nice to have known on both occasions so that we could have given Heals and Tubby

Shoaib Akhtar faces the Australian media at the Gabba about his bowling action.

a special send-off in Harare and Sydney. They say a player knows when the time is right, so I guess our world record-holding wicketkeeper knew that enough was enough. He has been a wonderful ambassador for Australian cricket. As great players leave the game the clock keeps ticking, opening up new and exhilarating opportunities for the new kids on the block.

With allegations flying around about the bowling action of Pakistan's 'Rawalpindi Express', the series had been built up to boiling point before a ball was even bowled. Like every Test match though, all the pre-Test controversies, speculations and opinions were forgotten when Glenn McGrath bowled the first ball of the series at 10 a.m. this morning. For the second consecutive Test match Steve Waugh went against Australian tradition and decided to bowl first on a Gabba pitch, promising good pace, seam and bounce. With three genuine new ball bowlers in our starting 11 everyone was pumped up when we took the field this morning.

By stumps, that early enthusiasm was dented a little as it was a tough first day of Test match cricket for the summer. The pitch didn't play as many tricks as we had hoped for but the bowlers stuck to the task pretty well. While it was not the perfect day, it could have been a lot worse when Inzamam and Yousuf were compiling their menacing partnership. Thanks to Damien Fleming's three vital wickets in the final session, the feeling in the changing room was positive at the end of the day.

With some of the journalists around the country calling for drastic changes in our batting order, the pressure was on from many angles for a high-class performance with the bat tomorrow. Obviously, we need to secure the final four Pakistani wickets as quickly as possible in the morning before being at our best to combat the aggressive and talented visiting bowlers. It is hard reading some of the criticism in the press but at the end of the day we all know that runs and victories are the only currency of value in the competitive world of international cricket. For the team's sake, a big first innings score will be vital for our prospects in this all-important first Test of the summer...

Our two debutants both had good first-up days in their cherished baggy green caps that were presented to them in an emotional ceremony by Australian cricket legend Billy Brown. It always sends a shiver down the back of the spine when a teammate is presented with his baggy green for the first time and this morning was no exception. Bill Brown explained the tradition of the baggy green and the pride for which it should be worn. He was inspirational in sharing his thoughts about playing cricket for Australia.

Last night at our team dinner Patrick Rafter came along as a guest of the team. What a sensational bloke! It was a buzz meeting a great Australian achiever, who has made such a mark in his chosen career. It was quietly inspiring just having him around as he seems like a champion of the highest degree. Stephen is keen to introduce a few new initiatives this summer, including inviting different Aussie achievers to our team dinners. Last night it was Pat Rafter, and it will be interesting to see who else accepts a dinner invitation during the summer.

The Dominators

Justin's View... *Day 2 First Test v. Pakistan*

6.11.99 As days at the office go, today was a fantastic one for the Australian cricket team. The balance of the game could have gone either way this morning. With the Pakistanis resuming at six for 280 either side could have pushed home a fresh advantage. Thanks to some excellent bowling and fielding in the first session, and an unbelievable first-wicket partnership between Slats and Blewey we are in a comfortable position this evening.

Everyone in the team knows there is still a mountain of work to do tomorrow but at least we have the foundation there to take charge of this Test match. When we took the field this morning our game plan was to contain the Pakistanis with a patient line and length. Barring a very aggressive innings from Moin Khan we achieved what we set out to achieve with Scotty Muller picking up his first Test wickets for Australia.

With two overs to face before lunch, Wasim Akram and Shoaib Akhtar looked in ominous form with the new Kookaburra ball. There is no worse time to bat than just before one of the major breaks in play but our two openers, Slats and Blewey, got through to lunch without losing a wicket. As if to set a trend for the day they then batted through the last two sessions to have us wicketless at stumps.

Where Slats was at his ruthless best in his approach, his partner was as solid as the proverbial double-brick house. In the last four Tests they have enjoyed three century opening partnerships in setting up the good guys for bigger and better things. Good mates off the field, these two are writing their own pages of history in terms of successful opening partnerships for Australia.

We are all hoping they continue on in the morning and, if the rest of us can contribute to the cause, then by stumps tomorrow night there could be more smiles than at a three-year old's birthday party. We have plenty to play for with the stage perfectly set for a ruthless display of Test match batting by the besieged Aussie top order.

Shoaib Akhtar, the 'Rawalpindi Express', sends down a fast one on the first day of the first Test in Brisbane.

Justin's View...

Days 3 & 4 First Test v. Pakistan

8.11.99 In terms of pure entertainment, this Test match has been a beauty. Never before can I remember seeing so many boundaries hit by both teams in a game of cricket. First it was Inzamam, Saeed and Yousuf in Pakistan's first innings, followed by Slater, Blewett, Mark Waugh and Gilchrist yesterday, followed by Shane Warne this morning. The blasting show continued this afternoon with Anwar and Yousuf again taking the aggressive option to pull their team back from the brink and back into this Test match. Being more than 200 runs behind in the first innings, many lesser teams would have disintegrated. Not Pakistan though, who played with a boldness reserved for a very tough and skilful cricket team.

In reality it was not only the punters who thought the game might be over this afternoon. After taking three early wickets it looked like we might steamroll the Pakistan batting line-up like the one-day team did in the World Cup final at Lord's. Our confidence was sky-high as we threw everything at Anwar and Yousuf. Unfortunately a couple of dropped catches, spells of loose bowling and periods of combative batting have robbed us of the early opportunity to take a decisive one-nil lead in this series.

With Stephen's wife Lynette already ten days overdue for their second child, it would be fair to say that Mrs Waugh was very upset with her brother-in-law for dropping Saeed Anwar early in the innings. Her reasoning was simple. If Junior had taken that catch at second slip, an early result was on the cards and therefore the chances of Stephen being home for the birth would have become more of a reality. If you gave him the same catch a thousand times I would back him to take it 999 times. It is funny how the pressure of Test cricket can play its little tricks.

As it now stands, the final day tomorrow promises to be a thriller. We need to take six Pakistani wickets to bat again and chase a score for a one nil lead. On a fantastic batting pitch, I believe we still hold the upper hand in this Test match. The fewer runs we need to chase the better, but whatever the task we are confident that we can do it. This is a great Gabba batting strip and by getting through the new-ball attack of Akhtar and Akram we will be in a very strong position.

By this time tomorrow we will know for sure who is the victor of this epic and entertaining battle.

The Dominators

Justin's View... *Day 5 First Test v. Pakistan*

9.11.99 It just goes to show that no matter how much planning you put into it, the unpredictability of Test cricket has a way of undoing all of the talking and preparation in just one ball. Before the start of today's play we had run through everything that we thought would be necessary to bowl out the Pakistanis as cheaply as possible. Steady, patient line and length to the dangerous Anwar, fullish out-swingers to the inexperienced Razzaq, and a disciplined line to the remainder of the Pakistani batsmen. Our planning was as thorough as usual with all the wise and adept men in our changing room contributing to our objectives for this final morning. The Test match was on the line, but we were as prepared as a good army unit and ready to chase anything our talented opponents would set us.

With the stage set at 9.30 a.m., we settled into our fielding positions for Warney's first delivery of the day. Everyone was pumped with enthusiasm as the team's spirits reached fever pitch for a Test match victory. The shouts before the first ball was delivered were the standard calls from Junior Waugh at slip of 'C'mon Warney nice and tight mate.' Gilly encouraged the team with 'Plenty of energy boys.' At silly mid-off Punter was shouting 'Big start boys, big start' and my words at shortleg were 'How about a wicket first ball Warney, start us off mate, first ball mate, first ball.'

After a solid session in the field the previous day everyone tends to be a little stiff and sore first thing in the morning. Today was no exception as Warney let go his first ball. From his hand travelled a rank full toss, which was very different from the type of ball that we had planned on bowling to the Pakistani batsmen. As I jumped for my life at short leg all I could hear was Warney shouting 'Oh no,' followed by shouts of joy from everyone barracking for the Aussies at the Gabba. Out of the corner of my eye all I could see was Punter throwing the ball into the heavens and running like a lunatic towards our superstar leg-spinner.

As Razzaq trudged off the field, head drooped, and I stood arm in arm with my teammates in the huddle, I had to laugh at the irony of this crazy game. All night Razzaq would have played over in his mind a thousand scenarios of how he was planning to play Warne, McGrath, Fleming and Muller when he arrived at the crease this morning. His thoughts would no doubt have centred on saving his team in a heroic debut Test innings. He would have dreamed of top-spinners, flippers, wrong 'uns, out-swingers and bouncers but I would bet he never even considered a rank full toss, especially on the first ball of the day. He would have contemplated even less hitting this same rank full toss into the unexpecting hands of one of the undisputed great fieldsmen of the world.

LEFT: A 'pigeon' among the crows, as Glenn McGrath walks along the ground on day four of the 3rd Test between Sri Lanka and Australia at Colombo.

BELOW: Steve Waugh, catching not praying during training in the lead up to the Galle Test, Sri Lanka.

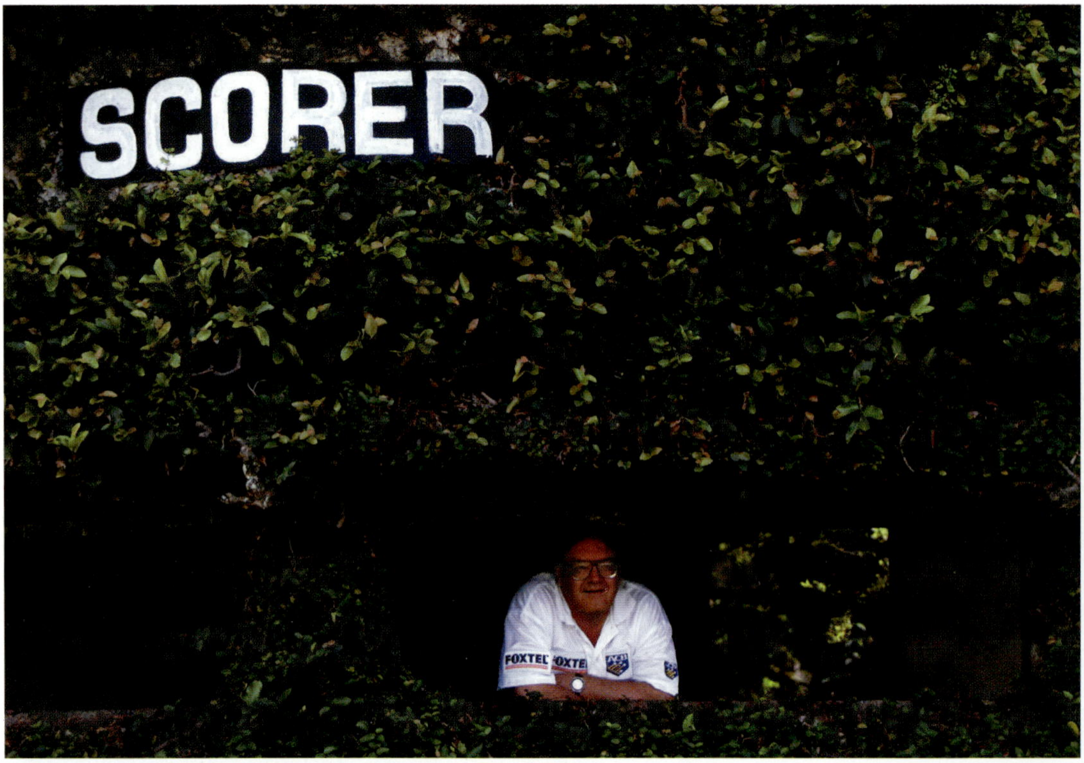
SCORER
FOXTEL
FOXTEL

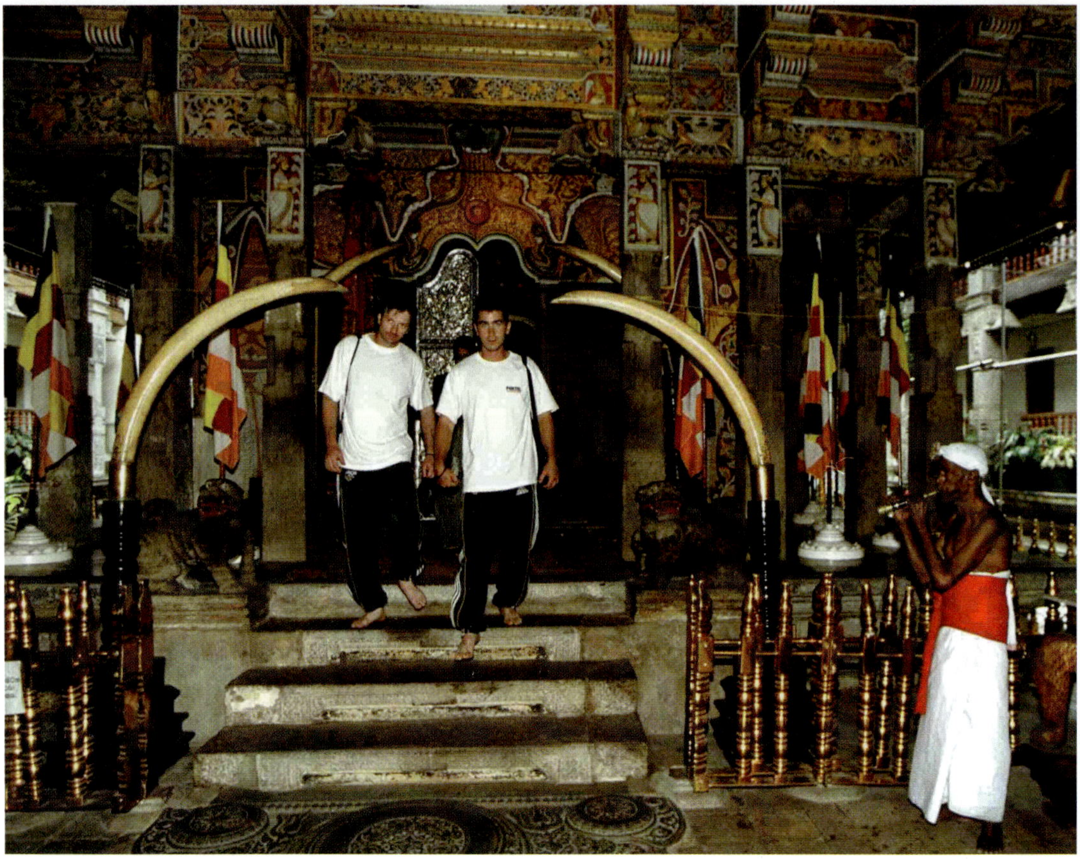

ABOVE LEFT: Mike Walsh Australian scorer in the scorer's box, during training at Colombo Oval, Colombo, Sri Lanka.

LEFT: Bare footed Steve Waugh and Justin Langer take in the sights at the Temple of the Sacred Tooth, Kandy, Sri Lanka.

ABOVE : Shane Warne celebrates as Colin Miller (in background) catches Arjuna Ranatunga of Sri Lanka, and Ian Healy runs in to congratulate, during day one of the second Test between Sri Lanka and Australia at Galle, Sri Lanka.

RIGHT: Few Australian overseas cricket tours go by without the loyal support of these two Australian cricket junkies. Lukey Sparrow (on the right) flies all around the world to cheer on the team, who make him feel a part of the touring party.

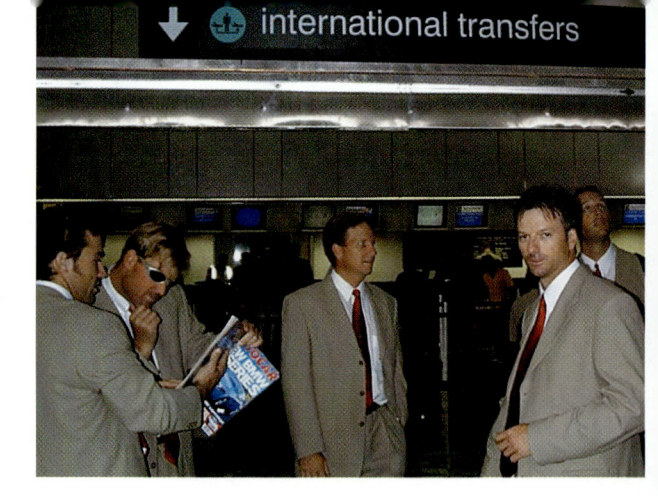

RIGHT: Michael Slater and Shane Warne choose their next car while Ian Healy, Steve Waugh and Dave Misson look around the airport terminal at Johannesburg while on their way to Zimbabwe.

ABOVE: Glenn McGrath who had already made friends with an elephant in Sri Lanka, meets a six month old rhino at a wildlife sanctuary, near Bulawayo in Zimbabwe.

LEFT: This magnificent lion at Chipangali Wildlife Sanctuary, outside Bulawayo suddenly emitted a jet of urine during the team's visit, hitting captain Steve Waugh. It was taken as a good luck omen.

ABOVE RIGHT: Preparing for the uncertainty of a thirteen hour train trip just two days before the first Test match in Harare, Zimbabwe. What a journey it turned out to be!

RIGHT: Arriving at Victoria Falls - hats and all - after the adventure of a lifetime.

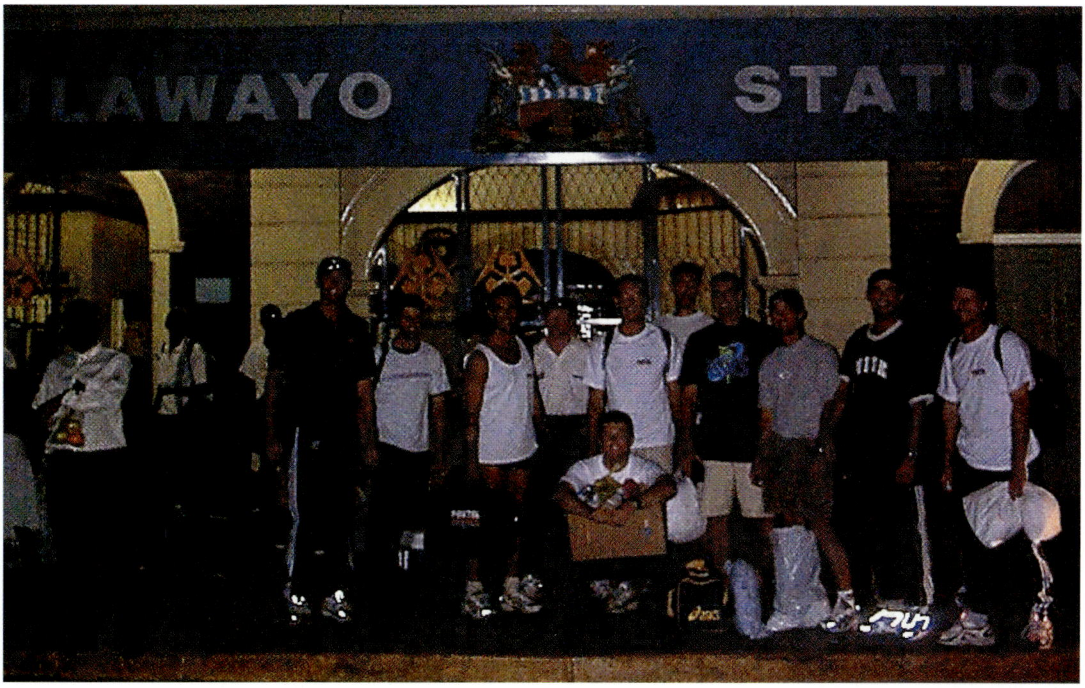
LAWAYO
STATIO

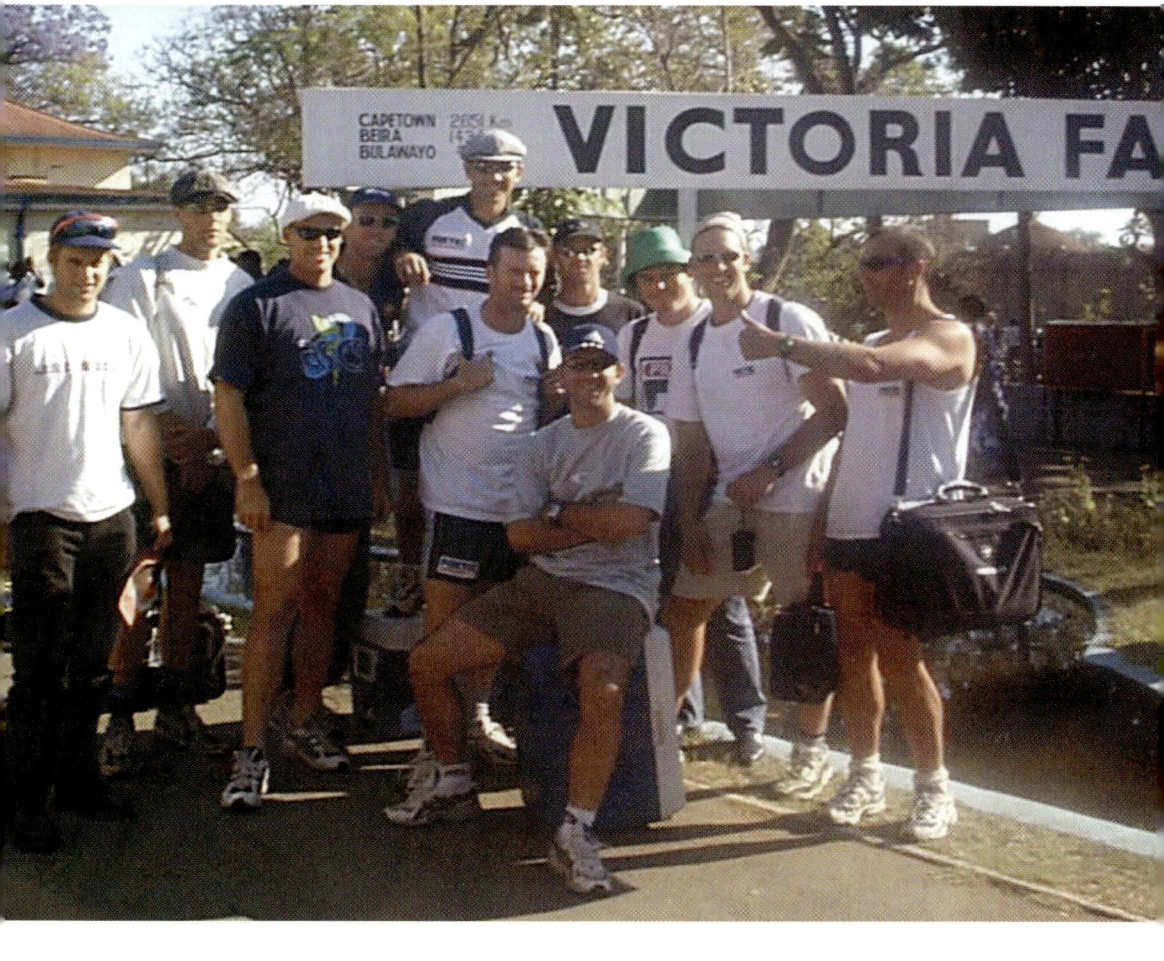
CAPETOWN
BEIRA
BULAWAYO
VICTORIA FA

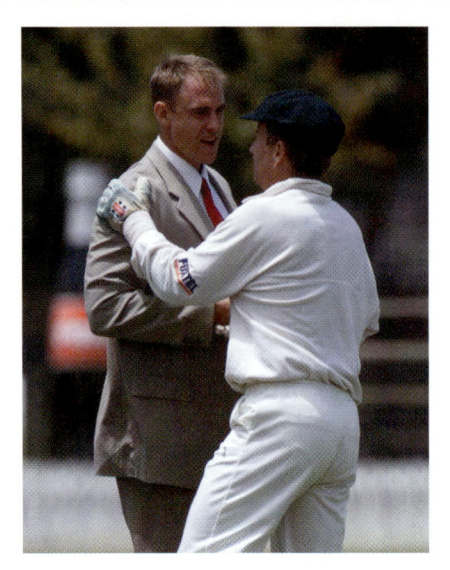

TOP LEFT: Errol Alcott, the team physio, known to all by the nickname 'Hooter', is an important and popular member of the Australian team.

TOP RIGHT: From left Bruce Ngwenya, Nicholas Singo and Trevor Phiri in the scoreboard at Queens Sports Club, Bulawayo, Zimbabwe.

ABOVE: A view of the cricket ground at Harare Sports Club with the 'Keg and Maiden' pub in the background. Shane Warne is bowling on the first day of the one-off Test match against Zimbabwe.

LEFT: Matthew Hayden (in suit) says goodbye to Ian Healy during the drinks break, as Hayden prepares to fly back to Australia to play Sheffield Shield cricket.

Heals and Warney are in no doubt. You're out! Another wicket falls during the one-off Test match between Zimbabwe and Australia at Harare.

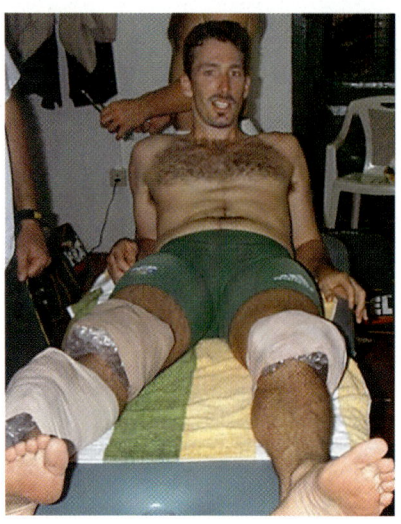

ABOVE: Damien Fleming celebrates with team mates after Ricky Ponting has caught Grant Flower off his bowling on the first day of the Test match against Zimbabwe.

LEFT: Flemo on the bench being treated with ice packs to reduce the pain to his knees after an epic bowling spell.

It is an amazing game in this regard, as there are so many different things that can happen on every single delivery leaving a bowler's hand. Who could have guessed the result of the first-up loosener of the morning? It is impossible really, although I will say we were more than happy with the outcome that kick-started the momentum for a sensational first session of Test match cricket.

Glenn McGrath bowled as well as he has bowled for a while with a disciplined line and length and Damien Fleming continued his outstanding and improved performance in Test cricket with five wickets. Their consistency under pressure proved the catalyst in the rapid demise of the Pakistani tail. Needing just over 70 runs, our openers, Blewy and Slats, continued their consistent partnership run with a faultless display of tough, and ruthless batting which secured our second consecutive 10-wicket Test victory.

In the changing rooms afterwards it was a little more sedate than usual with Steve Waugh taking the first available flight back to Sydney to be at his wife Lynette's side for the arrival of their second baby. Before he left the Gabba, Ian Healy was in the rooms to hand over the stage to Ricky Ponting who delivered his first Test match rendition of our team song *Under The Southern Cross I Stand...*

Although it was little sad to win a Test without Heals up on the table singing the song, Punter proved to be an excellent substitute for our now ex-wicketkeeper. There is nothing like winning a Test match for Australia. As Punter screamed our victory war cry, I could not help but smile at a job well done after five hard days of Test cricket against a very capable opposition.

P.S. The skipper had reason for a double celebration with the arrival of his first son, Austin.

The Australian team celebrate their win over Pakistan in the first Test at the Gabba.

Test No.3 Second Test v. Pakistan

HOBART 18–22 NOVEMBER 1999

This was one of the best Tests I've ever seen. It was tight all the way through and, with the tension at a high, decided by that brilliant last day.

Michael Slater followed his 169 in Brisbane with a fine 97 in the first innings here against some hostile bowling from the quicks and excellent off-spin from Saqlain Mushtaq. Slats had a great season and his performances went a little unnoticed. Even though he is an attacking player and takes risks, he also makes runs in pressure situations. He did well in tough conditions against Murali in Sri Lanka. He was never on top but he battled hard. Back home he began to reap some rewards. The great thing about Slats's contribution to this team is that when he makes runs he makes them quickly and that helps Australia set up a game. This Australian team scores at a fast rate and much of the on-field credit for that goes to Slats.

The critical part of this game was the last day and that 238-run partnership between Adam Gilchrist and Justin Langer that took Australia to a brilliant win. Yet, I thought that the turning point of the match came earlier, in Pakistan's second innings. I reckon that there is a critical moment in most games where the balance goes one way or the other and in this game I thought it was Mark Waugh's brilliant catch off Warney that got rid of Inzamam-ul-Haq. Warney had been bowling well with little reward before Inzamam rocked back to cut him. He got a top edge and Mark, at slip, put out a hand and grabbed it. An edged cut off a spinner is probably the hardest catch for a slip fieldsman. You are standing close because a spinner is bowling and a cut is played off the back foot which means the ball leaves the bat a metre closer to you than for a front foot shot. This happened early on the fourth day when Pakistan were already 334 ahead and Inzamam, after a night's sleep, had added only two to his overnight 116 not out. If that chance had gone down, Inzamam could have gone on to a really big score and put Australia out of the game. That is the thing with Mark Waugh. He can produce one moment of magic that turns a game. Not many players can do that.

Australia was 5 for 188 at stumps on the fourth evening, needing another 181 to win. An early wicket on the last day and Australia would probably lose. I ran into Justin in the hotel on the fourth night and he said the wicket was great. He was positive about his own batting and our chances, saying that if we could get a start in the morning a win was not out of reach. That confidence is typical of the team at the moment. They have that attitude that they are never going to lose. I am sure this game was decided when that bold confidence began to take hold. Lang was up for the challenge and Gilly always gives the impression of being nerveless. He plays the game the same way whatever the pressures.

An ecstatic Adam Gilchrist raises his bat and helmet after hitting the winning runs in the second Test v. Pakistan at Hobart.

Gilly's shot-making in that first hour of the last day was awesome and it obviously lifted Justin. Wasim Akram made some strange tactical decisions, especially opening the bowling that day with Azhar Mahmood instead of Waqar Younis. There are always internal politics in the Pakistan side and we all know that Wasim and Waqar have clashed a few times over the years. The Pakistanis can be a real rabble but they are a talented rabble and that is why they are dangerous. They must have looked back on that game and thought they deserved to win it. Yet they flew to Perth 0–2.

The main controversy on the final day was whether Justin nicked that one off Shoaib. The snickometer said he did but I'm not a great fan of that innovation. In general I think technology helps and I'm all for it but the snickometer is a bit loose. Did Lang hit it? At first he said he could not believe the fuss from the Pakistanis. A few days later he said he might have got a feather on it. I don't think it matters either way. If you go through the game you'll find other decisions which went against Australia. Justin got a poor decision in the first innings and Ijaz Ahmed was given the benefit of the doubt early in the second innings when he appeared to edge a ball down the leg-side. He went on to make 82. So who knows? And the way Gilly was batting he might have got us home even if Justin had been given out.

Justin Langer survives the Snickometer controversy during the second Test in Hobart.

This was a watershed game which I'm sure gave the Australians tremendous confidence, especially because the two batsmen who took us to the win were not big names. Justin had been under pressure and Gilly was playing in only his second Test. The Australians' self-belief grew significantly with this great win. From here on they believed they could win from any position and I'm sure that self-belief got them through a couple of tough Tests in New Zealand later in the summer.

Justin's View...   *The Run-Chase*

19.11.99 Hobart has always been a favourite touring place for me. Although it is generally colder than most other Australian cities, it has a relaxing feel that reminds me of a big country town. With great food, friendly people and magnificent scenery and water views, Hobart is an enjoyable city to play cricket in.

Bellerive Oval looked a treat this morning at training with the grass green and lush, and the sky as blue as a Sri Lankan sapphire. Although the pitch looks very flat, there is plenty of moisture under the surface. This is a sign that there is likely to be some assistance for the bowlers early on the first day. No decision has been made as to whether Scotty Muller or Colin Miller will carry the drinks, but either way we will go into this game with a talented and disciplined bowling attack. After the experience of the first Test our bowlers will be keen to build as much pressure on the Pakistani batting order with patient and aggressive fast bowling.

On the batting front, all the guys are ready to fight hard against the talented Pakistani bowlers. Traditionally a batting paradise, Bellerive has many fond batting memories for every player in our top order. Like every Test match we will all be ready for a tough initiation in the morning but again we understand that the rewards will come if we can work hard through the tough periods. With such a balanced bowling attack, the Pakistanis are bound to throw everything at us during this Test but at the end of the day that is what Test cricket is all about.

The Pakistanis have everything to gain from the next five days as they are one down in this series, so it will be no surprise to see them firing from the first ball of the day. After beating South Australia for their first victory of the tour this week, they have had the confidence boost they needed to kick-start their tour. In our favour is the fact that we can win the series with a victory in this second Test match. With our confidence high and the spirits of the team as good as they have been for a long time, we are ready to give the visitors a battle to remember. Who knows how the pitch will play in the morning: either way we will need to be as sharp as a razor to win day one.

From a personal point of view, the media have been giving me a grilling in the lead up to this Test. There has been much speculation and opinion about whether I am the right person to be coming in at number three. While it is always a difficult time for any player when the press corps singles you out for your performances, I know that I hold my own destiny in the palm of my hand. By scoring runs, I will be in the team for as long as I want to be. If I fail then I will be dropped: basically it is as simple as that. No one has a god-given right to be selected in the Australian cricket team and with the enormous depth of players around the country there is invariably going to be pressure on every player.

The Dominators

This morning at breakfast Stephen cornered me in the hotel restaurant and in a nutshell told me not to listen to any more of the press. He also gave me his 100 per cent backing and support, urging me to go out and back myself and enjoy the challenge of batting under pressure in the baggy green. This is one of the skipper's greatest strengths in that he backs his players and supports you to the very end. It is no surprise that the players in the team would run through a brick wall for him if it meant making a difference to the result. It is also no surprise that this team is gelling together so well when the men at the top are such respected individuals who make you feel like you are an important part of the machine. Tomorrow, it will be time to put all of the pre-Test speculation behind me and get on with my job of scoring runs for Australia.

Last week in Brisbane, Pat Rafter joined us for our team dinner before the start of the Test. Tonight Bill Brown, Arthur Morris, Bill Johnston and Doug Ring, four members of the 1948 'Invincibles' team, were our guests for the night. All four of them were great entertainment as they recalled how it used to be in their day. The funny thing is that although we are now paid more, spend more time warming up, and warming down, and take a plane rather than a ship to England, nothing much has changed. Sitting with Arthur Morris, one of our greatest-ever Test batsmen, he talked about criticism from the press, playing the spinners and playing with the great Sir Donald Bradman. It was fascinating listening to his stories over a plate of pasta and a dozen oysters Kilpatrick. From the way he recalled the past, it seems nothing is very different in the game today. Everyone had a great night, as we sat transfixed by stories of the wonderfully rich history of cricket.

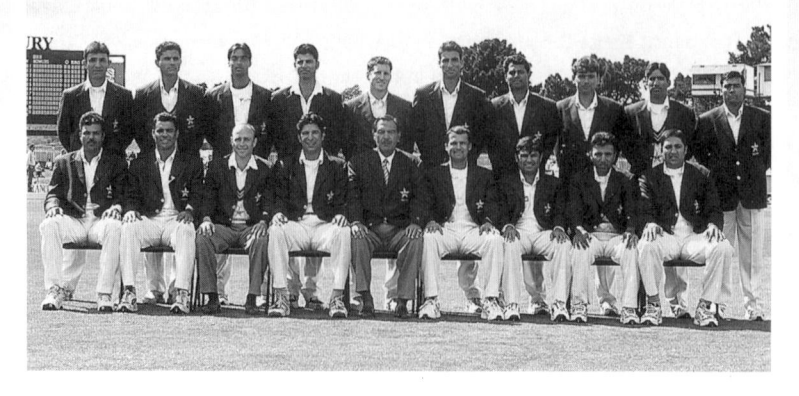

The Pakistani team at the Bellerive Oval prior to the second Test match.

Justin's View...

Day 2 Second Test v. Pakistan

19.11.99 At stumps tonight this second Test match hangs in the balance with both teams winning one day each. After a great day for the good guys yesterday, the Pakistanis came back at us like hungry tigers this afternoon. Saqlain Mushtaq and Waqar Younis showed the Australian public why they are two of the best bowlers in the world.

After a long absence from the Test team, Waqar displayed the traits of his golden years, reverse-swinging the old ball at menacing pace. His statistics in Test cricket are simply awesome and if not for injury problems over the last few years he could be even further up the list of the greatest ever wicket takers in the game. Today he was pumped-up like a heavyweight boxer as he roared into the crease like a runaway steam train.

At the other end, Saqlain had the ball on a string as he mixed his pace and spun the ball both ways. I have never seen an off-spin bowler genuinely spin the ball back into my pads like a leg-spinner, without an apparent change in his action. Muralitharan from Sri Lanka has the ability to straighten his off-spinner but Saqlain actually turns it the other way. When your brain has been programmed to play an off-spinners action with the ball turning away from the bat it is difficult to get used to the ball jagging in the opposite direction.

We knew from day one of this series that the Pakistanis have the ability to play destructive sessions with both the bat and ball. For four sessions of this Test match we have dominated the game. As we expected though, a couple of excellent spells of bowling from a couple of these Pakistani stars and we are now going to have to fight as hard as ever to stay on top of this match.

Saqlain Mushtaq — a bowling force to be reckoned with.

Traditionally, Bellerive gets flatter and flatter as the game progresses so no matter what our target, we will be able to chase it with confidence. For Western Australia, I have played in two successful run chases on the last day. With a fast outfield and even pitch we will back ourselves to win from any position, although we will obviously look to bowl tightly tomorrow to cut down our target to as small a destination as possible.

With Slats in scintillating form, anything could happen when we pad up for our second innings. He is playing with a confidence reserved for Mohammed Ali, as he dances, slashes and powers his way to runs galore. He is on fire, a fire that could ignite a productive run chase in the next few days.

The Dominators

Justin's View... *Day 4 Second Test v. Pakistan*

21.11.99 During my career, I have played in many games where the seemingly impossible became possible over the course of one session, one good partnership or one inspired bowling spell. The old cliche 'It's a funny old game' originated from the unpredictability of the game of cricket because you just never know what is around the corner.

Who could ever have predicted the situation of this match after the first four sessions of play. The Pakistanis were bowled out for 222 in their first innings and after lunch on the second day we were cruising at 1-140. Then thanks to a destructive spell by Waqar and a wily contribution from Saqlain, the game was back in the balance. As the contest progressed, the pitch flattened out and the visitors made the most of the favourable conditions, smashing us around the park for a day and a half.

Now at stumps on this fourth night, with 90 overs remaining in the game, we need 180 runs and the Wasim Akram-led Pakistanis need five wickets to even the series. What will happen tomorrow remains to be seen. All I know is that if we can apply ourselves for one ball at a time, for as many balls as we can, we still have a big chance in this Test match. Gilly's ability to score runs quickly will be in the back of our opposition's mind when play resumes at 11 a.m. He has been in incredible form with the bat of late and it would not surprise me at all to see him send a few shivers through their camp before the match is over.

For my part, I am still saying my prayers and thanking God that my season isn't over after being hit on the right forefinger by an Akhtar beam ball. It is hard enough facing his pace when he is landing the ball on the pitch, let alone when he doesn't even give it a chance to bounce. Although he was very apologetic after the delivery, I was lucky my finger wasn't shattered into a thousand pieces around my bat handle. At that pace, I didn't see the ball until I felt it hit my hand. It is rare to face a delivery like that (luckily!), so I really had no idea what to do with it. I am just thankful God was smiling on me this afternoon.

Tomorrow is a big day for both teams. With the threat of rain hanging like a blanket of doubt over the outcome of this Test, the motto for Gilly and me will be 'You just never know'. It seemed unlikely when Punter left the scene this afternoon for his third consecutive duck, but the way this game has been going I think there may still be a twist in this tale.

'It's a funny old game this cricket!'

Justin's View...

Day 5 Second Test v. Pakistan

22.11.99 What a day!

When Gilly met me at the crease yesterday I looked at my good mate from the west and said 'You just never know mate, you just never know. If we can hang in here until stumps we might have half a chance tomorrow.'

'We might even make Test cricket history here', I said with a laugh.

Admittedly I was talking more out of optimism than realism, but even so my heart told me we were some sort of chance. With our most senior batsmen licking their wounds in the Bellerive changing room I had a funny feeling that something special was still to come. The loss of our fighting skipper and Bellerive's golden boy in a few balls had dampened my enthusiasm for a Test victory, but I decided it was time to fight like a wounded tiger to stave off an early defeat.

Luckily Gilly and I were able to fight through to stumps last night, but with a full day's play remaining, our chances of survival, and the bookies odds, were stacked heavily against us. Walking off the ground I couldn't help but notice the scoreboard which read Gilchrist 45, Langer 53. My partner had scored his runs so quickly that a strange confidence was building inside me.

Overnight, I felt unusually calm about the prospects of the following day. With rain forecast for the next 24 hours I had a feeling grey skies and wet roads would greet me when I opened the curtains of my hotel bedroom this morning. As I have seen before in Hobart, another abandoned day's play would mean a one-nil lead going into the final Test match in Perth. This would be a WACA administrator's dream and a comfortable buffer for my teammates and our supporters.

What transpired on day five though was far away from my wildest imagination. Firstly, blue, clear skies smiled through my bedroom window when I dragged myself out of bed this morning. A competitive and entertaining rain-affected draw was now out of the equation. Instead, a fight of wits and skills and a potentially much tenser finale was now on the cards.

Just five days ago I could never have dreamed that today would happen. Winning a Test match and scoring a Test century, while sharing an unbelievable partnership with a good mate against a world-class opposition, with my dad cheering me on from the grandstand. Wow, somebody please pinch me!

As the day progressed it didn't only turn out to be a special day for Gilly and me personally but also for the Australian team and our sensational supporters. Personal glory is always sweet but it never matches the euphoria of sharing such a triumph with your teammates. The scenes in the Bellerive viewing room were incredible as our veteran left-handed teammate of two Test matches hit the winning runs with a trademark 'hoik' of the highest degree. The moment was sweet, as everyone savoured the elation of this historic Test match victory.

The Dominators

Winning a Test match always means a great deal to anyone wearing a baggy green cap. Today, winning was as perfect as I can remember, considering that this particular Test match was without doubt one of the toughest and most intensely competitive that I have ever been involved in. The tension was so high for the full five days that the sheer exhilaration afterwards was momentous. Equally, the disappointment painted on the faces of our opposition was as relevant to this drama as the smiles of delight etched under 12 baggy green caps.

For my part, the batting was great fun but not as much fun as my partnership with Gilly, who made my job easy. Every minute of our time together made the odd bruise, the odd strain and any previous doubt and fear worthwhile. My partner was magnificent as he played with a fluency and confidence reserved for a champion sportsman. He is in superb form as he goes from strength to strength with every outing in the Test match arena. His skill on day five in Hobart simplified my role, as his ability to score runs freely kept the pressure down to a simple battle between bat and ball rather than a battle of wits and slow run rates.

The success of our partnership resulted from sticking rigidly to our game plan. In short, this meant playing one ball at a time with sharp concentration. Before every ball we were speaking to each other and encouraging ourselves to concentrate on 'this ball' and 'keep watching this ball like a hawk'. Our communication helped inspire each other as we kept pushing ourselves to the limit to win an unlikely Test match. To say we were 'pumped up' is something of an understatement. As each run, each minute, was ticked off the ledger, the energy in the centre of Bellerive was as fierce as the local power station. It was inspiring, exciting and one of the greatest experiences of my cricketing career.

Justin Langer leaps for joy after posting a century in the run chase at Bellerive Oval, Hobart.

What started out as an optimistic hope turned into reality as the minutes passed by. As I counted down the runs ten at a time, my partner opted for the approach of playing out time. He

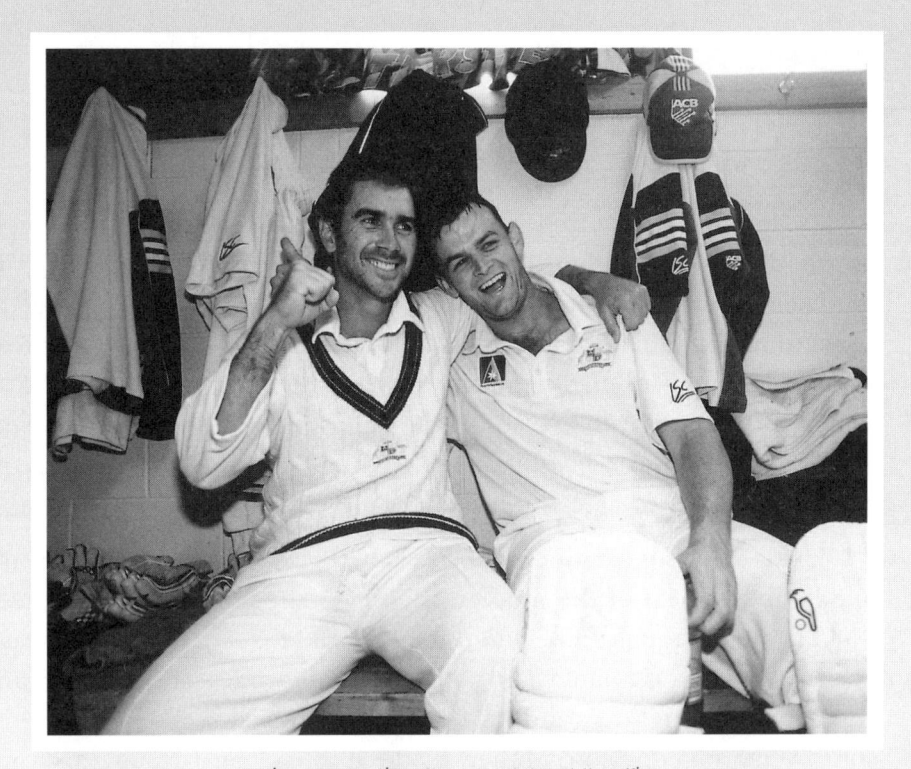

With my mate Gilly after a good day at the office.

would say to me 'C'mon let's bat well for the next seven minutes and get to 2.30' while I would come back with 'Seven runs and we only need 140.' Our different approaches kept us going individually and ultimately as a partnership.

Today really was like living a dream. Playing in a winning Test match for your country is always a joy, but playing a big part in winning a Test match for your country is unbelievable. The pride on our captain and coach's faces was inspiring as we entered the changing room. Their pride in the team's performance made the moment even more significant than that of a normal victory.

The one other thing I remember so clearly about this victory was the feeling during the lunch break today. Our teammates were so optimistic and excited that it wouldn't have seemed right to leave the field without having won this Test match and Test series. The feeling within the team was one of unwavering belief in the result.

Without being able to read into the future, I believe that this run chase could turn out to be a huge stepping stone for this team. If the Australian team has had a perceived weakness in the past, it has been in chasing a target. A big step was taken today to dispel this theory. By winning here, we will now feel that we can win anywhere.

Test No.4 Third Test v. Pakistan
PERTH 26–28 NOVEMBER 1999

As happens so often these days, controversies off the field overshadowed the lead-up to this game. Before the match, the 'can't bowl, can't throw' controversy erupted. Many people jumped to the conclusion that Shane Warne had been the one to say those words of teammate Scott Muller during the Hobart Test; this despite a lack of evidence except that the voice on the tape sounded like his. Because it supposedly involved a headline-grabber like Warney the story took off, yet it was really the biggest non-event of all time.

Firstly if Warney had said it, so what? Players say things out in the middle in the heat of the moment that later they might like to retract. But it is a tense, tough game and things get said that are not really meant. For that reason, if Shane had said it he would have been honest and courageous enough to admit it. But his word was not taken and so the controversy raged. Scott Muller made it worse by virtually accusing Warney when he spoke into the stump microphone during the tour game against India in Brisbane. Who do I think said it? Joe the cameraman. Does anyone really think Kerry Packer would risk his licence by allowing the Nine network to use Joe as a scapegoat and lie to the Australian public on *A Current Affair*? I don't think so.

The Pakistanis were probably never much of an opposition in this Test. They were prone to collapsing under the disappointment of playing well in the first two Tests and coming away with two defeats. With little to play for in Perth they were vulnerable. The momentum was with Australia and that is how the game panned out.

Before this match we brought Brett Lee into the 12. The word was out that Brett was an exciting prospect, very fast with enormous potential. He'd bowled well in the Prime Minister's game against India and seemed to have something special. I had a few reservations because although he was bowling fast he had not been getting many batsmen out. There was a big push for this kid but I was not sure that he was ready. After

Allan Border's Big Picture

the PM's game we decided to give him a taste of the set-up in the Australian side. Stephen was very keen for Brett to play in Perth, but we held him back. Damien Fleming had been bowling brilliantly since Zimbabwe and we saw no real need to change. Michael Kasprowicz was also in very good form and we thought he deserved a chance, especially because he had experience of Perth and could do the into-the-wind job for us. Kasper did what was required of him by taking seven wickets in the match.

Michael Kasprowicz celebrates one of the seven wickets he took in the third Test at the WACA.

The highlights from Perth were the continued good form of Glenn McGrath, Langer and Fleming, an underrated player and in this period often our best bowler. The bonus was the return to form of Ricky Ponting. After three ducks in a row, Ricky got an early half volley on leg stump and opened his account by clipping it for 4. All of a sudden the bad run was over and the form he had been showing in the nets appeared in the middle. His 197 was a superb innings and the beginning of a stretch of excellent form.

Flem is a good sort of bloke to have in the team. He is fairly quiet but he has a dry sense of humour and often comes out with funny lines in the dressing room. He does not get too carried away with things and in the past couple of years has bowled very well in most games. I remember Sachin Tendulkar saying to me a couple of years ago that he thought Flem was a very dangerous bowler and that is as good a compliment as you could hope for. After shoulder injuries early in his career Flem built himself up there and then began to take great strides towards becoming a world-class fast bowler. The word 'fast' is used advisedly. Although Glenn McGrath argues that speedguns do not do justice to tall fast bowlers, Flem has often been measured as our fastest bowler, at least before Brett Lee arrived. Whatever the correct readings are, Flem has been a very useful member of what is a very fine team.

Australia went on to win this game easily, by an innings and 20 runs to take the series 3–0, although it was a closer contest than that scoreline indicated. The critical thing was that Australia won the important moments far more often and deserved the victory. The team's pledge to try to win all six Tests in Australia that summer was halfway to fulfilment. With the win in Harare, it was now four from four and confidence was high.

Before the Perth Test we had the Warne–Muller controversy and after it the news that the umpires and match referee had sent a videotape of Shoaib Akhtar off to the ICC illegal deliveries panel. With the use of slow-motion replays you could mount cases against a lot of bowlers. Shoaib may have a chink in his action when he tries for extra pace. Because he runs in so fast things can fall out of sync pretty easily and that's when the kink in his action might appear. But generally I think his action is fine.

Justin's View...   *Third Test v. Pakistan*

25–28.11.99   Overwhelmed by the incredible public support after the Hobart Test match I was determined to finish the Pakistan tour with another big performance on my home ground. This motivation was enhanced by the focus within the team to beat the Pakistanis three-nil in the series. Our goal before the match was to play tough, disciplined and clinical cricket. As with the run-chasing theory, Stephen was particularly keen to dispel any theory of an inability to perform in so-called 'dead rubber' Test matches.

Therefore, when the last Pakistan wicket fell on Sunday afternoon, it would be fair to say this overall team goal was perfectly achieved. With Michael Kasprowicz and Brett Lee coming into the squad, we went about our business from the moment the skipper lost the toss on Friday morning. Although the pitch looked hard and flat, I wasn't unhappy to have seen Wasim Akram win the toss and bat first. Traditionally there is always some additional life in the WACA turf early in a game and, paired with the steep bounce, it is always challenging batting during the first session.

Coming to the WACA is always a formidable task for any opposition. The extra pace and bounce is foreign to most other surfaces in the world so it invariably takes time to adapt to the differing conditions. As with the Aussies visiting the spinning pitches in the subcontinent, the overseas batsmen must find it nerve-wracking when they see the first ball flying past their ears off a reasonable length.

From ball one of the Test match we were fired up and with the opportunity to beat one of the most talented teams in the world three nil and we went hard at our opponents. Continuing their great form, Flem and Pigeon bowled superbly, as did Kasper who has plenty to prove after his roller-coaster last 12 months of international cricket. He is a fantastic team man who was a popular re-selection.

After bowling out the visitors cheaply, it was a wonderful feeling spending time in the middle of my home ground with my supporters encouraging me like I have never seen before. Having a partnership with Ricky was almost as much fun as it was with Gilly only a few days before at Bellerive. Although he had made three consecutive ducks, Punter had the faith of all his teammates when he joined me at the crease. He has been hitting the ball sweetly in the nets since arriving home from Zimbabwe, so we all knew a big score was just around the corner.

His effort was sensational as he smashed the Pakistani attack to every advertising board on the ground. His cutting and pulling were awesome, as were his drives in front of the wicket. Batting with him was a buzz, as again, one of my teammates punished the

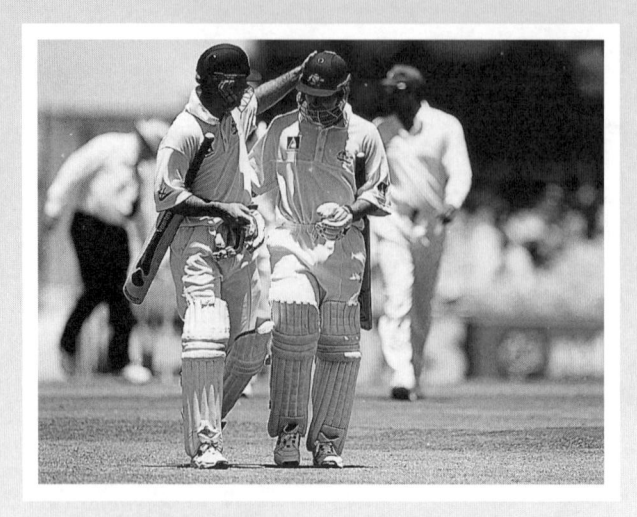

*Ricky Ponting and Justin Langer leave the field
after a record-breaking partnership against Pakistan in Perth.*

opponent while I lent him support at the other end. Experience can't be purchased and I truly think my experience at the WACA gave me a huge advantage when it came my turn to bat. Besides one-too-many hook shots against Akhtar, I was in batting heaven playing on the pitch that has taught me so many lessons about playing fast bowling.

With a lead that must have been as daunting as dental surgery for the beleaguered Pakistanis, our bowlers finished off the job with a ruthless display of fast and leg-spin bowling. In another disciplined display, our ambition of winning the first three Test matches of the summer became reality early on Sunday afternoon.

After all of the pre-match preparation, every player in the team feels fantastic about this result. For John Buchanan in his first series as coach and Steve Waugh in his first series as captain in Australia, the summer could not have started better. Sticking rigidly to our game plan from ball one, it was very fulfilling seeing everything fall perfectly into place.

Although everyone was ready to celebrate in grand style, our new coach called a meeting at the hotel before the party began. Going against tradition of an after-match free-for-all celebration, the half-hour review of the series made us all realise that there is plenty of room for improvement. This is very exciting as we have just beaten Pakistan three-nil and yet we all know we can play a lot better. Exciting times lie ahead in Australian cricket!

Test No.5 First Test v. India
ADELAIDE 10–14 DECEMBER 1999

India's first visit in eight years had created a lot of expectation, especially with the best batsman in the world, Sachin Tendulkar, coming in his maturity. The last time he had faced Australia he belted us—in India in 1998. But back then Shane Warne's shoulder was about to collapse. This time Warney was fit and bowling well again. It was going to be a great contest between two masters, not to mention McGrath, Fleming, Rahul Dravid, Sourav Ganguly and Anil Kumble.

Shane Warne smashes a ball to the boundary as he races to 86 runs off only 100 balls at Adelaide.

Another fine drive by Steve Waugh.

Michael Kasprowicz stayed in the Australian side because of his seven wickets in Perth and the fact that he deserved another crack at India after taking five wickets in an innings in the third Test in India last time. Australia batted first and were in trouble at 4 for 52 before another of those rearguard middle order partnerships turned things around. This time it was Ponting and the usual suspect, Steve Waugh. They took the score to 291 before Ponting was out for 125.

Steve went on to make 150, giving him that world record for hundreds against all opponents that his brother Mark missed in Harare. Shane Warne repeated his batting effort from Brisbane by making another 86, this time off 100 balls with 13 fours and a six. Australia's 441 after having been 4 for 52 underlined the depth and strength in the batting. Not everyone is in form at the same time but there always seem to be one or two batsmen who can make big scores and take the side out of trouble.

India replied with 285 and at times looked quite good. But our bowlers, especially McGrath and Warne, applied tremendous pressure. As hard as they fought, the Indian batsmen could not break free. Greg Blewett battled hard for 88 in the second innings but never looked comfortable. Set 396 to win, India collapsed under the pressure to be all out for 110 and give Australia a win by 285 runs. Flem took 5 for 30 in a wonderful display of sharp swing bowling. Again, Warney was in the headlines the next morning, for dropping a catch at first slip, which would have given Flem his second hat trick in Test cricket.

This match followed a predictable pattern. India's bowling was exposed as a little thin, its batting as too dependent on Tendulkar and the top order as too vulnerable to short fast bowling on bouncy pitches. In Adelaide the Australians bowled well to Tendulkar and even though he was out in both innings to debatable decisions I could see reasons for those decisions. So, five wins from five and a definite psychological edge established over the Indians early in a three-game series.

Justin's View...   *First Test v. India*

9.12.99 After an eventful couple of weeks, it is back into Test match action when the first ball leaves the hand of Pigeon or Ghekko Srinath at the Adelaide Oval tomorrow morning. Since the final day in Hobart, life has been unbelievable for yours truly. With two winning Test matches, two centuries and so much public support, it has been overwhelming. It has been a dream come true, a dream I am looking forward to continue living for as long as I possibly can.

While life has been hectic and we have all had some success over the past month, the past counts for nothing when our series with the talented Indian cricket team kicks off at 11 a.m.. The Indians are something of an unknown quantity because most of us have had little or no Test cricket battle time with our new opponents. Only two of this Indian squad have toured Australia in the past, so our preparation has been a little less thorough than for other teams.

In the one-day arena our countries have met on numerous occasions, leaving us with memories of limited over techniques and temperaments rather than a detailed analysis of their Test cricket strengths and weaknesses. Obviously the great Sachin Tendulkar will be an important player in this three-Test contest, but we will also target the gifted Ganguly, Dravid and Ramesh when we have the ball in our hands. In the bowling department Srinath, Prasad and Kumble are world class performers who are sure to keep our top order on its toes.

There is no better place to play Test cricket than the Adelaide Oval. From the beautifully picturesque ground where the cathedral overlooks the proceedings, to the manicured green outfield and perfect playing surface, Adelaide Oval is a favourite to many past and present players. There is always a special atmosphere about this Test match, which makes it one of the most memorable and enjoyable matches in the calendar year. Curator Les Burdett deserves all the credit and accolades that come his way as his ground is the perfect setting for any game of cricket, particularly the annual Adelaide Test match.

At training this morning, there was a special feeling within the team. The recent series against Pakistan has been a huge confidence booster for everyone involved and while there is still room for improvement we are looking to continue providing the Australian public with plenty to cheer about. The battle of Warney and Sachin promises to be a beauty, but I must admit I can't wait to see the little Indian master lock horns with Glenn McGrath, who is the best fast bowler currently playing the game. This duel could be one of the defining contests of this exciting Test match series against our largely untested opponents.

The Dominators

Justin's View... *Day 1 First Test v. India*

10.12.99 Do you call it an escape act or do you put it down to a very strong team, which has the ability to find something extra when the going gets tough? At 4/52, we were staring at a first session of play that could have put the Indians in a position of strength in this first Test. Fortunately for the Aussies, our durable skipper Steve Waugh and his gifted partner Ricky Ponting at first played with grit, before blossoming to compile an awesome partnership in the second and third sessions of play.

Statistics will tell you this was the fourth Test in a row in which we have had a 200 partnership in an innings. This is a fantastic feat for any cricket team as partnerships are the foundation for the success of any outfit. In our preparation, we regularly talk about the importance of partnerships with both the bat and the ball. This in mind, it is no coincidence we have won our last four Test matches.

Steve Waugh's century today made him the first player in the history of the game to have scored a ton against every Test-playing nation in the world. This is an outstanding achievement. There is no doubting the incredibly tough and disciplined mind of the Iceman.

Steve Waugh accepts the applause of the crowd at the Adelaide Oval as he reaches his 100.

As you can imagine, he was thrilled with this milestone, punching the air like a champion boxer after another autograph cricket stroke through mid-wicket. His mastery with the bat is the best in world cricket as he goes from record to record with every passing month.

If not for an unfortunate and unnecessary run out late this afternoon, both Punter and Tugga could be on the way to a double century when play recommences in the morning. As always, the Adelaide Oval was looking a perfect picture today, making it the ideal setting for their brilliant partnership. While both guys would have loved to be walking out together in the morning, the skipper will no doubt continue to grind the visitors into the ground.

Ricky's second consecutive century was brilliant with his straight driving being the feature of today's knock. Isn't it funny how quickly fortunes change in this complex and intriguing game that we play. Only two weeks ago Punter was coming out to bat at the WACA after three consecutive ducks. Now two innings later, he has added another two Test centuries to his name. This is why we play the game because it certainly has a way of keeping you on your toes all the time.

Justin's View...

Day 2 First Test v. India

11.12.99 Another century and a half for our well-decorated skipper, a swashbuckling 86 from our vice-captain and a superbly disciplined effort in the field has us on top in this first Test against India. On a day of tough Test cricket, we hold the upper hand on an Adelaide Oval pitch that is sure to deteriorate over the next three days. Already a few balls have started to stay a little low, a factor sure to play to our advantage as this game progresses. With 441 invaluable runs on the board, batting will become more difficult as this dry pitch starts to crack and crumble.

India will always feel a sense of confidence while their captain and batting genius Sachin Tendulkar is at the crease, but we know that a game does not revolve around one player alone. Our very own superstars McGrath and Warne were superb in keeping the little 'master blaster' quiet today. His tactics of batting slowly were a little surprising, although I can only guess he knows exactly what he is doing. While he is still at the wicket India are dangerous, so one of our main objectives will be to remove him as quickly as possible in the morning. If Glenn and Shane can continue with today's brilliant form, I get the feeling something is going to happen on day three tomorrow.

Always an important day in any Test match, day three is like the third quarter of an Aussie Rules football match. Early wickets in the morning will have our momentum running like a steam train towards another Test victory, while a Tendulkar-led partnership will have the Indians clawing their way back into this game. It is going to be a tough day tomorrow but in front of this festive Adelaide crowd, whatever happens it is going to be a lot of fun.

The Adelaide Oval is the perfect setting for any game of cricket, particularly the annual Adelaide Test match.

The Dominators

Justin's View... *Day 3 First Test v. India*

12.12.99 As a batsman there is nothing worse than getting out just before stumps. Not only is it disappointing for the batsman involved, but it also puts the team under unwelcome pressure. This in mind, I was as dark as an African night sky when Anil Kumble got one of his fast leg-spinners to bounce viciously with only eight balls remaining for the day. Out for 38 and surely leaving behind a big score on one of my favourite cricket grounds in the world.

Talking of leg-spinners, our lovable rogue bowled as well as I have seen since his major shoulder operation. He was fizzing the ball today as he used to in his glory days. It almost looks as though he is growing in confidence with every innings as he storms towards Dennis Lillee's wicket-taking record of 355 Test poles. While he has been bowling consistently since his operation, Warney has been getting that extra spin this summer which has made him the greatest bowler of this era. With Shane bowling like a magician and Glenn McGrath at his best, we are always going to be tough to beat for any opposition.

Tomorrow we will be looking to bat the visitors out of the match before throwing everything at them in the afternoon. Admittedly we are in a very strong position in this game but we will take nothing for granted until the last wicket is taken. Any team which has Sachin Tendulkar leading the way can never be taken lightly, so there is still plenty of work to be done in the next two days.

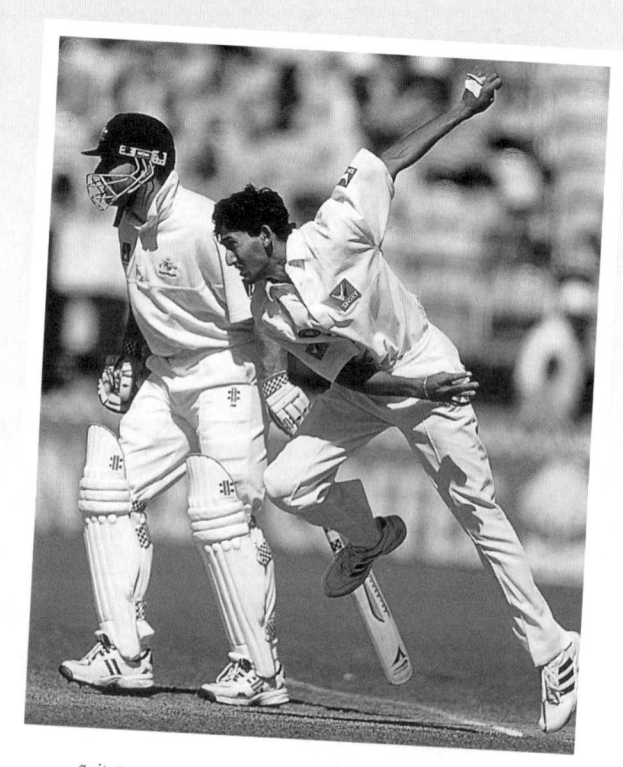

Ajit Agarkar sends down another thunderbolt to the Australian batsman at Adelaide Oval.

Justin's View...

Day 5 First Test v. India

14.12.99 That makes it five in a row!

After setting the visitors an intimidating target on a deteriorating pitch, they were always likely to struggle. Thanks to another typically disciplined effort from our four bowlers, we were able to celebrate another lunchtime victory here in Adelaide. With five consecutive Test victories and room for improvement, the feeling within the camp is very exciting. We are playing great cricket and are well on the way to reaching our pre-season target of an undefeated Australian summer.

The only thing that went wrong today was a dropped catch from our superstar leg-spinner and vice-captain Shane Warne who was visibly disappointed by his rare mistake. In typical fashion, Flemo laughed off the error of judgement even if it robbed him of his second hat trick in Test cricket. By three o'clock this afternoon, all was forgotten as we sang one of the best *Under the Southern Cross I stand...* that I can remember. It is amazing how a victory can eliminate any personal disappointments. In fact, at the end of the day this is why we play the game. The sweet taste of team triumph is as contagious and attractive as any personal glory.

Looking ahead and there has been a lot of talk about the form of Mark Waugh over the last few days. Having been through the same media scrutiny recently I can sympathise with what he is going through. With the team playing so well, I truly believe it is only a matter of time before Junior comes good with the bat. He is possibly the most gifted player in the team who is just as likely to come out on Boxing Day and smash another elegant century just like he did three Test matches ago in Brisbane. Amazingly, the frame of mind of Mark is fantastic. While Steve is known as the Iceman for his constantly cool exterior, Junior might have to go down as the Iceman Mk II as he doesn't seem to be overly concerned about his perceived form slump. In fact, like any champion, he is confident that runs are around the corner. He will probably get them when we really need them in the next two Test matches.

Blewey in repose at Adelaide while waiting for the next Indian batsman to appear.

Justin's View... *Christmas Day*

25.12.99 As a youngster, I have vivid memories of watching my heroes playing Test cricket on Boxing Day in Melbourne. Tattooed into my brain is an image of Dennis Lillee storming in to bowl the last ball of the day to the great Viv Richards. As we sat glued to the television set, we couldn't help but jump for joy as one of Australia's greatest fast bowlers sent the ball crashing into the West Indian champion's off stump. Every Christmas holiday was taken up playing backyard Test matches and watching my heroes in the baggy green performing on the hallowed MCG turf.

Now as a player, every opportunity I have had to be involved in a Boxing Day Test is like another dream come true. With a traditionally massive and appreciative Melbourne crowd, the feeling out on the ground is very uplifting. The noise is like nothing I have experienced before, exept maybe a Jimmy Barnes concert at the Entertainment Centre. The atmosphere is incredible and with the team playing so well at present, we hope to repay the support with another enthralling display of Test match cricket.

It has been a fun few days for the team, with everyone's family here in Melbourne for the whole Christmas week. Last night we had a fantastic Christmas Eve party at Warney's house. Everyone, including all of the kids, enjoyed a great night, with Australian sporting legends Mervyn Hughes, Sam Newman and Rexy Hunt joining in the festivities.

In every State, we have invited different sporting heroes to join us for our team dinners and last night it was Sam, Rex and Merv, who helped inspire the boys for the upcoming Test. Pat Rafter, four of the 'Invincibles', Rechelle Hawkes, Kim Hughes and Rachel Harris have joined us during the summer as an initiative by our skipper. It is an excellent idea as it is always interesting to hear from other elite sportsmen and women about their lives in a different field.

Steve Waugh is congratulated by Damien Fleming after reaching his century, on day three of the Test v. Zimbabwe at Harare.

RIGHT: A beautiful drive by Steve Waugh produces four more runs on day two of the Test match in Zimbabwe.

BELOW: A triumphant Australian team with the Southern Cross Trophy, after winning the one-off Test match against Zimbabwe at Harare.

BOTTOM RIGHT: Steve Waugh, the second highest Australian Test match run scorer, recovers after yet another test match century.

It is not often that a wicketkeeper is seen bowling, but Ian Healy did just that during the tour match against the Zimbabwe President's XI at Bulawayo. Note the expressive spread of his left hand!

LEFT: Scott Muller is presented with the baggy green by Bill Brown of the Invincibles before the first Test – Australia v. Pakistan at the Gabba Brisbane.

BELOW: Scott Muller takes his first Test wicket.

OPPOSITE TOP: Shoaib Akhtar appeals for a wicket as the unconcerned Australian batsmen take a quick run.

ABOVE LEFT: Michael Slater loses his balance as he tries to avoid a bouncer from Shoaib Akhtar at the Gabba, Brisbane.

ABOVE RIGHT: Adam Gilchrist hits another boundary in the first Test v. Pakistan.

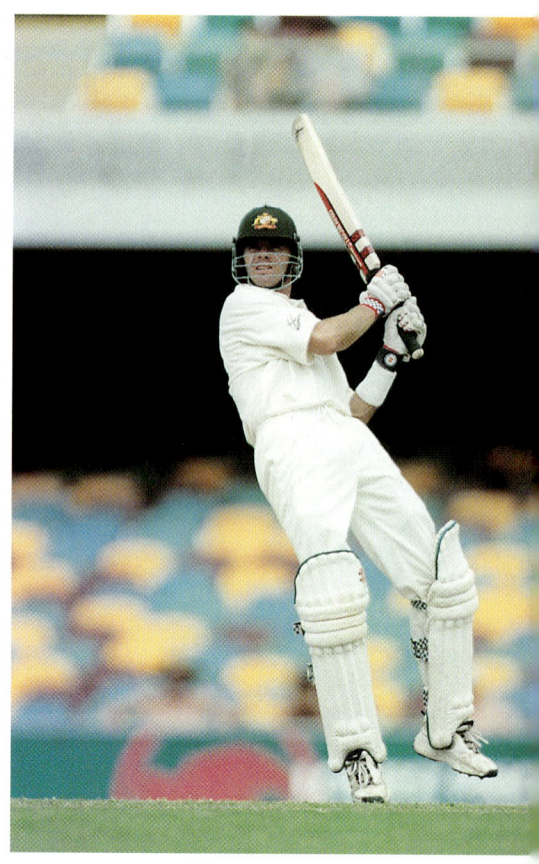

ABOVE LEFT: First Test – Australia v. Pakistan, Michael Slater acknowledges the applause of the crowd as he reaches his century.

ABOVE RIGHT: Another stylish shot by Greg Blewett sends the ball racing to the boundary.

RIGHT: Greg Blewett and Michael Slater relax in the dressing room after the victory over Pakistan in Brisbane.

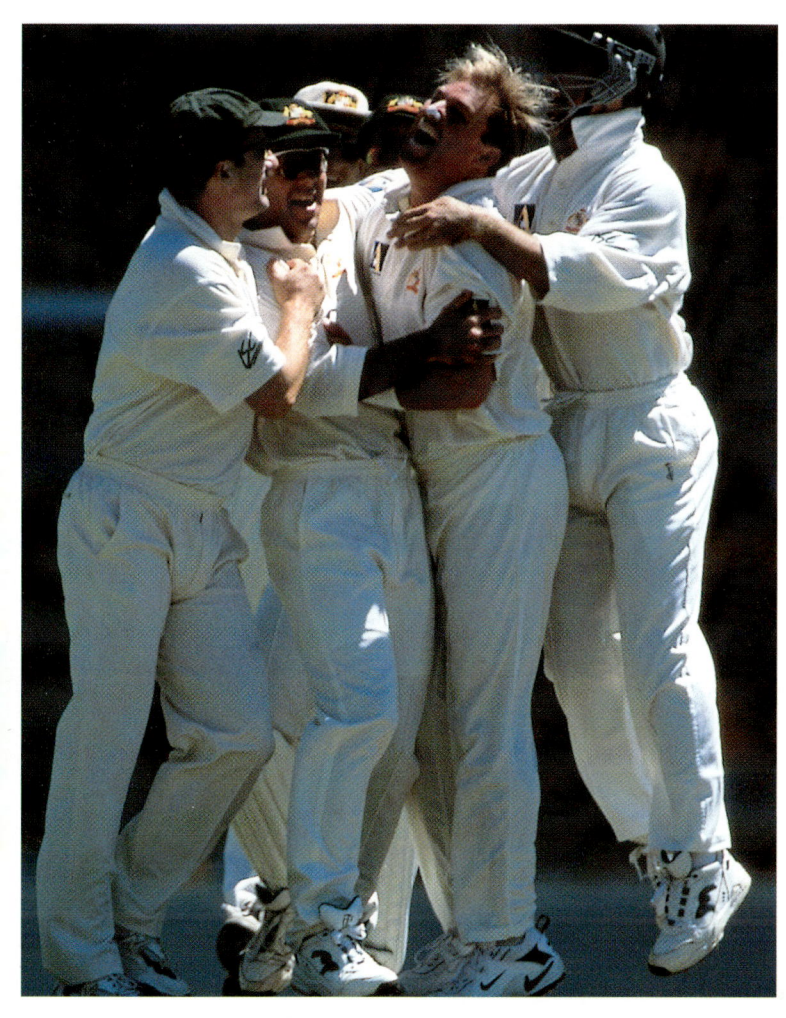

LEFT: The Australian team celebrate another wicket by Shane Warne at Brisbane.

BELOW LEFT: The Pakistani team leave the field as a massive hailstorm hits the Gabba during the first Test v. Pakistan.

BELOW RIGHT: Shoaib Akhtar looks ruefully at the stumps after being bowled by Damien Fleming.

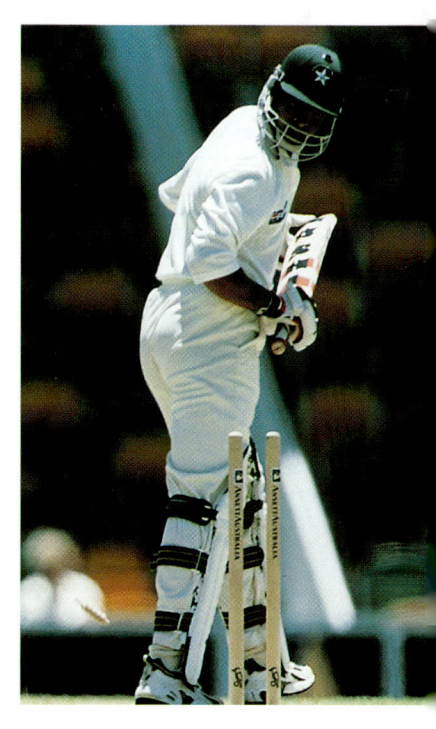

RIGHT Scott Muller follows through after sending down another fast ball during the second Test v. Pakistan at Bellerive Oval, Hobart.

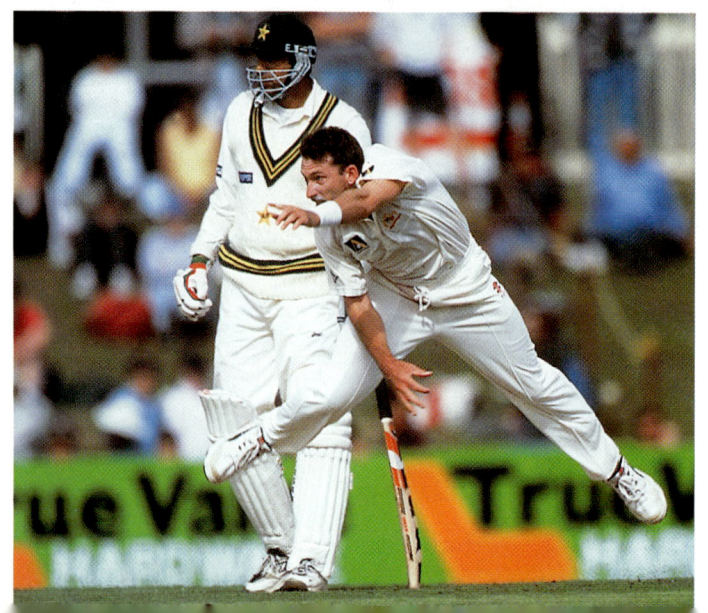

ABOVE: A general view of Bellerive Oval, Hobart, one of Australia's most attractive cricket grounds.

LEFT: Damien Fleming appears to be appealing for a wicket as part of his natural bowling action in the second Test v. Pakistan at Hobart.

Today it was a huge Christmas lunch together at the hotel (with Father Christmas and all) followed by training at the MCG. Admittedly it took a while to get going after lunch, but after a decent warm-up we had a productive session that has us all charged up for the morning.

Although the final 11 won't be announced until the morning I am sure that if Brett Lee is included to make his debut he will be ready for the challenge. Having played against this NSW fireball in a Pura Milk Cup game earlier this week I can testify that this young man is very, very impressive. He reminds me of a youthful Jason Gillespie in that he not only bowls very fast but he also looks to have phenomenal control of where the ball is going. Add to this an ability to swing the ball late both ways and the ingredients are all there for a very promising career for Mr Brett Lee.

Apart from his bowling ability Binger is also a very affable young man who looks hungry for answers to how he can be the fastest bowler in the world. He is receptive and respectful and looks likely to become an important part of the future of Australian cricket. His inclusion in the twelve is a further indication of the depth and strength of the Australian cricket stables, which continue to produce future champions. As I have said throughout this summer, this is a very exciting era to be involved with the Australian cricket team.

Whatever way the selectors decide to go we will soon find out, but, I have to say, the media circle suggests Michael Kasprowicz will be the very unlucky man who might miss out on playing this match. He is an integral part of this team, who gives his all every time he has a cricket ball in his hand. Being a different type of bowler from Brett Lee, it is encouraging to have a selection dilemma as the selectors have for tomorrow. Either way it can only be a major positive as both bowlers are potential match-winners.

Let's hope the Melbourne weather is as kind to us as the support from the cricket-loving supporters, as we look to win our sixth consecutive Test match.

Justin enjoys Christmas Day in Melbourne with family and friends.

Test No.6 Second Test v. India

MELBOURNE 26–30 DECEMBER 1999

Time for Brett Lee. Leading up to this game Brett had blitzed Western Australia in a Shield game in Perth. Geoff Marsh, now a selector, had seen that performance and sent word east that we had something special. We were on a winning roll and were playing a team whose batsmen did not handle fast bowling that well. Brett came into the side at the perfect time and made the most of the opportunity with a near-perfect debut.

After Australia made 405 with solid contributions from Slater, Ponting and Gilchrist, Brett bowled very fast to finish with 5 for 47 in his first innings in Test cricket, the equivalent of a century on debut. It looked then as if we had discovered another star player just when the team was playing as well as at any time in recent memory. What a bonus to be able to add express pace to a team that already had a great seam bowler in McGrath, a clever swing bowler in Fleming and the man many regarded as the greatest spinner of all time.

Tendulkar made a brilliant 116 but the next best score was 31. Not good enough against a ruthless team like Australia which rarely misses a chance to take control. Some teams play well before making a critical mistake at a vital moment. The Australians tend not to do that. Instead they work away, put the opposition under pressure and then, when they are looking vulnerable, apply the killer blow. It might only take one great delivery or a catch like Mark Waugh's in Hobart for the game to swing Australia's way. The best sides operate like that and the Australian team is undoubtedly the best in the world at present.

Tendulkar let rip at one stage in that innings as he began to run out of partners. I thought at the time that he might have made more of an impact in the series had he played like that more often. He gave the impression he would rather not be captain and that that responsibility inhibited his batting. Indian cricketers are treated like gods at home and the pressure on someone like Tendulkar is immense. It was no great surprise when he stood down from the captaincy soon after returning from Australia.

Allan Border's Big Picture

Tendulkar made 52 in the second innings as India chased 376. Steve Waugh showed what confidence he had in his bowlers by declaring the second innings at 5 for 208. In earlier days we might have ensured we set that psychological barrier of 400, but not any more.

On the final day Warne and Tendulkar provided an hour or so of brilliant cricket, a fascinating contest between two great players. Tendulkar came down the pitch to Warne and hit some great drives but Warne kept his cool and gradually worked his man into a vulnerable position. It took a few overs but eventually Warne deceived Tendulkar with an innocuous-looking top-spinner. A lesser bowler might have crumbled under the pressure after a couple of those fiercesome drives, but Warne was good enough to draw on his skills and tactical nous to lure the great batsman into a trap. That final top spinner might have looked a nothing ball but it was the perfect delivery at the perfect moment.

Australia took the series 2–0 with one to play and overall had won six from six. A win in the third Test in Sydney and they would have achieved their aim of winning all six Tests of the home summer.

Brett Lee is on fire as he dismisses Agarkar to take his 4th wicket in Test cricket.

The Dominators

Justin's View...   *Day 1 Second Test v. India*

26.12.99 Although yours truly hardly troubled the scorers today, it was a thrill to have walked out into the middle of the MCG for the first day of this second Test against India. The Boxing Day Test is arguably the most watched Test match of the calendar year because of the great Australian tradition behind the event. Just being in Melbourne is a buzz at this time of the year. Moving up from the traditional backyard Christmas Test match at home, to the big league in the centre of the Melbourne Cricket Ground is unbelievable.

After last year's rain abandoned Boxing Day, fears of a repeat this year hung over the awesome stadium while the black clouds hovered above. The 50,000 spectators, 24 players, two umpires and heavens knows how many supporters on their couches at home sighed with relief as the morning rain cleared from the grey skies. A break in the persistent, early rain allowed the game to start just after an earlier-than-usual lunch break. While we were looking to bowl first if we had won the toss, I don't believe this was the worst toss to lose. Sure we had to work hard against the new ball but as it has turned out, we are in an excellent position to take hold of this game.

It was as much a relief as anything else to see Junior scoring some runs. A great player like him is very important to the balance of any team and I always felt it was just a matter of time before he broke the recent shackles. He played with his usual elegance before falling to a ball from the rapidly improving Argarkar. His partnership with Slats has the team feeling happy with the day's result.

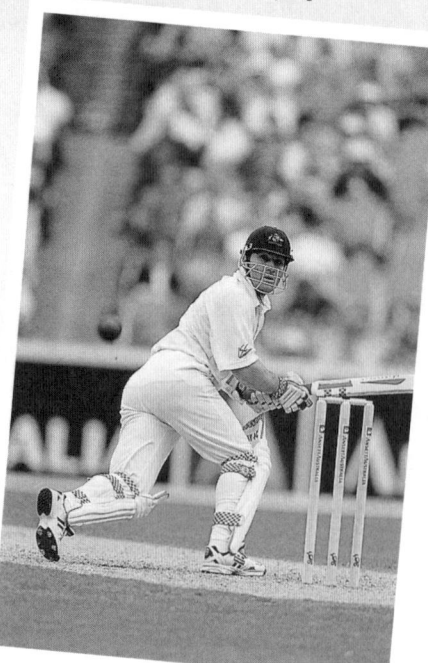

Slats (above) in partnership with Junior helped put the Australian team into a winning position.

While it was frustrating not to have played a full day of cricket, it was more positive than last season's abandoned day's play. With Warney determined to break Dennis Lillee's record on his home turf, the fact that we have batted first improves his prospects in this game. On a wearing pitch, our great blond 'leggie' is a deadly proposition, even for the Indians who love playing spin bowling. The next few days promise to be very exciting at the MCG.

Justin's View...
Day 3 Second Test v. India

28.12.99 Standing in the middle of the breathtaking MCG, I couldn't help but reflect on the air of greatness you sense on the lush outfields of one of the great sports stadiums of the world. As the drama of this second Test match unfolded in front of my eyes, it was exciting being a part of the battle between several of the modern game's best players.

From the member's end of the ground Glenn McGrath steamed in and bowled with the aggression and determination of a bull with the veritable red rag in front of his eyes. At the Great Southern Stand end, our blond superstar 'leggie' spun a web of controlled destruction that has him a sneeze away from Dennis Lillee's Australian wicket-taking record.

If this wasn't enough pressure for the Indians, the new kid on the block, Brett 'Binger' Lee, hit the international cricket world like a fierce tornado, taking five wickets in his first outing in Test cricket. His pace was ferocious and his direction exceptional, considering his lack of first class experience. From short leg, I gained far greater pleasure watching our latest speedster in action than I did facing him at the WACA a fortnight ago. When you have a bowler of Brett's pace and potential, it is hard to keep the smile off your face as you watch the opposition batsmen jumping around the crease like a team of firewalkers. He is an exhilarating and talented quick who bowled as fast in this Test match as I have seen since Shoaib Akhtar let loose before Christmas.

In my view, the introduction of Brett to our attack makes us a daunting opponent for any team. Like the West Indian attacks of the past, it is pure pressure for any visiting batsman. McGrath's accuracy, Fleming's swing, Warney's brilliance and Bingers' pace and aggression make scoring runs as tough as doing a bungee jump over the freeway. It is scary, it is uncomfortable and it is more a matter of hard work than fun.

Considering that Michael Kasprowicz, Jason Gillespie and Stuart MacGill, among others, are waiting in the wings, the depth of Australian cricket is outstanding, not only for the players but also for every Aussie supporter out there.

a happy Brett Lee faces the camera after taking five wickets in his first Test match.

The Dominators

Justin's View... *Day 5 Second Test v. India*

30.12.99 The threat of rain looked like it could have stolen our opportunity for a sixth straight Test victory today. With a few climatic nerves drifting through the changing room over the last few rain-interrupted days, the result looked like it might be out of our control. Thanks, though, to a supportive weather god and more wonderful contributions from every member of this team we are now two-nil up in this series. Whether it was Gilly, Punter or Junior with the bat yesterday, or our relentless bowling attack today, the fact is we are playing brilliant cricket together as a very united team. The sign of a good team is when someone always has the ability and desire to do the job required for his teammates. As we have seen this summer this is happening regularly with this squad of mates, rather than just teammates.

When Warney trapped a tired-looking Sachin Tendulkar lbw in front of his stumps, we all knew deep down that this would be our Test match. After a perfect spell of leg-spin bowling, even the great Indian batting master succumbed to the pressure. From my position at shortleg, it was apparent the Indian captain was feeling a little weary after what has been a tough tour for his team. He looked tired as he struggled to save his team from a second Test defeat. A number of times just before he was out he took a couple of deep breaths, a sign that he was really feeling the pinch. After the amount of time he has spent in the centre, plus the extra pressure of the captaincy, his downfall was a sign of the dwindling spirits of our opposition.

With wickets falling consistently throughout the day and only one wicket needed for victory after tea, the sun finally came out for the first time in this Test. Maybe this was symbolic of the confidence and inspiration oozing from this team. Finishing off this Test with the sun shining upon us was the perfect way to end what has been a happy Christmas week for the Australian Test team.

Again, *Under The Southern Cross...* helped finish off a wonderful Christmas celebration.

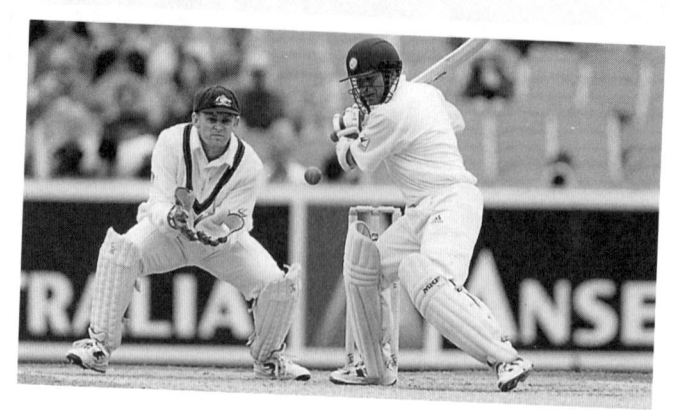

Adam Gilchrist behind the stumps as India's captain, Sachin Tendulkar, lines up a shot in the second Test.

Shane Warne congratulates newcomer Brett Lee on his fine bowling achievement at the MCG.

Justin's View... *Starting the New Millennium*

31.12.99 After a memorable second Test celebration at the Crown Casino last night, it was back on the road this morning for a short flight to Sydney. The symptoms of a heavy hangover were aggravated by the extras who had joined the Australian cricket team entourage. These extras included my two daughters, and Stephen's, Warney's, Buck's and Dave Misson's kids. After checking in to Quay West in Sydney, it was off for a light training run at the SCG. If you ask me, today's session was the perfect practice run. The batsmen had a bat against bowlers from around Sydney, and the rest of the time was spent stretching, relaxing and swimming in the SCG pool.

Obviously being 2–0 up in the series gives us the opportunity to lighten the load a little today. More importantly, the huge amount of cricket that we have played over the past five months helped convince Buck and Tugga to ease the load during today's training.

Because we had a Test match in two days' time, the team decided to stay in the hotel for a New Year's Eve celebration. This is not to say all the guys and their families didn't enjoy a festive night. The theme for the Millennium New Year's Eve was bad taste and while some of the boys stuck to their normal attire, Messrs Fleming, Buchanan, Misson, Warne and Langer were not to be outdone. With the magnificent Sydney fireworks outside the window of our manager Steve Bernard's suite, everyone had a ball as we celebrated the turn of the new century and the success of the summer thus far.

I hope that by the end of this week, Warney has broken the record, we have won this series three-nil and Mark Waugh has scored a hundred in his 100th Test match. Time will tell if all of this takes place, but I can say that at the end of day one the team is looking good again.

Test No.7 Third Test v. India

SYDNEY 2–4 JANUARY 2000

India have a terrible record away from home and by the way they played in Sydney, especially their fielding, it is not hard to see why. They all looked like they'd had enough and wanted to go home.

Glenn McGrath reclaimed the bowling spotlight in this game with five wickets in each innings, India making 150 in the first and 261 in the second. It was the usual perfect line and length from McGrath, great control and just enough movement to find the edge or sneak through the batsman's defence. Warne has been the inspirational bowler in the past decade and deserves great credit for helping the team reach its current high standing, but McGrath has never been far behind him in impact. Glenn is a great fast bowler and has been crucial in Australia's climb to the top. His ability to apply pressure to all batting line-ups consistently has given Australia a huge advantage in most matches.

Glenn is a very self-contained player. He worked with Dennis Lillee early in his career but these days he prefers to iron out any problems by himself. He is smart enough and knows his game well enough that it seems to take only a day or two, perhaps a glance at a video followed by a net session, and he has fixed any problem that might have crept into his action. The other notable thing about him is that he can remember in great detail every wicket he has taken. The guys reckon you can ask him to describe his 220th wicket and within a minute he'll have gone back to a landmark dismissal, say his 200th, worked forward to 220 and remembered it in detail. A little different from Merv Hughes, I'd have to say. But then it takes all kinds. Pigeon is brilliant at analysing batsmen, zeroing in on their weaknesses and working out a plan of how to bowl to exploit those weaknesses. Glenn McGrath can stand comparison with the other great Australian fast bowlers and his contribution to this team cannot be over-estimated.

Australia built a massive first innings lead of 402 thanks to a monumental 223 from Justin Langer and an undefeated 141 from Ricky

Ponting. Talk about cashing in! Ricky had gone from three ducks to his third hundred in as many Tests while Justin turned a scratchy half-century into a commanding career-best Test score. Ricky would miss the next Test series after injuring an ankle crashing into the SCG fence during a one-day international while Justin continued his improvement in New Zealand.

Three–nil to Australia over India, 6–0 for the summer and seven from seven including Harare. Steve Waugh's side was one win away from equalling the Australian record of eight successive Test wins, set by Warwick Armstrong's famous side of the 1920s.

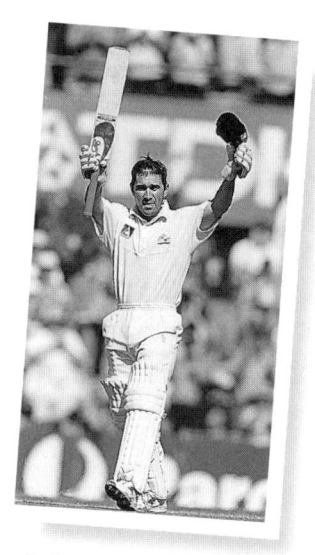

Justin celebrates another ton in the third Test v. India.

The Captain: Steve Waugh

Declaring earlier than he needed to in Melbourne was typical of the confidence Steve Waugh now brings to captaining Australia. In some ways he has been lying doggo. Because he was trying to establish himself in a struggling team, Steve was very quiet, perhaps a little introverted, in his early days. Then he was dropped and rebuilt his game with typical thoroughness. Similarly he began his captaincy career a little hesitantly. I talked to him in the West Indies early in 1999 when he was feeling his way. I remember saying to him that he had played so much cricket that he knew the game and therefore he should trust his instinct, go with his gut feeling more. He admitted he had been going by the book too much. For example, he had batted first in that series when the pitches had some juice in them on the first day. He batted because he had two leg spinners in the team and the theory is you want them to bowl last. But that theory did not work over there. That series ended 2–2 yet it probably should have been 4–0 to Australia. Now with the team on a roll and with 12 months experience in the job, Steve is a different man. He is very proactive in all his decision-making and he's confident enough to think laterally. He handles all the media duties really well and he has initiated a lot of changes. He has worked well with John Buchanan and between the two of them they have fine-tuned preparation to the point where during a tour they might not do much of a warm-up before a day's play, just the basics, which makes sense when you're playing that much cricket. Steve was part of the move for the guys to wear the baggy green caps in the first session in the field, then he took it further with the idea of wearing those skull caps, like the Victor Trumper cap of the early 1900s, in the Sydney Test against India. He has made the players more aware of the history of the game and the fact that they are part of that history.

Steve Waugh, determination in every step.

Steve has always played his cards close to his chest and been pretty quiet around the dressing room. But when Mark Taylor retired there was no doubt that Steve had the cricket brain and the will to win that you need to be a good captain. In the West Indies he might have been a little tense but later he allowed his personality to come through, especially his dry sense of humour. The World Cup was crucial to his development as a captain. We were all but out of the tournament and then he leads from the front and plays the greatest one-day innings of his life. We stay in the competition and go on to win the trophy. From there he has gone from strength to strength.

I like the fact that in Steve we have a captain who began his career in the bad old days, the mid-80s, when we weren't winning much at all. He can keep reminding the guys of how bad that was, that they don't want to go back to a similar situation. That experience added steel to his character. It will be interesting to see how they all cope when they go off the boil and cop some criticism because it will be new to them. Most of the team have come through in a successful era and are used to that. After New Zealand, Adam Gilchrist had played nine Tests for nine wins. You cannot ask him yet what it feels like to lose a Test match. With Steve's link to the last bad era he can keep the players' feet on the ground and keep pushing them. Certainly Steve inherited a talented team from Mark Taylor, but Tubby was such a successful and respected captain that he must have been a hard act to follow. Yet Steve has taken the team to even greater heights. That is an outstanding achievement.

One characteristic that has often distinguished Australian teams has been the commitment to the team cause. Other teams often give the impression they are a group of individuals pulled together by selectors and they could split apart at any time. The Indians are often like that. It cannot be easy when you might have three different languages being spoken on the field with some players not understanding others. I am not saying all Australian teams are perfectly united, but this one is very tight. They enjoy each other's company and are all prepared to work in the same direction. That unity builds a mental strength that helps you win. It is hard to measure what team spirit gives to a side, but if you are going into a game with that sort of camaraderie you are going in with an extra player.

Justin's View...   *Third Test v. India in Sydney*

2-4.1.00 Affectionately known as the 'Iceman', I have never seen our captain more nervous than when he told the team of his plan to help commemorate the first Test match of the century. Tugga was visibly apprehensive because he wasn't sure how his teammates would react to wearing the same skull caps as the team of 1900. His idea, backed by the ACB, was that we would be presented with replicas of the predecessors to our baggy greens to wear during this historic Test.

After getting over the shock of the new look, every player was thrilled and very proud of the captain's idea.

Before the game, the morning was much more hectic than the standard pre-game preparation, but it was an absolute privilege. Being presented with our new replica caps by the Prime Minister, Mr John Howard, was a great honour for the 12 guys in this first Australian Test team of the century. I felt a little sorry for Colin Miller who was the 13th man for the Test. Consequently, he missed out on receiving a cap but I guess that is part of missing selection in the final team. The caps are fantastic, and something I will cherish for the remainder of my days.

After the cap presentation, Mark Waugh was honoured for his outstanding achievement of 100 Test matches for Australia. Not one for speaking in public, he stole the show with a moving acceptance speech in front of his home crowd. Any player who reaches the century of Tests is a legend and Junior is certainly one of these.

Luckily, we have already won this series because had the team been less relaxed the events of the morning could have hampered some of the guys' preparations. As it was though, we had a very enjoyable lead-up to this historic third Test against India.

When it came to cricket time, Sachin Tendulkar won the toss, and surprisingly to some, decided to bat on a well-grassed and harder-than-usual Sydney pitch. Before the game, the New South Welshmen in the team had said they had never seen an SCG pitch like this in all their careers. With the pre-game hype and a chance to bowl on this lively surface, we were very happy about their decision. The chance of winning every Test of the summer plus the opportunity for Warney to break the record had 11 players in the middle of the SCG trembling with an adrenalin hit.

When the energy within the team is all going in the same direction, the pressure on the opposition is fierce. By stumps today the Indians were in all types of trouble. This didn't surprise me because such pressure can be suffocating for any opponent, no matter how talented they may be. Had there not been a long rain interruption, we could easily have been batting before stumps on day one.

As the rain was falling during the afternoon, Pat Farmer, Australia's truly inspirational ultra, ultra long distance runner visited the changing room. Having seen him

Allan Border's Big Picture

Brett celebrates the wicket
of Vijay Bharadwaj during the third Test
against India at the SCG Sydney.

on *This is Your Life* I was ecstatic to have a chance to meet the man face to face. What a fantastic bloke and Australian he is. Among other things, his message was that you could achieve whatever you set out to achieve by giving it your all and never giving up on your dream. He also shared with us his own motivational strategy: he gets through his immensely long runs by always picturing the finishing line in his mind. Seeing the finishing line helps him get through every tough moment along the way. Considering there would be plenty of tough times in his kind of sport, his message was very strong.

His words of motivation helped me get through a few tough periods during this Test. There were times early on day two when I felt terrible with the bat in my hand. During the struggle, I kept telling myself to hang in there, and by doing so there would be a Test century for the taking. My finishing line was initially the hundred, but that mark turned into a bigger and more productive innings as the words of Pat Farmer rang in my ears. Scoring a Test century is a marvellous feeling, especially when it goes a long way towards putting your team in a commanding position.

With the help of Punter, who has had a brilliant last four Test matches, I always knew this game wouldn't last very long when our opponents had to bat for a second time. When India took the new ball at the end of day two I was amazed at how much life remained in the pitch. If I was still playing and missing on 150 then I thought it was going to be more than a battle for the Indian batsmen who must be down in confidence.

My prediction came true when Glenn McGrath, Damien Fleming and Brett Lee exploited the lively pitch perfectly. When Sachin pushed an easy catch to me at cover, the game again was as good as over. With an extension of a half an hour on day three, we were able to clean up the Indian line-up and the Test match was ours in three days.

After winning six Tests this summer and seven now in succession, our celebration fitted the feat. At around 1.00 a.m. Punter led the team through *Under The Southern Cross....* Rather than the normal changing-room rendition, it was out into the centre of the SCG for a chance to sing our song for the last time this summer. With plenty to reminisce about, Punter gave us one of the best ever versions of our victory song which is a part of Australian cricket folklore.

This summer has been so much fun. The team is very close and very, very determined to win Test matches. John Buchanan has been brilliant, Steve Waugh inspiring and the rest of my teammates awesome in their individual and combined efforts. To be part of such a team is a privilege, an honour and a living dream come true. I only hope there are many more times like these to come.

Our goal at the start of the summer was to win every Test match. When Steve offered this challenge to the team in Brisbane in November, there were a few cautious glances around the room. Now, after the goal has been attained, there seems no reason why we have not just scratched the surface. Time will tell!

Allan Border's Big Picture

Shane Warne bowling at the third Test v. India at the SCG.

Ricky Ponting, Glenn McGrath and Justin Langer after the game
wearing their 1900s replica skull caps and enjoying a well-deserved beverage.

Justin's View...   *The NZ Tour, Continuing the Climb up the Ladder*

6.3.00 Touring can be pretty tough, especially for the guys who have wives and kids at home, but when you visit a place like New Zealand it is significantly easier to handle. Arriving in Auckland on Thursday night, it became quickly apparent that this tour is going to be just like travelling around Australia. Having been here seven years ago, I didn't remember how similar our two countries are. There isn't the cultural shock of armed bodyguards like Pakistan, or metal detectors in the hotel foyer like Colombo. Nor are there the social dilemmas of South Africa or the beggars on the streets of India. The air here in New Zealand is fresh and clean, as are the streets, parks and beautiful green countryside.

The five guys joining the one-day touring party couldn't have picked a better day to arrive as it happened to be the day New Zealand were rejoicing in the triumph of winning the 2000 America's Cup. The streets of Auckland were similar to the celebrations of New Year's Eve at Circular Quay in Sydney. There was much festivity and rejoicing with street parties erupting all over the city.

Touring can be tough, especially for the guys who have to leave wives and kids at home.

Unfortunately, the celebrations were not as joyous for the Australian touring party as the one-day team lost their last game of the six-match series. Although it was disappointing to lose their final contest of the tour, their efforts over the last three weeks have been nothing short of superb. For that matter, the performance of the one-day squad since they won the World Cup final on June 20 in London has been admirable. Walking into their change room when we arrived, there was a real sense of confidence and good humour as the boys rolled past their world-record achievement of 13 straight one-day victories.

It is strange coming into the tour late, but that is now accepted practice. Both teams understand the protocol and get on with their business, even if it is difficult for a few guys missing selection in both forms of the game. The business now for the Test squad is to prepare for the upcoming Test series where we have an opportunity to break a few records ourselves. So far, we have won seven Test matches in a row; it would be perfect to leave these closer shores with another three Test match victories under our belts. By playing our best cricket, there is no reason why this cannot be achieved. After the way we have played our Test cricket this summer, anything is possible.

Justin's View... *Preparation in New Zealand*

9.3.00 Our preparations kicked off during the last four days with a practice game against Northern Districts in Hamilton. On the same ground on which we will play the third Test match, all the team gained excellent centre-wicket practice. Throughout the game all the bowlers took a few wickets and worked on their rhythm and length for the first Test in Auckland.

Although our fast bowling brigade looks in good shape, you would not be a fast bowler for anything. If it isn't a back injury, it might be a shoulder problem, a stress fracture or a torn intercostal muscle. If you are Damien Fleming, it might also be your knees crying out for mercy and screaming for a break from the rigours of international cricket. After a gruelling schedule of one-day and Test cricket, Flemo is feeling the pinch, or at least his knees are giving him more trouble now than a grumpy mother-in-law.

While his injury is not permanent or overly serious, he will not be playing in the first Test starting at Eden Park in Auckland on Saturday. Naturally, he would love to have the new ball in his hand on Saturday morning, but everyone in charge has agreed that a week's break will be the best remedy for our experienced swing bowler.

With the Eden Park pitch likely to turn square, Flemo's unfortunate injury makes the job of the selectors a little easier. Colin Miller was set to play in this Test match anyway, so now Stephen, Shane and Buck will not have to lose any sleep over which one of the other fast bowlers would carry the drinks.

Brett Lee has taken the international scene by storm since his Boxing Day debut and after the way he bowled this week in Hamilton he looks set to have the New Zealanders jumping around the crease. His extra pace and raw aggression add a certain fear factor to our attack. Having him in the side makes fielding much more exciting as he tries to terrify opposition batsmen.

Possibly, the most significant contribution for the week has come from Damien Martyn, who smashed a brilliant hundred in his first first-class game for Australia in five years. His innings ensures that he will wear the baggy green cap on Saturday; something he has been working very hard to achieve for a very long time.

Our preparation has been superb with everyone taking plenty of valuable practice out of the last four days at Hamilton. Not only did every player spend time in the middle, but we also won our first game of this tour, a factor that is as important to a team's lead-up as any individual's effort. Confidence is contagious and winning is a habit that we are determined to keep going. There is so much for us to play for that we will be as ruthless as possible in achieving our goal of winning our first Test series in New Zealand for 24 years.

Justin's View...

The Perfect Pitch for Warney's Record

10.3.00 It has been nearly two months since our last Test match together and, while the team has a different look about it, the feeling has not changed one bit. When we last walked onto the Test arena we wore replica caps as a symbolic gesture for the first Test match of the last century. Tomorrow at Eden Park in Auckland, it is back to our own baggy green caps and back to the business of Test match cricket.

One of the players, wearing his baggy green cap with as much pride as anyone, will be my West Australian teammate Damien Martyn. After a long absence, he is now back in the Test team. After a great deal of soul-searching, he has worked hard on all aspects of his game to be where he is today. Not that long ago he was questioning whether he would ever play cricket for Australia again and yet he is now established in the one-day team and on the verge of playing a permanent role in the Test team. His perseverance and determination will make his journey out into the middle of Eden Park sweeter than many people could imagine. I will have a tingle down the back of my spine when I see my partner since junior cricket days walking out with me in the morning.

With every happy story comes a bad one and it was disappointing to hear that Ricky's ankle may take longer to recover than everyone first thought. After an unfortunate fielding accident during the one-day series at home, his operation yesterday revealed that his leg might be in a worse state than we had feared. Luckily for him, and us, there is little cricket on the itinerary over the next six months, so the lay-off could be a blessing in disguise for one of our most decorated young cricketers. Our thoughts are with him, and he will be missed within the team, not only for his batting prowess but also for his influence on all the players.

Last time I played here in Auckland I scored a pair so you can be sure there is plenty of extra incentive for yours truly. With the chance to win our eighth straight Test match and Warney only five wickets away from DK's record, this team will be firing come 10.30 tomorrow morning.

A fielding accident during the one-day series at home, and an operation on his leg put batsman Ricky Ponting out of this Test. We'll miss his batting prowess and his influence on the players.

Test No.8 First Test v. New Zealand
AUCKLAND 11–15 MARCH 2000

Throughout my career Australia encountered tough times in New Zealand. The Kiwis lift their game when they see an Aussie and Stephen Fleming's improving side was always going to give Steve Waugh's team plenty of challenges; as tough or even tougher than Pakistan had offered. As well the Kiwis were on their home turf where the weather and the wickets suit them more than they do us. At home the Kiwis play a clever psychological game. They play the underdog card very well, talking as if they will just be happy not to get thrashed by Australia while all the time hoping the Australians believe it and become complacent. Coming off seven wins in a row, the Australians could have been vulnerable to this sort of propaganda.

The series did not begin too well for Australia. We were bowled out for only 214 in the first innings of the first Test after winning the toss. The Eden Park pitch was a slow turner, the sort of wicket that has troubled Australia in the recent past. In Daniel Vettori, New Zealand has a class spinner. Justin Langer made an attacking 46 off 47 balls but it was really Mark Waugh who saved the day with a clever and calm 72 off 144 deliveries. Again this was Mark Waugh using his special gifts to make a critical contribution. While a very good batting team struggled in the conditions, Junior got his head down and played a very, very fine innings, worth a big hundred on a flatter, faster pitch.

Langer and Gilchrist helped Australia to 229 in the second innings after McGrath took 4 for 33 to have the Kiwis out for 163. Justin again attacked the bowlers, especially Vettori. His 47 proved again that he had developed the confidence and the nerve to attack bowlers in tight situations in Test matches. In the space of a couple of months Justin had moved from a tentative, limited player to an attacking number three, to the player we thought he could

Justin Langer at practice.

become. It is a great tribute to his determination that he was able to turn things around. Back in September he had few ideas about how to play Muralitharan. By March he was playing Vettori very well and belting everyone else.

Another important effort in that second innings came from Damien Martyn who had replaced the injured Ponting. Many people say Marto was the most talented batsman of his generation, but he lost his way and had been out of the side for about six years. However, he had been playing well in one-day cricket and we felt he had worked hard to resurrect his career. I have always had a soft spot for Marto because he has a special talent. He didn't realise it early in his career because he was a bit of a wild child. Everything had come easily to him. He was in the under-age teams and was captain of the Australian under-19s. For a while he wasted his gifts, but he has matured lately and is developing into a fine international player. Marto's improvement was another example, like Langer and Lee, of a player reaching new levels in the past year. On this tour he played very well under pressure and in conditions far different from those at his home ground in Perth.

Damien Martyn has matured into a fine international player.

Vettori ended with 12 wickets for the game but New Zealand could not reach the 281 they needed in the fourth innings. They were bowled out for 218 with Colin Miller taking 5 for 55, a terrific effort by him and a just reward for the excellent cricket he had given us since he came into the side for the tour to Pakistan in 1998.

This win meant the team had equalled the Australian record of eight Test wins in a row set 80 years earlier by Armstrong's team. Fittingly, the wicket that brought the historic win made some history of its own.

The Warne Phenomenon

When Adam Gilchrist caught Paul Wiseman off an attempted sweep, finally Shane Warne had broken Dennis Lillee's Australian record for Test wickets. I had the feeling that the coming record had been in the back of Warney's mind all summer. I'm sure he was disappointed that he didn't break it in Australia. I thought that a lot of his bowling was geared around getting that record and that he was not quite as relaxed as normal and didn't bowl to his usual standard. At one stage I said to Warney that he should not worry about not getting the record in Australia because the big moment will be when he gets close to the world record. Now he has the record he will be fine and can start chasing Courtney Walsh's world record. When he nears that he will probably face the same tensions.

Shane Warne, whose ambition was to be an Aussie Rules football player, leaves the field after taking his 356th Test wicket.

They are hard to avoid. With the huge coverage the game receives these days, especially with statistics so thorough, any player learns quickly when he is coming up to a milestone. With a national or world record the spotlight burns.

I'm sure Warney has achieved more than he thought he would. In some ways I think he still wonders how he ended up a great cricketer when his ambition was always to be an Aussie Rules player. Not even he expected to make the impact on the game that he has and I'm sure there are times when he wonders how he arrived where he is now. Although there is still a little of that original knockabout kid left in him, Warney has changed over the years. Anyone would with all the success and the fame it has brought. He is more guarded about people now, wary of who he lets get close to him and he's more savvy about his image. When he goes out now he's more aware of the attention whereas in his earlier days he was just a fun-loving bloke like thousands of his age. I suppose that is part of the process of getting older and being under the spotlight for so long. When you're on a pedestal as he is you learn you have a long way to fall if things go wrong. That whole process has taken its toll but I think he is still the good solid bloke he was at the start. Dennis Lillee went through a similar thing. At the height of his career Dennis had a huge profile, but back then there was not the massive media coverage the game receives now. For example, people in India never saw much of Dennis. There was no worldwide television coverage then as there is now. The whole coverage of the game is a lot more intense now and that has meant that Warney has been in that fishbowl more and more. The Warne phenomenon has been amazing.

There are many similarities between Warne and Lillee. Shane has the same ultra competitive streak that Dennis had. When they are out there competing they have a fierce desire to win and that always separates the great from the very good. Dennis had such commitment that he could wear himself out. As a fast bowler, Dennis needed to work on his physical fitness very carefully whereas Warney has survived on some pretty strange diets and hasn't been as attentive to his fitness as Dennis was, although he is improving in that area. Warney goes through periods when he might beef up a little, but generally speaking he looks after himself pretty well. Now he is 31 he is going to need to do extra physical work to maintain standards. They are also alike in the way they carry themselves off the field. It might be a slight comment here and there, a look in the eye, a swagger—something that makes their presence felt. Both enjoy the spotlight and use it to remind their opponents that they're still around.

Warney's arrival on the scene was the most critical thing that happened to Australian cricket in the past six or so years. For me it was a breath of fresh air. For quite a while we had good fast bowlers—Alderman, Lawson, Reid, McDermott, Hughes—but when Warney came onto the scene it was an entirely different ball game. As captain I had to learn how to use a leg spinner, when to bowl him and when to give him a rest. He was amazing because he could keep things tight as well as take wickets. Things always happened when he came on. All of a sudden I was able to make very positive decisions rather than playing cautiously as we had to in my early days as captain. Things happened so quickly with Warney in the side. The pace of the game increased because he was always threatening to take a wicket and I'd spend most of my time deciding whether to put in another fielder around the bat or in an attacking catching position somewhere else. We were often well on top with Warney bowling and it changed things for me and the team very dramatically. I really enjoyed the '93 Ashes tour. We had variety and quality and it was just a fantastic way to play cricket. From the 1989 Ashes series on, we handled most teams well except for the West Indies. But after Warney arrived in January 1992 we were definitely on the way to the top.

Glenn McGrath, a superb spearhead with the new ball.

Glenn McGrath deserves special mention because he has been a superb spearhead with the new ball. If we had had Warne and some modest quick, we would not have been so successful. But with Warne and another strike bowler of the calibre of McGrath we had a powerful combination. Perhaps we could have won games with Warne alone from 1993 through to about 1995. He was phenomenal then and we could probably have built a strong side around him as New Zealand did around Richard Hadlee. But I doubt that we would have been able to sustain that for long. After Hadlee the Kiwis had Danny Morrison for a while and now Vettori but neither is a Hadlee. Luckily we have had not only Warne and McGrath but also Fleming, Gillespie and MacGill on occasions and now Lee. The development process over the years has been very successful and has continued over these 10 Tests. It has been great to watch. How appropriate that it was Warne who took the wicket that put him ahead of the great Lillee's record and the team on an equal footing with Armstrong's legendary side.

The Dominators

Justin's View...   *Day 1 First Test v. New Zealand in Auckland*

11.3.00 At 4.17 p.m., the scoreboard suggested that we were in a lot of trouble on day one of this first Test against our archrivals. All out for just over 200 in the first innings of a Test match is nothing to boast about. Nevertheless, I would rather be in our shoes than theirs. By stumps, we had taken four wickets; a bonus considering this Eden Park pitch is almost certain to become harder and harder to bat on. New Zealand will have to bat last on this surface, so it would be fair to say that every run we can set them will almost be equivalent to two runs on this spinners' paradise.

When Tugga won the toss this morning, we knew advantage number one had gone our way. With the pitch turning in the first session, the ball can only spin more and more as the game wears on. This in mind, we would have liked to have scored more heavily in this first innings but we are still feeling confident at the end of day one.

Thanks to Mark Waugh's outstanding innings, the New Zealanders will have to bat as well as they possibly can to take a lead on the first innings. With Pigeon and Brett Lee chiming in with three of tonight's four wickets it would be my prediction that Funky Miller and Warney will cause more Kiwi headaches for the remainder of this Test match. At the pace he bowls, Colin Miller, the experienced journeyman, could hold the key to this Test.

PS Damien Martyn's catch at third slip this afternoon was as good a catch as you are likely to see on any cricket field.

Chris Cairns swoops down to send me back to the crease.

Allan Border's Big Picture

Justin's View... Day 2 v. New Zealand in Auckland

12.3.00 Losing the younger of our twins just before stumps has left this Test match in the balance. With three scheduled days to play, the pressure is on for both teams. Junior has looked in such great touch over the last two days that he could have batted the Kiwis out of this first Test. As it was, he lost his wicket to the impressive young Daniel Vettori, who is enjoying the conditions here at Eden Park.

Although we are currently in the stronger position, we will have to play tough cricket from here on to ensure a first Test victory for this series. The pitch is undoubtedly spinning like a subcontinent surface, so any run chase will be difficult for the home side. Such is the difficulty level of batting on this pitch that I can't imagine any of the New Zealand batsmen will be sleeping comfortably tonight. I can't remember the pitches in Sri Lanka spinning as much as this pitch and, considering we have a hungry Shane Warne and experienced Colin Miller ready to win this Test, we are still in the box seat.

A fruitful partnership between Marto and Gilly in the morning can only magnify our chances of an eighth-straight Test victory. The longer they can stay at the crease, the more frustrated the New Zealanders will be and the more excited our world-class bowling attack is sure to become.

The experienced spinner, Colin Miller (above) and the ever-hungry Shane Warne are ready to win this Test.

The Dominators

Justin's View...   *Day 3 v. New Zealand in Auckland*

13.3.00 After spinning his destructive web, Warney is now only one wicket away from breaking the Australian wicket-taking record. More importantly for the Aussie Way, we are only five wickets away from winning this first Test match. The only barrier to this potentially perfect story is that the Kiwis only need 130 runs to steal an unlikely victory on this challenging Eden Park pitch.

To his credit, New Zealand's middle-order batsman Craig McMillan played courageously this afternoon to give our opponents a sniff of victory. He was not at all perturbed about hitting our spin twins back over their heads and, although he took some chances, his calculated risk-taking has left this game in the balance. On another day of drama in which Daniel Vettori became the youngest spinner in the history of the game to take 100 Test wickets, this Test match looks likely to be a nail-biter tomorrow.

From our point of view, an early wicket in the morning will be crucial. There is enough experience in the team to know that we can get plenty of assistance from this pitch. This suggests that opportunities to wrap up this game are sure to arise if our bowlers can put enough balls in the right areas tomorrow.

After Gilly's superb batting this morning, the target of 280 was one that we were comfortable with. As always, the game of cricket should never be taken for granted, so we knew not to relax and expect an easy victory. Both teams realise that this game is still alive and kicking and while I still believe we are in the box seat we will have to be at our best tomorrow.

The first half-hour will be tension-plus, but the team that panics least will win this Test, and with our experience and talent, I will back us to come out of the match triumphant.

Adam Gilchrist and Colin Miller rejoice after another wicket falls at Eden Park.

Allan Border's Big Picture

Justin's View...   *Day 4 v. New Zealand in Auckland*

14.3.00 An abandoned day's play gave Matty Hayden and me the chance to present our illustrious skipper with New South Wales's wooden spoon for the 1999/2000 Pura Milk Cup season. People outside the team may not realise it, but within the team there is a fierce rivalry between the states. For years as a younger player I listened to how good the New South Welshmen were as a cricketing state. The Waugh boys particularly have enjoyed boasting about the strength of their home state and the unbreakable spirit of the baggy blue cap. I would love to have had a dollar for the number of times I have heard Stephen brag that 'Australian cricket is strong when New South Wales cricket is strong.'

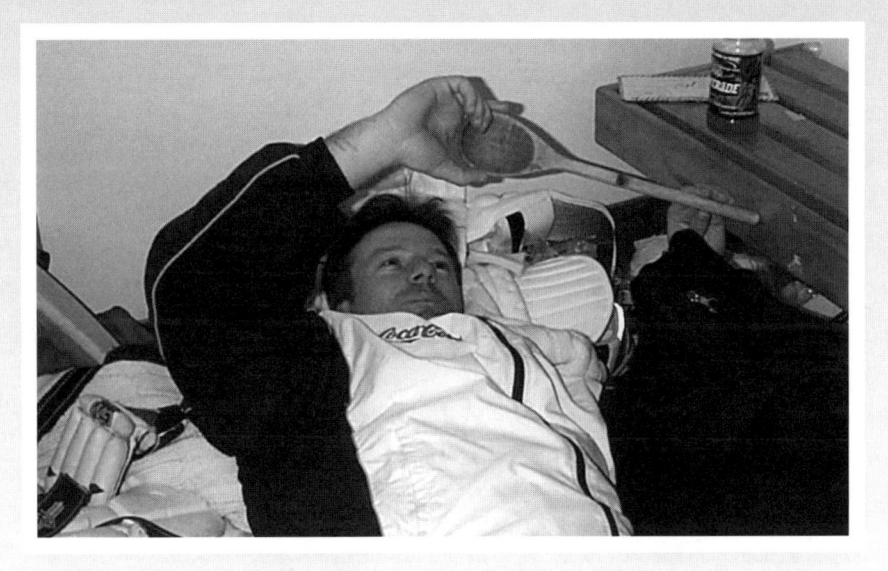

Tugga examines the wooden spoon, presented by non-New South Welshmen to our deeply partisan skipper for his home-state's Shield failure of late.

Without wanting to rub it in too much, a few of the boys who don't play for NSW have enjoyed the last two lean years for the Blues. While it is all in good humour, the banter in the changing room provides plenty of entertainment. To the horror and disappointment of the twins, the presentation of the wooden spoon helped ease the tension of today's abandonment. Many of the squad took great delight in presenting the Blues with their second consecutive wooden spoon.

After a sleepless night last night, day four certainly did not pan out as expected. Rather than spending the day fighting out the remainder of this exciting Test match, our time was taken up reading books, playing tennis-ball cricket, kicking the football and speculating about what will happen when play finally gets under way. As if there isn't enough pressure surrounding this match; we now have to wait until to tomorrow for the climax of Test match number one.

The Dominators

Justin's View...   Day 5 v. New Zealand in Auckland

15.3.00 It would have taken a bold judge to predict that this Test match would last the full five days. Obviously the rain played a major part in this drama, but when Warney broke D K Lillee's record this afternoon by taking the match-winning final wicket, a huge tension was broken all around.

Walking onto Eden Park this morning the game lay in the balance. Had the New Zealanders scored the 130 required runs they would have pulled off one of the great run chases in Test cricket history. The tension was like a tight rope in our changing room. The abandoned day only added to the drama being played out on the field. When Shane finally secured wicket number 356 for himself and number 10 for us, the feeling was one of both triumph and relief.

Funky Miller celebrates our win with scorer, Mike Walsh.

Beating New Zealand always means a lot to us and, considering there was so much riding on this result, the feeling going into the match was magnified tenfold. Warney had the record to beat, we had the record winning streak to play for and we were keen to win the first Test of this series.

Overall, we know we didn't play our best cricket in this Test match, but in a way this is a positive result. Not having played Test cricket since the first week of January it was good to shake out a few cobwebs over the last five days. At the end of the day, I think we stuck to our task well and struggled through the toughest periods of the game. We can play better cricket, but we still leave Auckland victorious.

While Warney was today's hero, Funky Miller's dangerous off-spinners, Glenn McGrath's brilliance and Brett Lee's sheer pace ensured the victory. In the batting department we have room for improvement but Junior, Gilly and Marto, in his comeback Test, showed great signs of touch and control.

Leading one-nil in this series is a distinct advantage and with an improvement in our consistency the prospects for winning nine consecutive Test matches is becoming a definite possibility. John Williamson, a friend and hero to the team, helped us celebrate the victory. Every time we win a Test, his song *True Blue* blares from the team's jukebox. Joining us at the team hotel tonight, he sang a few songs to help make this victory even more memorable and enjoyable. After a huge celebration, our thoughts will be blurry, but very encouraging when the sun comes up in the morning.

Allan Border's Big Picture

Justin's View... *Post Test Match Shenanigans*

As part of tour tradition, one of the first duties of the fines committee is to buy the worst clothing outfit possible. The collection of garments becomes affectionately known as the 'daktari'. This daktari is awarded every week to one of the boys who may have stepped out of line in one way or another, on the field or off the field. This week it happened to be Slats. Unfortunately, our dynamo opener miscued a pull shot while receiving throw-downs at practice. This would not usually be a problem except that this particular stroke cannoned into the side of Michael Kasprowicz's jaw. At our post-Test match fines meeting, Slats was unanimously voted as the daktari winner and he was ordered by the team to wear his newly acquired outfit at the end of the Test match.

Last seen wearing it in the wee hours of the morning, he provided us all with plenty of entertainment, upholding the tradition with great pride and enthusiasm.

Slats got the daktari for a practice shot that hit Kasper on the jaw.

Call it male bonding, call it what you like, but our social committee of Warne, Gilchrist and Hayden come up with all types of events and pranks to heighten the team atmosphere. This week, not only was the daktari awarded, but the fines masters decided on a different way to enjoy a night out with the team. The plan was for everyone in the touring party to buy a piece of headwear for one of their teammates. There were no limits with some of the boys getting off lighter than the others.

Glenn McGrath always looks menacing with a new ball in his hand but I don't think I have ever seen him looking as spooky as he did tonight. Thanks to Steve Waugh's taste in headwear, our premier fast bowler would have scared his newborn son with his new face-mask. Matty Hayden looked more like a goofy Indian chief, while our physiotherapist, Patty Farhart, standing in for Errol Alcott, combined both daktari and headwear. Nice look!

Imagine the Australian cricket team eating dinner in a Napier restaurant looking like this. It was a sight to remember. The things we get up to make the mind boggle; I guess it is good clean fun if nothing else.

A hooded Pigeon courtesy of Steve Waugh, hatter to the famous.

Justin's View...

21.3.00 On every tour, a number of warm up games are played for the team to gain valuable match practice. Today the number of these fixtures is decreasing as a result of the general increase in cricket played during the calendar year. This week, Central Districts played good hard cricket and provided excellent competition but, in the final analysis, the last three days have been hard work for other reasons. Firstly, the pitch on day one was as lively as John Travolta's dance moves and, secondly, a three-day game in the middle of the Test series did nothing for team motivation. Having played so much cricket over the last six months it was tough for a number of the guys to get pumped up for this particular encounter. While it gave Michael Kasprowicz the opportunity to have a long bowl, you could tell by the team's body language that it was not the most inspired effort by the Australian cricket team.

On a positive note, Mark Waugh continued his excellent form with the bat and there was valuable time spent in the middle by Marto and yours truly. In the bowling department, it was heartening to see Damien Fleming back playing after a week's rest for his sore knees. He took no time at all to find his rhythm as his five-wicket haul in the first innings reflected. Depending upon the Wellington pitch for the second Test, it will be a very difficult selection meeting for the tour selectors. As good a problem as it is to have more options than less, Brett Lee and Colin Miller, who both had great first Tests, will now be competing with a fit Flemo, who has been a star all summer.

An inspection of the Wellington conditions may make the decision easier, but all things being equal I wouldn't like to have to leave one of these guys out of the starting eleven. Whatever the selectors' choice, the team that walks out onto the ground on Friday is sure to be a tough one for New Zealand. With the opportunity to win the most ever consecutive Test matches by an Australian team, the motivation will be electric in our preparation and performance. It is not every day that you can be a part of history and after the buzz of Warney's record last week I wouldn't mind being a part of it again later this week.

Taking the flight from Napier to Wellington this morning was a little eerie, considering the size of the plane and the fact that we were flying to one of the windiest parts of the world, affectionately known as 'Windy Wellington'. We enjoyed our first taste of the weather conditions from high up above. I have had some rough flights in my time, but this morning's journey was up there with the roughest of them. I hope that the cloudy and windy welcome to New Zealand's capital city is not a sign of things to come this week.

All aboard for windy Wellington.

Allan Border's Big Picture

Justin's View...   *Towards Breaking the Australian Record*

23.3.00 As I said the other day, I am glad I am not on the selection panel for tomorrow's second Test at Wellington's Basin Reserve. With the pitch looking as though it could seam around early, the logical choice may favour our swing star Damien Fleming. History, though, suggests that the Basin pitch may spin and keep low later in the game. With five wickets in the first Test, Funky Miller will also be hard to overlook. It is going to be a tough call whichever way it goes, but I am sure the experience of Stephen, Shane and John Buchanan will produce the right decision.

The other selection issue concerns our in-form younger twin who has been troubled with a stiff neck. I hope the intensive treatment he has had all day will help him wake up pain-free in the morning. If today is anything to go by, he could be struggling to take the field and Matt Hayden could find himself back in the baggy green. Last reports suggest Mark is improving with every treatment: let's hope the news is equally as positive at breakfast.

Our preparation has been excellent for this Test match. Although it is very cold here in Wellington, and the wind factor is up there with the WACA's famous seabreeze, the team is on a high and looking forward to making this Test a special one. A number of the families have joined us for this Test so the feeling within the camp is relaxed but focused on the job at hand. A win here will mean we have won more consecutive Test victories than any other team in the history of Australian cricket. This factor alone will act as a huge motivation when the first ball is bowled at 10.30 in the morning.

Wellington's Basin Reserve.

Test No.9 Second Test v. New Zealand
WELLINGTON 24–27 MARCH 2000

This was another good Test match in which Australia's overall strength saw it through. Chris Cairns did in this game what he had threatened to do in the first. His 109 was a great innings and one of those rare occasions when a batsman successfully took to Warney. At 4 for 51 chasing 298, Australia was in trouble but another middle order partnership not only rescued the innings but also took it to a match-winning total of 419. Yet again the captain engineered the recovery, this time with Slater who made an excellent 143. Steve finished on 151 not out, along the way adding 199 for the fifth wicket with Slats and 114 for the sixth with Damien Martyn who made 78. That sixth-wicket stand gave Australia a handy first innings lead of 121 and, after dismissing New Zealand for 294 in the second innings, they had to make only 174 to win. The team managed that for the loss of four wickets with Langer and Mark Waugh making most of the runs.

Chris Cairns, an outstanding New Zealand player.

In this stretch of games, Australia either lost early wickets and was rescued by the middle order or Slater made a big hundred at the top and someone made runs later on. No team gets everything right in every game, but the great teams know how to fight their way out of trouble. With consistently solid performances from the bowlers, the batsmen were able to work around the inevitable failures and do the job in every game.

Slater the Enigma

If you look at the history of the game there are not too many opening batsmen who have played with the daring of Michael Slater and still averaged above 40. In some ways Slats's contribution was overlooked during this 10-Test period. Yet when you put it into context, you can see his great value to this team. A player like Geoff Boycott might average more

The ever-popular Michael Slater makes sure of this one in the second Test against New Zealand at Wellington.

than Slats but that is partly because Boycott was obsessed with averages—well one average, his own. Boycott was a great technician and was very good at saving games or setting up wins, but he never won many games and never had the positive impact on a team that Slats has had on this Australian team.

Slats now has 14 Test hundreds from 62 matches. His ratio of centuries to innings would be sensational if he had converted his eight 90s into hundreds. We all tend to develop such high expectations of some of our players that when they struggle for a little while we can forget the things they've done and some of the circumstances in which they've done them. Slats does go through periods where he gets out for low scores but that is partly the lot of the opening batsman. Against the new ball at Test level you have to expect to receive some very good deliveries. Given that, Slats's contribution has been tremendous. He sets a tone for the whole batting line-up. His approach is so aggressive that it tells other teams that the Australians are playing to win first and foremost. Relax for a few moments and the Australians will take the game from you. Winning Test matches is about taking 20 wickets and to do that you need batsmen who can score quickly to give the bowlers enough time. Slats can do that from the first over and his influence is therefore very important.

People from other countries absolutely love Slats and cannot believe he is not in the one-day team. As a selector I cop that all the time. His one-day record for New South Wales is disappointing and with competition for places high that is one of the reasons why he is not in the Australian one-day side. If Slats played in one-day cricket as he plays in Tests he would be perfect. But for some reason he believes he has to be even more aggressive in the one-dayers. He will work it out some time but by then it might be too late as one-day cricket is increasingly a younger man's game and his time is running out. I keep telling him he has to play four or five one-dayers for NSW and produce some substantial figures and that will see him break into the national one-day team. Slats certainly has the talent to play one-day cricket—he has so much talent it is scary—but he has to make one-day runs for NSW first. However at Test level Slats has been a tremendous player, a key figure in this team.

Justin's View... Day 1 Second Test v. New Zealand in Wellington

24.3.00 'Catches win matches' is a saying I have heard since I was a kid. Whether in a schoolboy game or a Test match, it always runs true. Had we taken all our catches today, the score line at stumps would surely be reading differently. Unfortunately, a couple of mishaps in the field allowed Chris Cairns to smash a brilliant Test match century, while Nathan Astle probably scored 40 more runs than he should have. The old adage about catches winning matches is more relevant at this level because your mistakes become very expensive due to the quality of the opposition.

New Zealand's all-rounder Chris Cairns played a fantastic cameo innings. He was brutal against Warney, hitting our superstar 'leggie' for a number of massive sixes.

As impressive as his six-hitting was his front-foot driving against the pacemen and a couple of excellent hook shots off Glenn McGrath were just as memorable. For a middle-order batsman who also opens the bowling, this century today must put him in line with the best all-rounders in the game. Considering he came to the crease with Warney bowling as well as I have seen him bowl for a long time, his innings was world-class.

At lunch, we looked in total control of this second Test match but as so often happens the momentum shifted rapidly the other way in the hour after the first break. The Cairns/Astle partnership dominated the second session and, as the pitch flattened out so did our early advantage. Eventually we dismissed the New Zealand tail, but having lost Blewey and nightwatchman Warney before stumps, the Kiwis may be just ahead on points. With the pitch looking like a batsman's dream we will have to put New Zealand's 300 into perspective when we bat tomorrow.

New Zealand's brilliant all-rounder, Chris Cairns roars up to the wicket.

Justin's View...   Day 2 Second Test v. New Zealand

25.3.00 Today is the first time in 10 years of first class-cricket that I have seen both batsmen run off the field during the drinks break for, how should I say it...a visit to the gentleman's toilet! It was not that Slats and Tugga were going through particularly nervous times against the New Zealand bowlers; rather it was a case of the freezing cold conditions playing tricks here in Wellington. At drinks, several of the New Zealand fieldsmen left the ground for a moment's relief, as did both our batsmen who felt their bladders were bursting at the seam. Having played county cricket for the past couple of years, I know players regularly have to contend with icy climatic conditions, but today was without doubt as cold as I have experienced on a cricket field. It was absolutely freezing and very, very windy.

The iceblock fingers and stiffer than usual, bodies of the Kiwi fieldsmen were to our advantage throughout this excellent day for the Aussies. It is always very difficult standing in the field wearing a couple of cricket sweaters, a shirt, a T-shirt and a couple of pairs of socks. In a funny sort of way, I almost felt sorry for our opposition as they battled with the bleak skies and frosty wind. Having said that, it was a delight watching Slats bring up his fourteenth Test century, with Tugga at the other end blasting his mandatory ton for a Test series.

An exhausted Slats in the dressing room after posting another ton.

Both New South Welshmen batted beautifully on a fantastically even batting strip. Slats was at his belligerent best in a return to form, which was always 'just around the corner'. He is so exciting to watch, and his style of play must be heart-breaking to any opposition bowling attack. At tea, it was impossible to predict just how many he would end the day on. Such was his dominance, it looked like he might break a few personal records himself. Apart from one false hook shot just after tea, Michael Slater was simply sensational.

His partner, our captain, answered all the questions raised at our team meeting this morning. We as a team talked about the need for hunger and determination to ensure we win this Test match. Yesterday, we were a bit slack in a few departments but, apart from two early dismissals this morning, today was different.

With a 20-run lead, Marto looking in awesome touch, Tugga as hungry as Jacks and Gilly still to come, we have reversed the momentum of this game. Tonight we are in a situation where we can nail home the advantage when the first ball is bowled in the morning. The longer we can bat the better, not only for the state of the game but also for the comfort of the warm changing room.

Justin's View...   Day 4 Second Test v. New Zealand

27.3.00 When it really counts this Australian team has the ability to step up to a higher level and intimidate the opposition by pure pressure and intensity. After letting the New Zealanders off the hook in the last hour yesterday afternoon, a more disciplined approach was required in the first hour this morning. With this in mind—surprise, surprise—Tugga threw the ball first to superstar McGrath and then to our wily and experienced off-spinner Colin Miller. Their job was to apply the brakes early on New Zealand, particularly Chris Cairns.

From ball one, the pressure out in the centre of the Basin Reserve was fierce. McGrath was brilliant and Funky Miller as tight as a guitar string, as we held Cairns and Fleming to very few runs in the first few overs. It was sheer intimidation: neither batsman could score a run on either side of the wicket. After Cairns's Ian Botham-like onslaught in the last session yesterday; the New Zealanders probably gave themselves a chance in this Test match. That ambition was short-lived. As has become a trademark of this Australian team, the early pressure and subsequent wickets of Cairns and Fleming quickly destroyed the opposition's hopes.

Thanks to a cameo performance with the bat by tail-ender Simon Doull, we were probably chasing 50 more runs than we were expecting. He swung the blade like a samurai warrior, frustrating our ambition of a very small victory target. Although the target had blown out a little, we knew the pitch was still flat and the outfield very fast. After our historic victory in Hobart earlier this summer, we now have very few

The team dressing room, a retreat from the cold and the scene of our victory celebration – notice the extensive John Buchanan preparation sheets up on the walls.

fears of any situation. This was proven again by our clinical run chase this afternoon. With Daniel Vetorri side-lined by a back injury, and the Kiwis hampered by a dwindling confidence, it was great to finish this Test in four days and stamp our authority on the series.

As usual, the after-match celebration was a comedy. Loud music, photographs, cold beer, sprayed champagne and one of the longest renditions of *Under The Southern Cross...* that has ever been performed. Taking over in the absence of Ricky Ponting, our patriotic, baggy green-loving captain asked every player to get up on the table, one by one, and describe their favourite memory of the last nine Test victories. At the end of each player's speech he led or, more correctly, roared a verse of our team song. The changing room was like a beer-drenched, echoing cave, as we sang the song with the gusto of a Pavarotti rehearsing in the shower. With John Buchanan, our managers, Steve Bernard and Mike Walsh, Patty Farhart and Dave Misson also invited to share their favourite memories, 19 verses of the song were sung, or screamed, depending on who was listening. It was a blast: a mixture of inspiration, humour and patriotic pride that will not be forgotten for a long time.

Voices hoarse and chests puffed out, we eventually left the Basin Reserve knowing that whatever happens, this experience of nine Test victories can never be taken away from us. Sure the record may be broken one day, but the feat of winning nine consecutive Tests is an achievement of which we are very proud. Playing in a team like this is a privilege. It is not only a dream team for raw talent and skill, but it is also a dream team of characters and character. Experience, know how, determination, perseverance, pride, wisdom and respect aren't for sale anywhere. That is why this team is so special. It has an awesome blend of cricketing skill and those characteristics that money can't buy but are rather earned as a part of being an Australian cricket player with a baggy green cap on your head.

Funky Miller taking the celebrations very seriously.

Test No.10 Third Test v. New Zealand
HAMILTON 31 MARCH–3 APRIL 2000

By this stage Australia had won nine Tests in a row and no selector wants to change a team in that sort of form. Yet it had become obvious that Greg Blewett had struggled for every run he had made all year. That was the way it looked to me. Throughout the summer he had not played with any fluency. Even when he made the 88 in Adelaide, he was battling with himself the whole time. The selectors just got to the stage where we thought enough is enough: he has had a good run, but it hasn't quite worked. It was another tough decision, but we also thought that Matthew Hayden had made so many runs for Queensland in both forms of the game for so many years and had done well on this tour that he deserved a chance. Matty works hard at his game and even though he was on the sidelines most of the time he has offered strong support to those in the 11. He had done everything he needed to and deserved his chance in this third Test.

The Australians went into this game knowing that if they won they would have won 10 in a row and would be one victory away from equalling the world record for consecutive Test wins. And guess whom Australia plays in that first Test next summer? The holders of that record, the West Indies. Despite the obvious motivation for the Australians I had the feeling the Kiwis were not shot ducks. They seemed to take offence that they were actually 0–2 down. Whereas other sides we have played have been well beaten after losing the first two Tests, the New Zealanders were not going to lie down and let Australia walk all over them. They had had a good summer by beating the West Indies and they wanted to finish it off with a win in Hamilton. Unfortunately they had to try to achieve that without Vettori whose shoulder had given way.

Again New Zealand made a modest first innings score of 232 with Brett Lee taking another five wickets. And yet again, Australia was in trouble in their reply, this time 5 for 29 when nightwatchman Shane Warne became the third of Shayne O'Connor's five wickets. After Mark Waugh battled for 28 off 55 balls, Adam Gilchrist joined Damien Martyn to save the innings. The two new boys added 119 for the seventh wicket with Gilchrist blasting 75 off 80 while Marto played steadily for an undefeated 89 off 136 balls.

Leading by only 20, Australia dismissed New Zealand for 229 in the second innings before setting out to make the 210 needed. Each of these Tests followed the same pattern with a lot of innings totals in the 210 to 250 bracket. This one in particular was evenly balanced until one player took the initiative. That man took the unlikely form of Justin Langer—unlikely that is until his remarkable make-over this season. After a promising 37 from Hayden, Langer attacked the Kiwis and succeeded in taking the game from them. At the end he was undefeated on 122 made off as many balls. This was brilliant batting, probably even better than his innings against Pakistan in Hobart.

Our attitude to chasing totals has improved a great deal. There was a period when anything around 120 to 140 was usually too much for us even in reasonable conditions. The attitude has obviously turned around and Steve Waugh and Mark Taylor deserve credit for that. They had obviously decided that we were not going to muck around when chasing small totals. We were just going to go out there and go for the bowling and take the game by the scruff of the neck. There is nothing worse than poking and prodding around like we did in the past. You can get yourself into a bit of strife as soon as you lose a couple of wickets. But if you score at five or six an over, pretty soon you're in sight of the target. This win in Hamilton was a suitably emphatic way to end what had been a brilliant run of 10 successive Test victories.

Justin Langer, pleased as punch after a not-out century.

Justin's View...   *Third Test v. New Zealand in Hamilton*

31.3.00 Back-to-back Test matches are always a challenge to both mind and body, but apart from the unfortunate dismissal of Matty Hayden before stumps we have had a fantastic day on this first day in Hamilton. Determined to leave New Zealand while still playing our best cricket, our bowlers were sensational throughout the day.

Up-and-coming superstar Brett Lee took his second five-wicket haul in Test cricket, with an awesome display of control and aggression. He is an excitement machine with a cricket ball in his hand. Like poetry, his run up is fluent and smooth, while his delivery, and resulting thunderbolt, is fierce and potentially harmful to the batsman hopping around the crease a pitch-length away. His inclusion in the team in December has added a new dimension to what was already a strong combination. His raw pace and youthful enthusiasm as a part of our armoury has helped turn our bowling attack into one sure to cause sleepless nights among opposition batsmen worldwide. He is a fantastic young man who looks certain to take the international cricket world by storm and should be around for a long time to come.

Before the tossed coin spun into the air this morning, our preparation for the game had been as thorough as ever. Winning this Test match means a great deal to every member of this team. During our team meeting last night all of the guys spoke about what this Test match meant to them, and how they were going to approach this final Test match of the summer. In short, most of the boys talked about playing their best cricket over the next five days. Although we have won the first two Tests, everyone agrees that we are still not playing as well as we can. As daunting as this may sound to the New Zealanders and their supporters, I honestly believe we can improve in many aspects of our game. This in itself is very exciting for the team because although we are winning we still have room for improvement. With this in mind, the sky is the limit for development of this already successful team.

Winning the toss this morning may initially have seemed a huge benefit on a grassy pitch. Having played at this ground a few weeks ago I think the pitch is likely to become flatter and flatter as the game goes on. In a perfect world, we wouldn't have lost any wickets at stumps, but as it stands, we are still in a great position going into day two. The bowlers did everything the skipper could have asked from them and now it is up to the batsmen to destroy the spirit and enthusiasm of the New Zealand team.

Justin's View...   *Day 2 Third Test v. New Zealand in Hamilton*

1.4.00 By the way we started the day, you could have believed it really was April Fool's Day. In what was possibly our worst session of cricket since the first Test in Sri Lanka, we offered the New Zealanders another brief sniff of victory.

The great thing about cricket is that you just never know what is around the corner. Sometimes, actually most times, the best-laid plans can come unstuck as they did this morning. Before a ball was bowled, we were hoping to bat only once in this Test match. After a fantastic display yesterday, it was our plan to score heavily in our first innings and bowl out the New Zealanders without having to bat again. On a pitch that seemed likely to flatten out, this was a distinct opportunity and one that seemed very attractive to every one of the people in Hamilton wearing green and gold.

Unfortunately, this perfect-world scenario was blown out of the water by drinks as we sat at five for 30, in the first hour of play. Who would have predicted this? One thing is for sure, the personnel in the Australian changing room were in some state of shock at what had occurred in the first 60 minutes. Thanks to a fired-up Chris Cairns and the deceptive Shayne O'Connor, we were in all sorts of trouble.

Enter Damien Martyn and Adam Gilchrist. What a partnership we witnessed for the next two hours! Replacing their green and gold one-day caps for their baggy green caps, my Western Australian teammates smashed the New Zealand attack to every part of the ground. Their batting was entertainment at its best, as they counter-attacked brilliantly under immense pressure. Scoring so quickly, they stole back the momentum of the game in the space of 20 overs. From the depths of despair rose two warriors who put us back into the game.

Unfortunately Marto stood stranded just 10 runs short of his maiden Test century. As disappointed as he was to miss out on this personal milestone, I would have to predict his first hundred is not far away. He was outstanding in defence and attack, with his balance at the crease being a feature of his classy innings. Again, today was a testament to this man who has fought hard to regain a place in the Australian Test team. He is an exciting and seasoned talent, who now looks so at ease with himself that it seems a shame we have not had the opportunity to enjoy his talent for so long in the Test arena. It is a great pity that he was not rewarded with a ton, as he thoroughly deserved to achieve that in this Test match.

As for the state of this game, I would say, as in the previous Test matches, it currently lies in the balance. Taking the wicket of Stephen Fleming before stumps was a huge bonus that may have us just ahead on points. The first session tomorrow will be vital for the result of this Test match. A couple of early wickets may lead to a three-day Test match, while a spirited fight by the Kiwis will leave us with a Hobart-like run chase.

Only time will tell, as you just never know what is around the corner in Test match cricket. That is why we love it so much.

Justin's View...   *Day 3 Third Test v. New Zealand in Hamilton*

2.4.00 Bad light robbed us of the opportunity to complete a historic Test victory in three days. After Chris Cairns again did everything in his power to drag his team out of deep trouble, we now sit just 73 runs away from winning our 10th straight Test match. For me it means a sleepless night but, if I am honest, the New Zealanders will be feeling the pressure more than we are. On a flat pitch we should achieve our target before lunch tomorrow, giving us the chance to fly back to Australia a day early.

Winning this Test match means so much to the team that we will be playing with the same discipline and desire as we have all summer. Having Tugga as my batting partner will mean there is no way anything will be taken for granted. He is a master of taking few foolish chances in his quest to win this series three-nil and finish the summer just as we started it. Ten straight triumphs is so close that it makes me nervous just thinking about it.

Chasing just over 200 runs for victory is a tricky little target, but thanks to a dominant innings by our comeback king and man mountain, Matty Hayden, we are sitting in a strong position. It was a thrill watching Haydos taking it to the New Zealand attack. When he is going, his presence at the crease is daunting. Taking over from Blewey for this final Test, Matt was determined to grab his opportunity with both hands and, after the way he batted this afternoon, I think he has done that. Batting with him in this type of situation was something we have talked about for a long time. Because we are now on the brink of another victory, the enjoyment factor of our partnership was colossal.

The lighter side of Haydos at the headgear event early in our New Zealand tour.

Justin's View...   *Day 4 Third Test v. New Zealand in Hamilton*

3.4.00 The climax of this tour, and the summer, could not have gone to plan any better than it did today. The only downside was Tugga retiring hurt when he was hit on the elbow when the game was as good as won. Scoring a Test century was a buzz of course, but not as enjoyable as singing *Under The Southern Cross...* in the Hamilton changing rooms with my teammates. This summer has been as golden as any of us could ever have imagined. In many ways, it is a shame that our unbelievable run of victories has to come to a halt until next summer against the West Indies.

Being a part of this team really is a great honour and privilege. We set out at the start of the summer to win every Test match. At first, this seemed an unlikely goal. Thinking back though, I remember the look in the eyes of Steve Waugh and John Buchanan when they set this challenge to the team. They truly believed, or at least acted like they believed, that we could re-enact the feats of 'The Invincibles'. After the Sri Lankan tour, a number of issues within the team needed to be addressed. They were, and by continually seeking improvement
we now expect to play like the best cricket team in the world.

Among all the highs of the last 10 Test matches, the thing that stands out the most in my mind is that it has been so much fun. *Under The Southern Cross...*, wearing my baggy green cap, with a team of great blokes and outstanding cricket players, this has to be a dream come true.

Conclusion

Although it is difficult to compare different teams I would have to say that this Australian team could be the best since I started playing in the late '70s. The best side I played with was probably the one from '89 to '93. Or was it the one in the late '70s to early '80s when we had Lillee, Greg Chappell and Rod Marsh? In those days we didn't win any games in Pakistan and we never toured India. We lost 3–1 in England in '81. We were beaten by the West Indies all the time. We were good at home but we didn't do anything spectacular overseas. Perhaps the '93 Ashes team was the best I captained.

We had Boon, Slater, Taylor and the Waughs, Hughes plus May and Warne at their best. But throughout all those years the West Indies were awesome; the side we could not beat. This Australian team is beating everyone but you have to ask whether the opposition is as strong as it could be. You can argue forever on that one but it is hard to see the current West Indies side coming anywhere near their sides of the '80s. England, New Zealand and Pakistan are not what they were 15 years ago although South Africa has come back into world cricket and done well. I think this Australian team is as good as we can make it and up there with any we've produced, but perhaps some of the other sides have declined in the past 20 years.

So to the next challenge of equalling and then breaking the West Indies' record of 11 consecutive Test wins. What a delicious irony to think that we might knock the record off against the West Indies who gave us so much grief for so many years. Although the West Indies are improving after a bad period I can't see them matching Australia just yet. Next summer we could set a record that would be hard to match, but winning all five Tests against the West Indies is a tough ask. Even the weather has to be kind. After that will come one of the few remaining challenges for modern Australian teams: winning a Test series in India. With Warne still fit, Colin Miller still bowling well and the improvement of young batsmen like Ponting, Langer, and Martyn together with Steve Waugh's excellent leadership, this Australian team might be the one to break that Indian hoodoo.

If it does, credit will have to go to many people. The Australian Cricket Board set up the Academy in the mid-1980s as we started to work our way out of that slump. The coaches at state and international level have worked hard and combined resources well. Australian cricket has made mistakes but not many bad ones and we remain well ahead of the pack. But it could all fall down if the Test side loses its way. Frankly, I don't think it will. It contains too many talented players with the right attitude. They are a special bunch of blokes. They are not just good cricketers. They have got a tremendous work ethic, they feed off each other so well and they are well led, well coached and well managed. Now for the West Indies.

The Dominators

When fans sit down, in years to come, their hands around a beer,
And discuss games, and feats and deeds, that made them clap and cheer,
They'll talk about the big ship's team, and Bradman's forty eighters,
The Chappell team that ruled the world, and of course The Dominators.

They're four great teams, who represent our cricket at its best,
They played and beat all other teams, in one-day and in test,
And though I'm not prepared to guess, that if they got to play,
Between the four, which team would win, on any given day.

But Tugga's side has proved to all, they're really quite a team,
And in the spring of ninety-nine, its cricket was supreme,
By winning ten tests on the trot, another record broken,
There could be more to add to that, but that's best left unspoken.

The Pakistanis were the first to tour, a hard resourceful side,
With pace to burn, and spinning guile, their batsmen true and tried,
And though one up, the first Test won, the Hobart Test looked lost,
Two fifty short, five wickets down, I thought the boys were tossed.
Occasionally, when things are tough, the steel comes to the fore,
And teams are measured, in future years, by facet not by flaw,
With Gill and Lang showing the way, the runs began to flow,
They backed their skills, showing true grit, their legend starts to grow.

Confidence grew within the team, a psychological plus,
Their style of play was hard and tough, efficient without fuss,
They tossed the Pakistans aside, and blew them off the park,
And then they took on India, a team who'd left its mark.

In ninety-eight, their Indian tour had ended in defeat,
That series left a mental scar they needed to delete,
And if they dreamed of rating now, amongst our greatest teams,
A trouncing of the Indians, would validate these dreams.

The showdown came in Adelaide, and then the MCG,
Where Brett Lee burst upon the scene, a nightmare fantasy,
Our stranglehold was tightened, at Sydney's final test,
Tendulkar's grip, the team's bête noire, was this time laid to rest.

And though the team felt satisfied, they'd crushed the enemy,
They had to beat another foe, and fight complacency,
The captain spoke of pride and guts, the task had not begun,
Until we'd taken on NZ, the job would not be done.

The Kiwi on its own dung heap is not an easy foe,
You have to fight parochial crowds, and pitches flat and low,
Plus vagaries of weather that will freeze you to the bone,
You have to dodge the negatives, stay focused in the zone.

Their focus chose to underline their deeds of such renown,
'Cause once again they won the tests, and stared the Kiwi down,
The end result, a realised dream, their plan was now complete,
Armstrong's record at last surpassed, ten tests without defeat.

At last they can be rated at the top of cricket's pile,
And though it's nice to contemplate, that feeling for a while,
The hardheads know, there's plenty more, the team has to achieve,
To lose the plot and lose their crown's a thought they won't conceive.

And while the team is in good hands, with Tugga in the chair,
With Shane and Mark, Pidge, Flem and Slats, no effort will they spare,
And Gill and Lang, Blewey and Punt, now starring on their stage,
Bing and Kaspa, you can be sure, will still maintain the rage.

And as I've said, there's more to come, their era isn't finished,
Their records will stand tests of time, ne'er to be diminished,
As time goes by, and deeds inspire, the words of commentators,
The fans will nod, in mention of, the name The Dominators.

Steve Bernard

TOP: Justin Langer, fielding close in, flinches as Waqar Younis hits out in the second Test v. Pakistan at Bellerive Oval, Hobart.

ABOVE: The attacking 'slips' cordon was the source of many wickets for Australia.

LEFT: Glenn McGrath prepares to send down another fast one for the waiting hands of the Australian in-fielders.

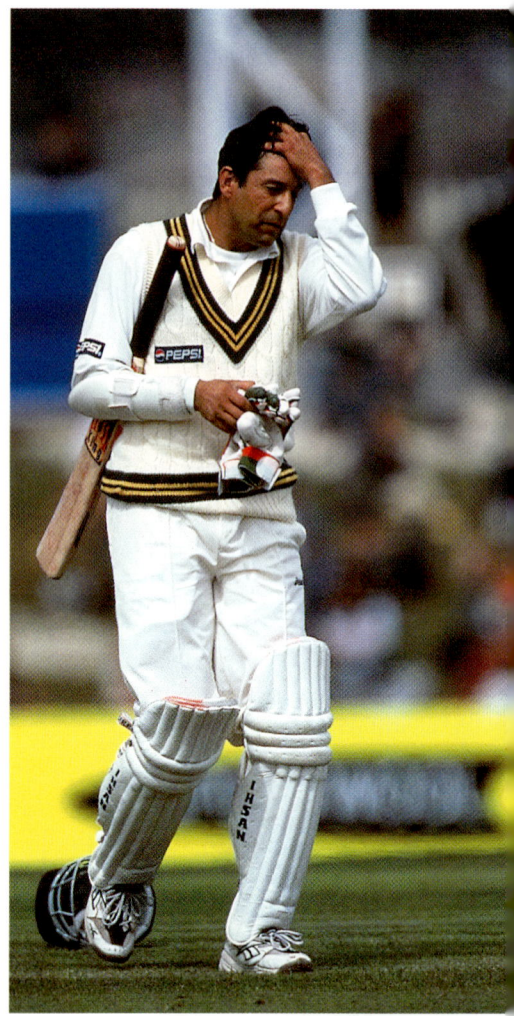

ABOVE FEFT: Damien Fleming's bowling action is captured in perfect relief in the late afternoon at Bellerive Oval, Hobart.

ABOVE RIGHT: Wasim Akram of Pakistan is dazed after being hit by a rising ball from Damien Fleming.

RIGHT: The so-called 'snickometer incident' in which Justin Langer survived a confident appeal for caught behind, off Wasim Akram's bowling, during his crucial 237 run partnership with Adam Gilchrist that ensured Australia won the second Test to go up 2-0 in the series.

ABOVE: Adam Gilchrist celebrates with Shane Warne after hitting the winning runs at the exciting second Test v. Pakistan.

RIGHT: Gilly leaves the pitch with a souvenir stump after hitting a match-winning 149 not out, at Bellerive Oval, Hobart.

ABOVE: A general view of the WACA ground, Perth, during the third Test v. Pakistan.

RIGHT: Ricky Ponting avoids bouncer on his way to amassing 197 runs.

OPPOSITE TOP: Ricky Ponting and Justin Langer scurry back for a second run during their record partnership of 327.

OPPOSITE BOTTOM: Adam Gilchrist dives to catch Yousuf Youhana in the first innings of the third Test v. Pakistan.

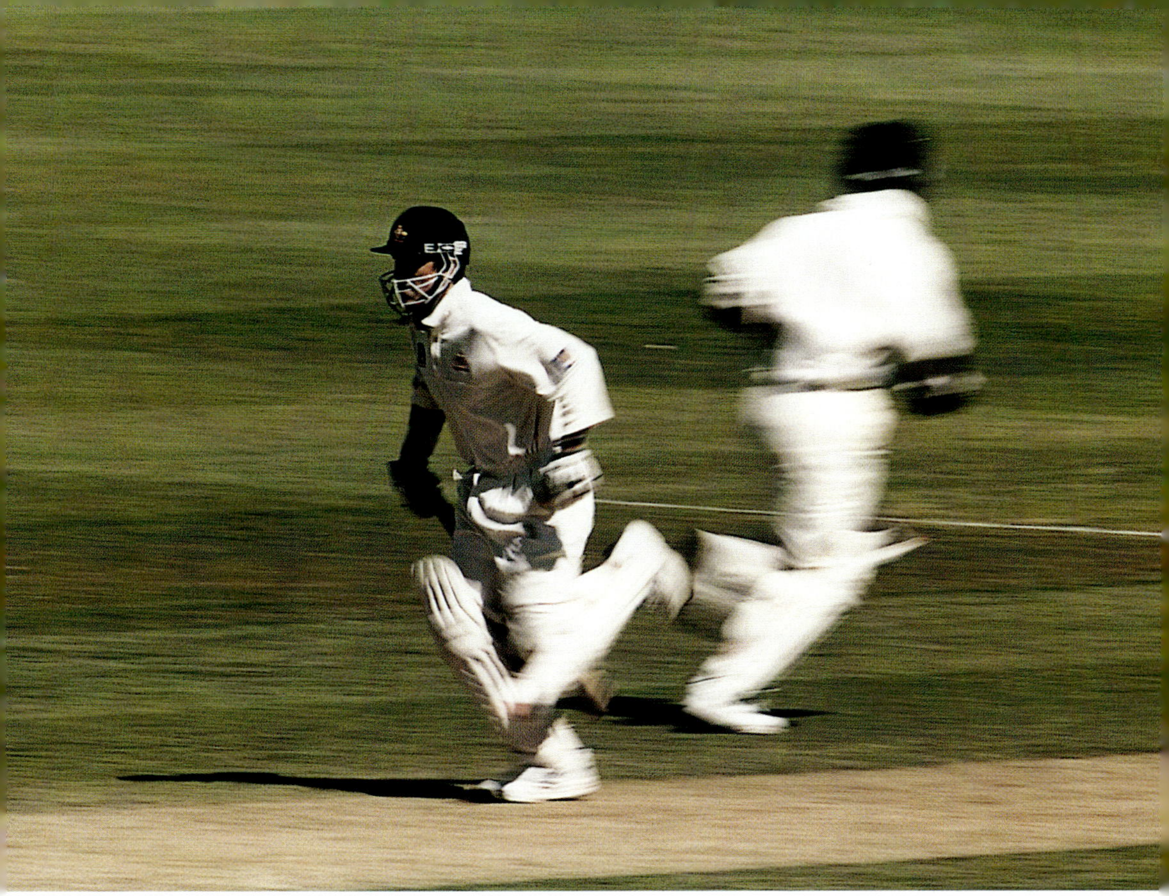

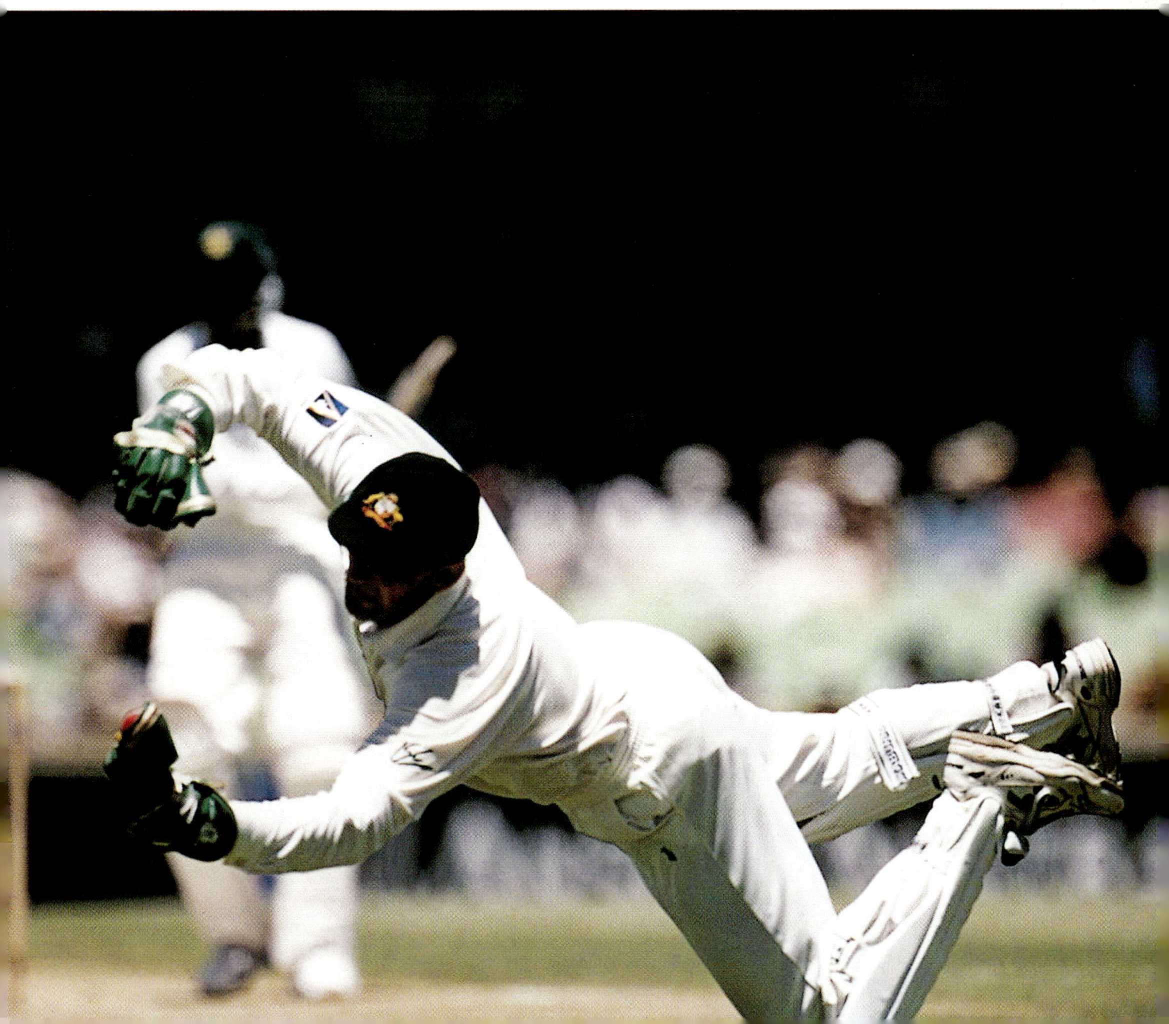

RIGHT: A tired Ricky Ponting removes his helmet and heads for the pavilion after scoring an epic 197 runs.

BELOW LEFT: Justin Langer, who shared the record breaking partnership with Ricky Ponting, pulls a ball to leg on his way to making 144 runs at the WACA in the third Test v. Pakistan.

BELOW RIGHT: Ricky Ponting and Justin Langer pause during their magnificent 327 run partnership.

OPPOSITE TOP: The Australian team celebrate the wicket of Izamam ul Haq.

OPPOSITE BOTTOM RIGHT: Steve Waugh (150) cuts a ball to the boundary in the first Test v. India at Adelaide.

OPPOSITE BOTTOM LEFT: Adam Gilchrist still at the ready, in the late afternoon.

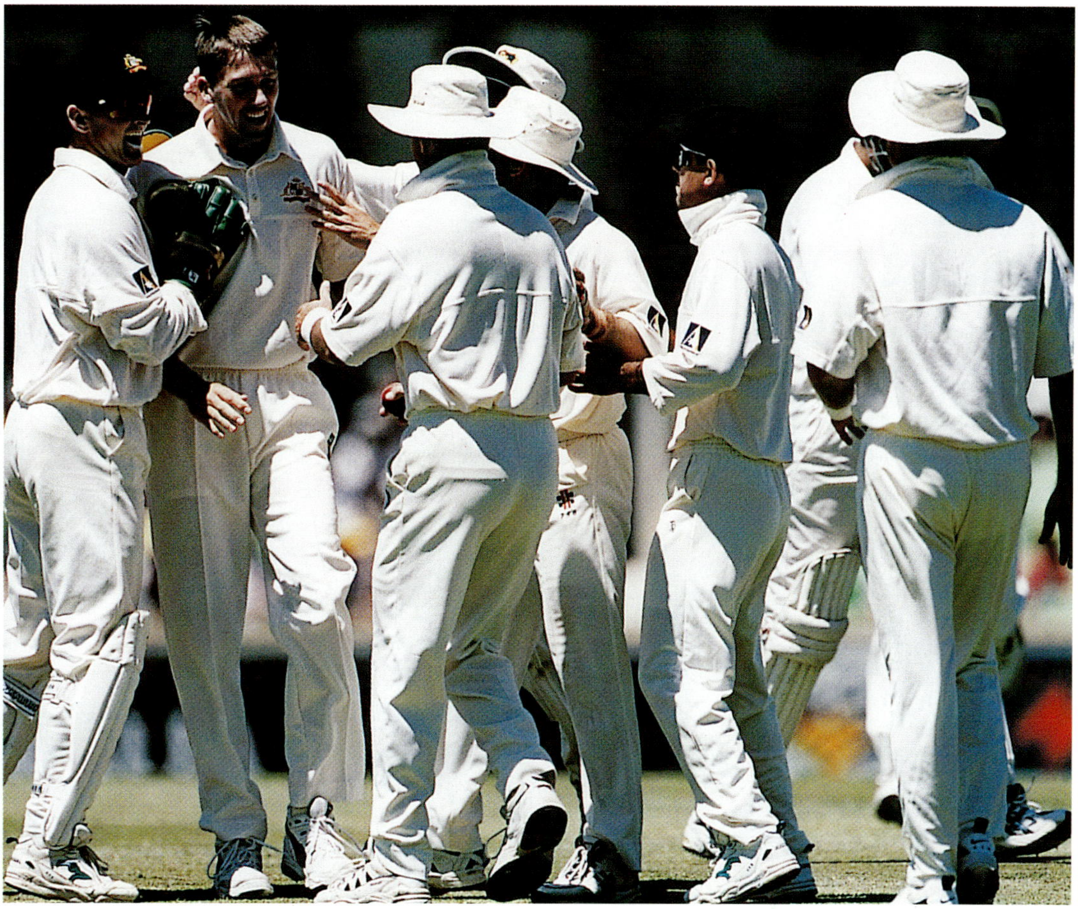

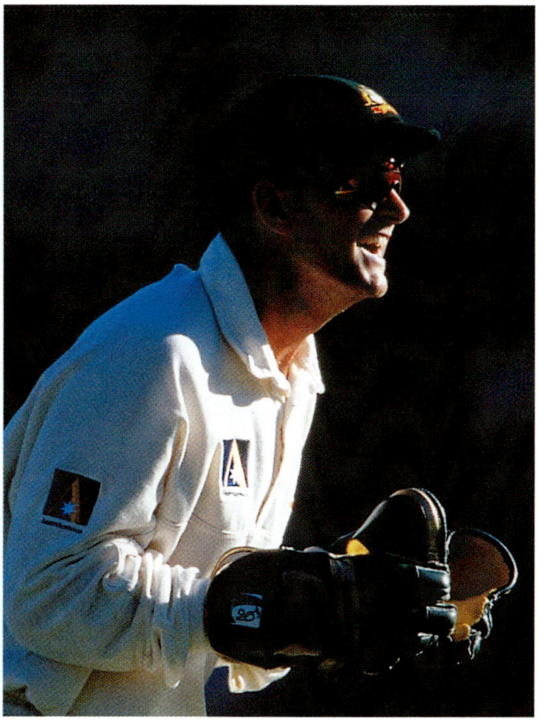

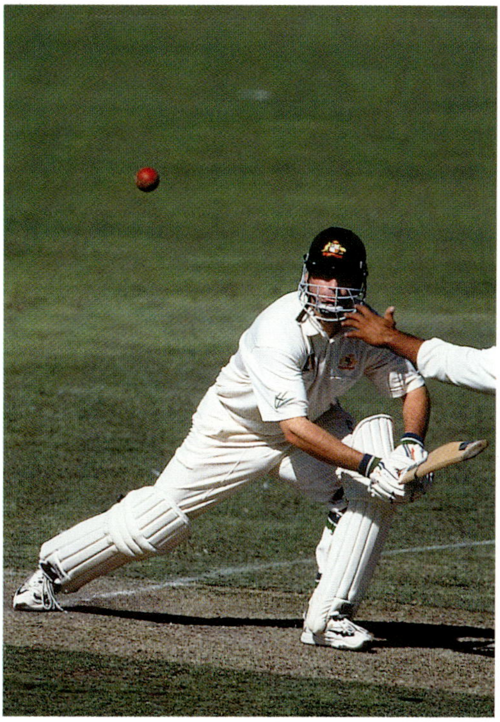

ABOVE: A rare moment when Shane Warne drops catch in the slip cordon during the first Test v. India.

LEFT: An exultant Ricky Ponting waves his bat as he brings up his 100 against India at Adelaide.

The Team

2

A Winning Combination

Members of The Dominators team bring with them individual strengths and talents and combine as one well-disciplined unit, accepting differences, sharing jokes and building up morale. Here then is a series of pen portraits of this magnificent team—whose record-breaking string of unbroken Test successes may take a long time to eclipse.

Greg Blewett	Glenn McGrath
Damien Fleming	Colin Miller
Adam Gilchrist	Scott Muller
Matthew Hayden	Ricky Ponting
Michael Kasprowicz	Michael Slater
Justin Langer	Shane Warne
Brett Lee	Mark Waugh
Damien Martyn	Steve Waugh

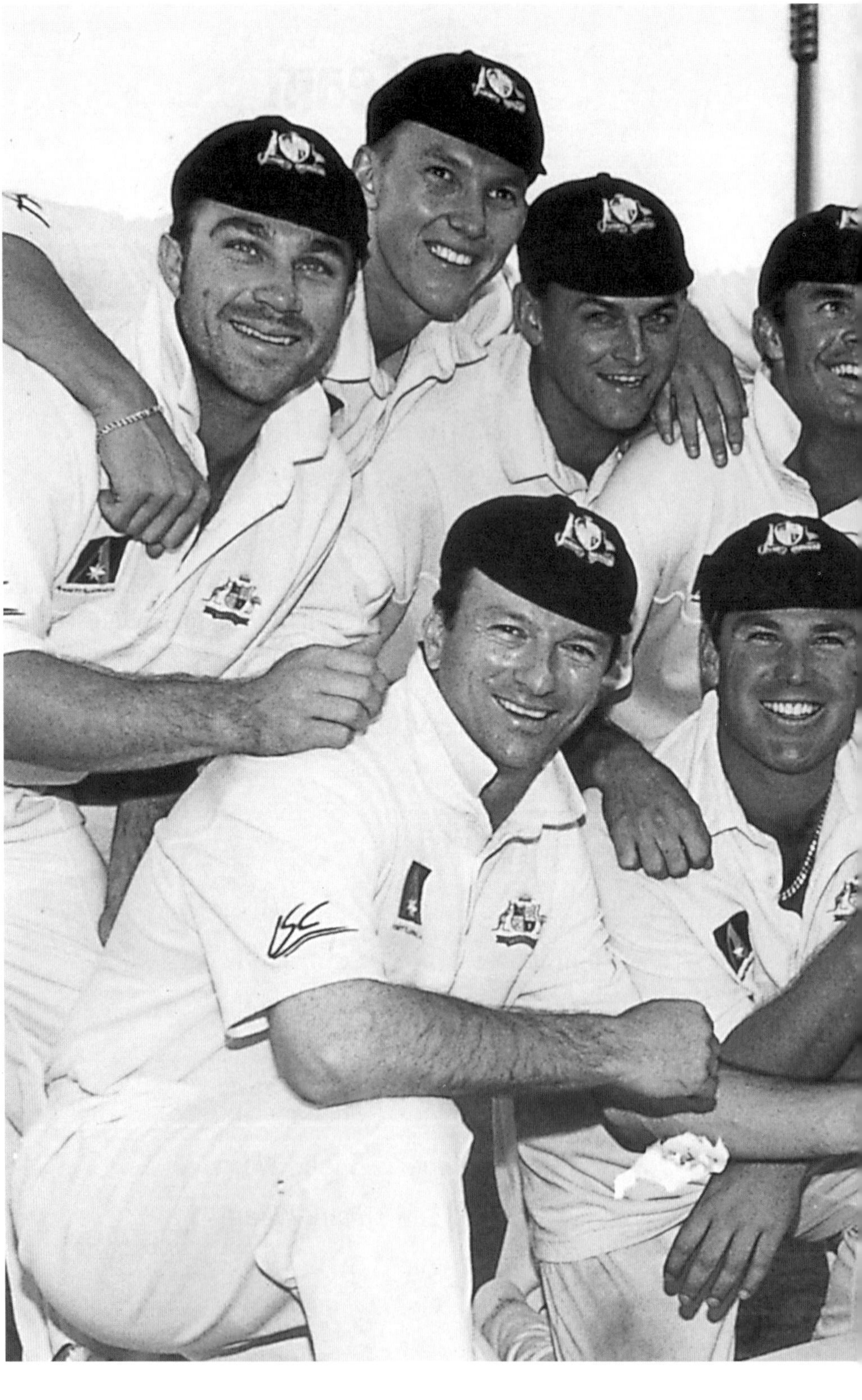

A triumphant team wearing their 1900 replica caps celebrate with the Border-Gavaskar trophy after their win against India at the Sydney Cricket Ground. Backrow from left: Michael Slater, Brett Lee, Adam Gilchrist, Greg Blewett, Michael Kasprowicz, Mark Waugh, Ricky Ponting. Front row from left: Steve Waugh (C), Shane Warne, Glenn McGrath, Damien Fleming, Justin Langer.

GREG BLEWETT

BORN: 29 October 1971, Adelaide, SA
FULL NAME: Gregory Scott Blewett
BATTING STYLE: Right Hand Bat
BOWLING STYLE: Right Arm Medium
TEST DEBUT: Australia v. England at Adelaide, 4th Test, 1994/95

Australian Cricket Academy 1990

Greg Blewett

Greg Blewett finished the 1999–2000 season on the sidelines in New Zealand, but I'd like to think he'll be back clamouring for our attention as selectors this summer. At his best, there aren't many guys better to watch. But the time has probably come for Greg to overhaul some aspects of his game. If he can overcome this setback, he'll be a much better player for it.

Blewey went to the Academy in 1991, and was always rated a good player, but his initial impact in international cricket was beyond all expectations. He came into calculations six summers ago when the selectors decided to try out a few of their young stars with an Australia A team in the World Series Cup: guys like Bevan, Lehmann, Hayden, Ponting and Langer all under Damien Martyn's captaincy. Greg was actually one of the last ones picked, but he forced everyone to sit up and pay attention with a hundred at the SCG, and sort of vaulted the queue to get into the Test side. Once there, he peeled off more centuries in back-to-back Tests against England in Adelaide and Perth; the first guy to do it since Doug Walters 30 years earlier.

Since then, Greg's often threatened to be a really great player. When he made 214 at Durban in March 1997 against the likes of Donald, Pollock, Klusener and Adams, putting on 385 for the fifth wicket with

Steve Waugh, he looked invincible. Then there was a beautiful 135 against England at Edgbaston a few months later, and a breathtaking 213 not out off 180 balls for the Australian XI against England in Hobart two years ago which was one of the best innings I've ever seen. Bellerive Oval's a place you can play that sort of knock, because the ball bounces consistently from first to last and you can always hit through the line with confidence, but I thought: 'Gee, no one can bat better than that.' In form, he's a very difficult guy to keep quiet, a graceful driver who gets the left elbow right up, and who pulls anything even slightly short.

By the same token, Greg's gone through too many periods where he looks out of sorts. His technique works well for him when he's confident but, when he falls, he can fall hard. Perhaps it's the case that his initial results were too good: guys who make a great start to their Test careers often come back to field within a few years. Players like Steve Waugh and Shane Warne are all the better for having had to fight every inch of the way when they started in Test cricket.

Last season, Greg seemed to struggle for every run he made. All credit to him, because he got some good scores, and he battled all the way through. But now that he's out of the team, he might want to rethink his commitment to opening the innings. He wants to go in first, but he's achieved his best results down the order, and he might be better value to the team at No. 5 or No. 6.

Greg's a good style of a bloke and c abilities, but this is the third time he's been dropped from the side,

An animated Blewey appeals for a wicket during day four of the Test against Zimbabwe.

and I hope he really takes stock. He has available to him in Adelaide one of the best technical people round, Greg Chappell, and it wouldn't hurt him to do a bit of soul searching about his methods. He's got the determination to come back, and he's young enough to see it through.

Blewey has always fitted well into the Australian teams he's played with. When the team divides into the Nerds and the Julios, there's no doubt whose side Greg is on: he's a Julio through and through. As one of the resident fashion gurus, he certainly lets you know about it if he sees you wearing dodgy shoes, or a shirt that's a bit ordinary! He's one of the keenest golfers in the side, playing off four, and has a technically perfect swing.

Greg's such a skinny bloke that he sometimes looks a bit of a pushover, but looks are deceiving. I played cricket against his dad Bob, who captained South Australia a bit over 20 years ago and was a real tough nut who didn't mind a word or two on the field. Greg's a bit similar, with heaps of courage, which comes out when he's fielding at short leg as did David Boon. He's got lightning reflexes in that position and is completely nerveless. At Leeds in July 1997, he caught John Crawley there off Jason Gillespie from a full-blooded clip off the toes: an outrageous wicket but a very important one.

A measure of Greg's determination was seen at Brisbane last season when he and Michael Slater went in just before lunch on the second day to take on Shoaib Akhtar and Wasim Akram. The Pakistani pair bowled like lightning and made us fight for every run, but Blewey and Slats laid the groundwork for a huge total by batting through the rest of the day, and they weren't separated until the score was 269.

Greg now has the job in front of him. Matthew Hayden has fought his way back into the Test side, so he's the current incumbent and deserves the opportunity to make a go of being Slats's opening partner. As I said, Greg might be better suited to a position in the middle order, especially if he tightens his technique against quality spin bowling, and works on a few ways of turning the strike over. We'll be watching his progress closely, and I hope he makes life difficult for us!

DAMIEN FLEMING

BORN: 24 April 1970, Bentley, WA
FULL NAME: Damien William Fleming
BATTING STYLE: Right Hand Bat
BOWLING STYLE: Right Arm Fast Medium
TEST DEBUT: Australia v. Pakistan at Rawalpindi, 2nd Test, 1994/95

Damien Fleming

Damien Fleming looks like the last guy you'd give a new ball to. He cuts a pretty ungainly figure, with his paddle feet and his short run, and doesn't impress you with his athleticism anywhere; he's pretty average with a golf club or tennis racquet, and I once saw him play in a netball game against his fiancé and he was way out of his league. Mind you, she does play for Australia!

But Flemo is a cricketer opponents underestimate at their peril, a swing bowler of surprising pace and bounce, and a dedicated and popular team man who's been forced to make a habit of overcoming injuries to get where he is. He's one of the unsung heroes of this Australian team, consistently picking up his two-fors, three-fors and four-fors, and maintaining the pressure with his excellent line and length. In between times, lots of swimming, weight training and uphill running have improved his strength and flexibility.

Experience of consistent success has been a long time coming for Flemo. He first played cricket at under-12 level with Springvale South 20 years ago, and hit district cricket for South Melbourne at the age of 16 way back in 1986–87. He made his Sheffield Shield debut in November 1989 as a tearaway paceman with one of those 'start-from-the-sightscreen' approaches and a big, high, windmill action. But he soon began to master the art of swing bowling and five years later was taking a hat-trick in his first Test appearance at Pindi Stadium in Pakistan. By then, however, he'd sustained a shoulder injury playing in league cricket in England, which has flared up periodically ever since and restricted him to only 19 Test appearances. He also suffers occasionally from hamstring strains, and tends to keep our physiotherapists busy during home seasons and on tour.

Fortunately, Damien's a pretty philosophical character, who sees the funny side of life and always has a smile on his face. When he was a teenager in Springvale, he had hair down to his waist and wouldn't have looked out of place as a member of Spinal Tap; nowadays, while the haircut's gotten a little more conservative, he still loves his headbanger music. Whenever he and David Boon got together in the dressing room, they made a helluva racket.

Damien's also one of the dressing room's resident wits, very quick with a one-liner, and probably has a career ahead of him as a stand-up comic. He even looks a bit like Jerry Seinfeld! On one trip to Sri Lanka, he kept everyone entertained by taking a videocamera into the streets. One scene had Flemo telling the camera: 'I promised myself when I came away that I'd get to know a little Sri Lankan...and here he is!' The camera pulled away to show Flemo patting the head of a little boy next to him.

Likewise, when he came back after missing a few games of the CUB Series last season with a virus, Flemo told us: 'I don't think I'll be in any doubt for the finals. You don't have to be too fit to carry the drinks. As long as you don't spill them...' He loves playing his guitar, to which he's been known to sing along, and wetting himself at any film with Jim Carrey in it, especially the Ace Ventura movies. If Flemo gets hit for four, you'll sometimes see him remonstrating with himself as he walks back to his mark, because he sets himself such high standards on the field; but otherwise, he's as relaxed as they come, and pretty much goes with the flow.

One of the most surprising features of Damien's record—it's probably a little surprising to him, too—is his Test batting average of almost 20. Flemo looks a bit agricultural and takes a big wind-up, but he can get stuck

The Team

in when he wants to and frustrate the best bowlers. He steps away a bit and slides a lot of balls over point, and he doesn't mind the odd Gordon Greenidge hook shot when he's feeling confident, but that's probably the right way for him to play; he's one of those guys who's inclined to get a nick when he plays too straight and sensibly. In the first Test against England at the Gabba in Brisbane two years ago, he floored the Poms with an innings of 71 not out, full of exotic shots including back foot drives over cover with one leg off the ground, which extended our innings from 7 for 365 to 485 all out. Nothing is quite so deflating for an opponent as tail-end runs, and it guaranteed us a big first-innings lead.

In the next Test at the WACA Ground in Perth a week later, Flemo bowled beautifully in conditions that suited him, taking 9 for 91 in a man-of-the-match performance and beating the bat countless times. Even Glenn McGrath had to play second fiddle to Flemo in that match, and it was all over half an hour before tea on the third day. In England next year, I'd back him to be one of our most consistent bowlers; certainly he was one of our 1999 World Cup stars in the Old Dart, playing in all 10 matches, and keeping his cool in the last over of the amazing tied semi-final with South Africa against big-hitting 'Zulu' Klusener. That throw down the pitch to Gilly to run Allan Donald out is now probably the most famous underarm since Greg Chappell's!

Flemo hit 30 in April, which can be a bit like the beginning of the end for some fast bowlers. But provided he continues to keep injuries at bay, I think that this cheerful Victorian has a lot of cricket ahead of him. His run-up and action are so economical and his control so good that there's no reason why he can't keep going for many years yet. And, for as long as he does so, this Australian team is bound to be a fun, happy...and loud...one.

Damien Fleming of Australia lunges to field off his own bowling, during day three of the tour match between the Sri Lanka Board XI and Australia at Colombo Cricket Club,

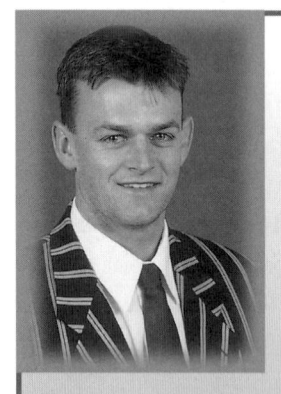

ADAM GILCHRIST

BORN: 14 November 1971, Bellingen, NSW
FULL NAME: Adam Craig Gilchrist
BATTING STYLE: Left Hand Bat
OTHER: Wicketkeeper
TEST DEBUT: Australia v. Pakistan at Brisbane, 1st Test, 1999/2000

Australian Cricket Academy 1991

Adam Gilchrist

Some Test cricketers have to wait an eternity before they savour success. Take ICC referee John Reid, for example, who was a fantastic all-rounder for New Zealand in the 1950s and 1960s and the best player in a very ordinary side. He didn't play in a winning team until he led the Kiwis to victory against the West Indies in his 27th Test. What must John make of a guy like Adam Gilchrist whose Test record is nine matches for nine victories? In fact, there can't be a player in history who's experienced anything remotely similar.

Adam could answer that he's played a very big part in those successes. The West Australian wicketkeeper/batsman has already made 41 dismissals (38 catches, three stumpings) not to mention 629 runs at 57.2. He's also made his runs at a helluva rate, striking at 76.6 per 100 balls; not bad for one-day cricket, let alone the five-day form.

One-day cricket, of course, is where it all started for Gilly. Australia first capped him four years ago in the Titan Cup in India when Ian Healy suffered an injury, then decided to make him a limited-overs specialist while retaining Heals as our first-choice Test stumper. It was a hard choice, because Heals's keeping in every form of the game had never been less than immaculate, but we just thought that a decision had to be made about the direction of the side, to make us a bit more dynamic in the 50-

over game while building up to the crescendo of the World Cup in 1999. Adam certainly provided that dynamism: he's already made almost 3,000 one-day runs at an incredible 90 per 100 balls. Steve Waugh then had the brainstorm of turning Adam into an opener in January 1998, and he made the first of his seven one-day hundreds in only his second outing.

I must admit that the first time I saw Adam, I wasn't completely convinced. Seven years ago he was a junior batsman from the Academy struggling to get into the New South Wales Sheffield Shield side and looked a bit fragile. Although he was a handy player, I wondered whether he'd make it. But Adam then took his fate in his hands. He reckons he plays his best cricket as a keeper rather than as a batsman alone and, because his state already had a good gloveman in Phil Emery, he shifted to Western Australia in August 1994. The Blues hierarchy are probably ruing that now; I had a lot of time for Phil, too, but they let a pretty special cricketer go.

There was nothing Adam could do, of course, about being Heals's Australian understudy. He just had to bide his time and make sure he was ready when the great Queenslander called it a day. To his credit, he did just that. You expected some sort of hiatus after Ian's retirement, with Adam feeling his way into the job at least for his first few Tests. But no sooner had he taken over than he became a vital cog in the Australian Test machine: his glovework has improved with every match, and his batting's been simply extraordinary.

There was some talk around a year ago that we should have let Heals play a farewell Test in Brisbane against Pakistan. As one of the selectors involved, I can tell you it was a very difficult choice. Ian had indicated to us in advance that the trip to Sri Lanka and Zimbabwe would be his last tour. When he returned to Australia, he then explored the possibility of playing his last game at the Gabba; understandably so, as he was within cooee of 400 Test dismissals.

Typically, though, Ian left it to the selectors completely. And our dilemma was that, knowing we had to introduce a new player, it was preferable to do so in the opening Test of a series. So that's what we did and, even though there was a lot of sentiment involved, and we copped some flak for the decision, I think events have proven us correct. The question you have to ask is: would Gilly have been capable of playing that great innings on the last day of the second Test at Bellerive Oval if it had been his Test debut? I'm sure it helped that he already had the experience of that 81 at the Gabba under his belt.

Gilly's 149 to help Justin Langer win the game at Hobart was astounding. At 5–126 chasing 349 last on the fourth day, I have to admit that I thought we were gone: we'd had a go but just had to accept being 1–1 in the series. Gilly, though, doesn't know any other way to play, and he turned the match on its ear very quickly. I don't think I've ever seen Wasim Akram treated with such disdain. In the end it was made to look almost inevitable. Under a normal run chase scenario, you don't really get excited until you're about 15–20 runs away. But even when we were 100 runs short in Hobart, you were thinking: 'We're going to do this easy.'

In terms of the team environment, Adam fitted in from day one. He's a solid citizen and, in time, a potential captain: bright, quick-witted, and unusually good on his feet. A lot of players go onto the public speaking circuit, but few of them are really comfortable doing it; Adam is very accomplished and articulate, with a great sense of humour and a flair for mimickry. While playing with Australia A a few years ago, he fronted the bar with his hair slicked back, hissing away about ordering 'a nice chianti', in an imitation of Hannibal Lecter from *The Silence of the Lambs*.

On the cricket field, though, Adam is anything but an impersonator. One look at his figures tells you that he's the genuine article. His 100 per cent record can't last forever, of course, but I'm sure he'll be fighting as hard as he can to maintain it.

Adam Gilchrist in the classic pose to receive at the Australia v. Pakistan second Test at Bellerive Oval, Hobart.

MATTHEW HAYDEN

BORN:	29 October 1971, Kingaroy, QLD
FULL NAME:	Matthew Lawrence Hayden
BATTING STYLE:	Left Hand Bat
BOWLING STYLE:	Right Arm Medium
TEST DEBUT:	Australia v. South Africa at Johannesburg, 1st Test, 1993/94

Matthew Hayden

It is not hard to conclude that if fate had treated Matthew Hayden a little differently he might have been one of the outstanding Australian players of the past 10 years. He has certainly been one of the outstanding interstate cricketers of the past 10 years. Year after year he has scored heavily for Queensland, yet somehow he has never managed to establish himself at the international level. Why such an obviously talented player should have failed in this way is one of the recent mysteries of Australian cricket. Some have wondered whether he lacked the technique or the temperament, or both, to succeed in the international arena. His admirers, though, are more inclined to blame the national selectors for not persevering with him long enough.

Tall and broad-shouldered, Hayden caused something of a sensation when he made the Queensland side as a 20-year-old opening batsman in 1991–92. He made 149 in his debut Sheffield Shield match against South Australia early that summer, hitting 23 fours, and went on to top the Queensland aggregates for the season with 1028 runs at 54.11. He repeated the performance in his second season, 1992–93, topping the aggregates with 1150 runs at 52.27, and on the strength of that he was chosen for the 1993 tour of England. At this stage many believed a new Australian batting star had emerged; an impression which the left-hander's initial form on the tour (he began with scores of 151, 122 and 96) seemed to confirm. It was no surprise early in the tour when Hayden was chosen in the Australian team for the one-day series against England. If all went well, he seemed sure to open the batting for Australia in the later Ashes Tests.

But all did not go well. Hayden stumbled in the final county match before the first Test, against Leicestershire, scoring 2 and 15, while in the same match his rival for the Test position, Michael Slater, made 91 and 50 not out. Slater got the nod for the first Test and went on to open for Australia throughout the series. It would not be the last time that a turn of fate seemed to deprive Hayden of his destiny.

Back in Australia, Hayden ran hot again in interstate cricket. In six matches for Queensland he hit seven centuries, scored 1136 runs and averaged 126.22; a feat which earned him a place on the tour of South Africa later that summer. He made his Test debut in the first Test of the series but failed in both innings and was not picked for another Test. Other, similar disappointments were to follow in the years ahead, but to his great credit Hayden never lost sight of his goal of making his mark in Test cricket. As always he remained a fine and powerful striker of the ball, but with maturity he seemed to play with more discretion, encouraging some to believe that his best years lay ahead. His return to the Test side after a three-year absence for the final Test in New Zealand in early 2000 (only the eighth Test of his career) was a promising sign. The heavy-scoring Queenslander may yet score heavily for Australia, too.

Matthew Hayden of Australia bowls, during training at Sinhalese Sports Club.

MICHAEL KASPROWICZ

BORN: 10 February 1972, South Brisbane, QLD
FULL NAME: Michael Scott Kasprowicz
BATTING STYLE: Right Hand Bat
BOWLING STYLE: Right Arm Fast
TEST DEBUT: Australia v. West Indies at Brisbane, 1st Test, 1996/97

Michael Kasprowicz

As a fellow Queenslander who's had a long association with him I may be a bit biased, but I must say that any success that comes Michael Kasprowicz's way really pleases me because he's one of the nicest guys around. Though Kasper doesn't push his own barrow much, and might have suffered as a result, I still think he has a huge future. He's still only 28, and gets better with every season.

Kasper made his debut for Queensland in January 1990 when he was a 17-year-old still attending Brisbane State High School. He'd been a schoolboy star in cricket and Rugby, and perhaps part of the thinking was that cricket should get in first to make a claim on his talents, but he was big, strapping and very quick for his age. We thought: 'We'll have something special here by the time this bloke is 22.'

Kasper developed quickly, and went to England in August 1991 on an Australian Young Cricketers tour, taking nine wickets in the First Youth Test at Grace Road. After a big Sheffield Shield season in 1992–93, when he took 51 wickets at 24, he was probably a bit unlucky to miss out on the last pace bowler's spot on the 1993 Ashes tour which went to Wayne Holdsworth.

As I had with Mark Waugh six years earlier, I recommended Kasper to Essex in 1994 as their overseas player, and he had a good season in which he claimed 60 wickets at 31. In hindsight, however, county cricket mightn't have been quite the right move for him at that stage of his career. He came home a bit jaded, which sometimes happens: you can burn yourself out busting a gut for a county, and consequently lack a bit of zip at the start of a season here (in fact, it happened a year later to Carl Rackemann, who lost a fair bit of the edge off his bowling after a hard year bowling for Surrey). Anyway, whatever the reason, Kasper lost his place in the Queensland side, and had the disappointing experience of being 12th man when we won our first Sheffield Shield in March 1995. But the need to fight his way back was a test of character which he passed with flying colours, because he gained his first Australian one-day cap the following season.

Kasper wasn't immediately successful when he was finally rewarded with his baggy green cap four years ago against the West Indies; he went wicketless in his first couple of Tests. But there have been times since when his talents have shone through. On his first tour of England in 1997, he bowled superbly at the Oval to take 7 for 37. With McGrath unavailable and Warne struggling, he then carried our attack in India seven months later. Sachin Tendulkar took to him a bit, as he took to everyone, but Kasper had his revenge at Bangalore when he picked up 5 for 28 and the man-of-the-match award.

Even though he's been in and out of the Australian team since then, I think Kasper has continued to develop. If I'd had a criticism of him in the past, it was that he could be a bit expensive and bowled a few too many 'four balls'. But since shortening his run, he's held it together far better without any cost to his pace. With the meteoric rise of Brett Lee and the probable return from injury of Jason Gillespie, he's probably fourth or fifth cab off the rank among Australian pace

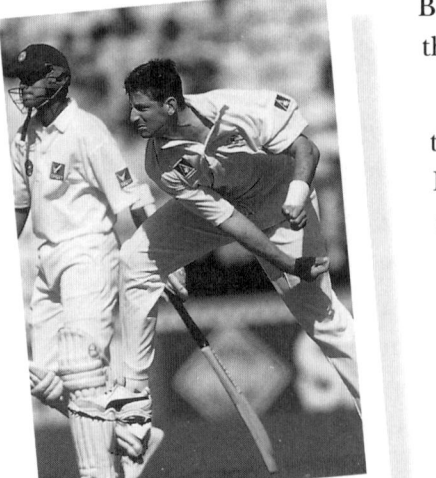

Michael Kasprowicz in action during the first Test against India at the Adelaide Oval.

bowlers at the moment, but he could be second or third. He's still relatively young, and probably only approaching his peak now. He's a great competitor, as strong as an ox, hits the bat hard, and can bowl either with the wind or against it: a quality that captains appreciate.

Kasper fits right into the current Australian dressing room, enjoys sharing in everyone's successes, and is one of many guys who'll laugh himself stupid at Jim Carrey's Ace Ventura movies. He's particularly close to Damien Fleming, and also to Queensland's Andy Bichel, with whom he shared accommodation for many years before Andy married Dion.

One of Kasper's lesser-known talents is that he's a great cartoonist. Every now and again, he'll sit down and start doodling, and before you know it he's dashed off a quick caricature of someone. He captures people's idiosyncracies really well, often with a ribald comment or two and a few appendages added! When he's done playing, he might consider a career knocking out cartoons for *Playboy*!

There's no doubt either that Kasper could have been an outstanding Rugby player, at least as good as his younger brother Simon who's a first-grade backrower for Souths in the Brisbane club competition. Kasper toured New Zealand with an Australian Schoolboys team in 1989, and would have made a terrific lock/breakaway. Even now he has good hands and fantastic skills, and for a big man moves really well. One look at that burger bum of his and you can guess what value he'd have been in a scrum, too! In fact, I look at a guy like Kasper—and also Steve Waugh with his writing and photographs, and Brett Lee and Damien Fleming with their musical talents—and think how much the game has changed since I was playing it. When I was wearing the baggy green, all we were good for was hitting and bowling cricket balls. Nowadays, the guys seem to have talents in all sorts of directions.

As I said, Kasper is one of the all-time nice guys in cricket. I always feel really pleased when either he or Justin Langer do well on the field, because I know how much work they've both needed to do to get to the top. Don't underrate Michael Kasprowicz. He still has a lot to offer Australian cricket.

JUSTIN LANGER

BORN:	21 November 1970, Perth, WA
FULL NAME:	Justin Lee Langer
BATTING STYLE:	Left Hand Bat
BOWLING STYLE:	Right Arm Medium
OTHER:	Wicketkeeper
TEST DEBUT:	Australia v. West Indies at Adelaide, 4th Test, 1992/93

Australian Cricket Academy 1990

Justin Langer

Justin Langer is a guy with character to burn. And he's needed all of it. Nobody's had it tougher getting to where he is today, when he is just about the most consistent number three batsman in the world. Even two seasons ago, when we were playing the Poms in the 1998–99 Ashes series, people were asking whether he was up to the task. I was commentating for BSkyB at the time—the Aussie in the England camp—and the question I got more than any other was: 'Why is Langer in this side, batting at first-drop? Where's Bevan? Where's Law? Where's Lehmann? Where's Blewett?' But, from the selectors' point of view, Justin's case was always about more than cricket ability; he had the courage, the work ethic, and the personality of a guy who could make a real go of Test match cricket, given the opportunity.

Giving him that opportunity hasn't been easy. The first time I played with Justin was in the Adelaide Test against the West Indies in January 1993. Though he was a last minute replacement, because Damien Martyn and Dean Jones were unfit, he turned out to be the guy who really held us together on the last day, grinding out 54 in 253 minutes. He was just about on the plane for England later that year when he had the misfortune to pick up a pair in a Test at Eden Park and not get picked.

For the next five years, that was the story of Justin's career: he was always the last guy picked, and the first one dropped, and sat through tours of Pakistan, West Indies and England as a constant first reserve. But the great thing about Justin was that he wore the disappointment so well. You never heard any complaints, and he was always the first guy to take pleasure in other people's successes. I remember the party after we won the Frank Worrell Trophy back from the West Indies five and a half years ago; although he hadn't played any Tests on the trip, he partied as hard as anyone. Justin had the Aussie flag round his neck all night like a Superman cape, and ended up getting a tattoo on his backside to mark the occasion.

All Justin needed was a bit of luck, and he probably got it in Pakistan about two years ago. He was picked at number three in the first Test at Rawalpindi, and was lbw for a duck to an unplayable in-ducker from Wasim Akram. We stuck with him for the second Test at Peshawar and he got a virtually identical delivery from Shoaib Akhtar that also hit him on the pads. It looked pretty close to me, and Justin must've thought it was curtains, but the umpire let him off and he finally made the breakthrough: his maiden Test hundred after five and a half years and ten widely-spaced Tests.

Since then, he's not looked back. He's now made seven Test hundreds, boosted his average to 41.75, and played several crucial smaller innings. In very tough conditions on an underprepared pitch in Auckland six months ago, his attacking 46 and 47 were worth a hundred each. And the way he finished that tour with the second-fastest Test hundred by an Australian—122 not out off 122 balls at Hamilton—suggested that we still haven't seen the best of him at international level.

Justin Langer walks to practice before the
second Test at Bellerive Oval, Hobart.

One influence in Justin's transformation, I think, has been his seasons in county cricket. He played for Middlesex in 1998 and 1999, getting heaps of runs and often batting very aggressively, and is now captain. We Aussies are apt to sneer at the county circuit a bit. But, if you enjoy playing cricket all the time, it can be a great education. I suspect that being treated as a senior player in what is otherwise a pretty ordinary team, and depended on for runs day-in day-out, has probably been really good for Justin: he's written a terrific book about his experiences called *From Outback to Outfield*, and turned himself into a bit of a journalist by writing his Postcards series on the Baggy Green website.

By the same token, there's always been something a bit special about Justin. He comes from a good gene pool; I played against his uncle Robbie, who was a tough, aggressive number three for Western Australia 20 years ago, very unlucky not to play Test matches. And Justin's a handy guy to have on your side; he has a black belt in martial arts, and the other guys in the Aussie side have to be pretty careful what they say to him! He's also a solid family man with two kids, having married Sue in April 1996, and I think in time will come into calculations as a Test captain; he's a bit of a Steve Waugh disciple, and a lot of Steve's confidence and determination has rubbed off on him.

No matter what Justin achieves, he's already gone down in history with Adam Gilchrist as a result of their match-winning, sixth-wicket stand of 238 against Pakistan in the second Test at Bellerive Oval last summer. Justin had been under a bit of media pressure about his recent scores—though his name hadn't really come up at the selection table—and we were looking pretty sick at 5 for 126 chasing 369 in the fourth innings late on the fourth day. But Justin confided to Gilly when they got together: 'You never know.' And they took it from there, eventually making it look easy. Justin made 59 and 127 in that game against a top-line attack, batting nine and a half hours in the match often under enormous pressure, which testifies to his fantastic concentration and survival instincts. He's a really gutsy cricketer and, personally, I can't help but feel pleased for him, knowing all the checks and setbacks he's experienced since his Test career began.

BRETT LEE

BORN:	8 November 1976, Wollongong, NSW
FULL NAME:	Brett Lee
BATTING STYLE:	Right Hand Bat
BOWLING STYLE:	Right Arm Fast
TEST DEBUT:	Australia v. India at Melbourne, 2nd Test, 1999/2000

Brett Lee

Twenty-three-year-old Brett Lee hit international cricket with the force of a cyclone last summer, coming from nowhere and bowling like the wind against India, Pakistan, New Zealand and South Africa to bag 60 international wickets in next to no time. But while it might look as though we rushed him into the big time on the basis of only a handful of first-class games, the truth is otherwise.

I first saw Brett as a 16-year-old, when he came to bowl to the Australian team in the SCG nets, and he was that quick it was scary. He was a bit wild, and his direction wasn't so hot, but we all went: 'Gee, where's this kid come from? We should pick him now!' But although he made his first-class debut for the AIS Cricket Academy on a New Zealand tour in April 1995, we held off until we'd seen a bit more of him, and also until he dispelled a lingering question mark about his fitness. He had one of those half-and-half actions—not quite side-on, not quite front-on—which place great strain on a guy's back, and he needed to sort that out before he really became a contender for higher honours.

Brett was picked in the Australia A team to play South Africa in December 1997 and looked very promising indeed, but a few weeks later hurt his back diving in the field during a grade game for Mosman.

He went on an Academy tour of Zimbabwe in March 1998, but stress fractures then kept him out of the game until just before Christmas that year, and we finally decided to try him out on the Australia A trip to California in September 1999.

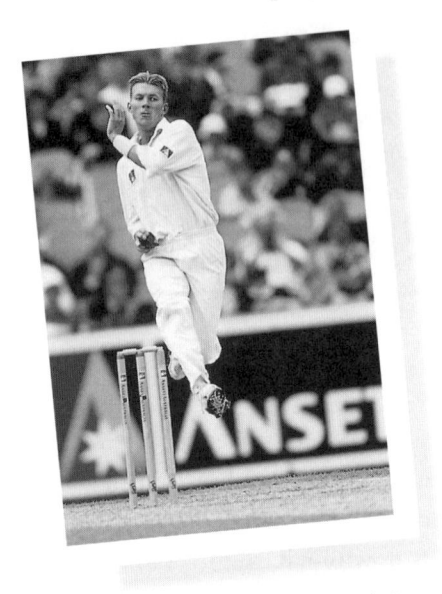

As coach for those five matches against India A in Los Angeles, I was pretty impressed with him. His action had straightened out and he obviously had huge potential, but I remained unsure that he was ready for the top level. There was a bit of a push for him from his Blues skipper Steve Waugh and we picked him for the third Test against Pakistan in Perth: we thought it would be beneficial for Brett if we steered him into the Australian system early so he could knock around with experienced guys like Steve and Glenn McGrath. But we didn't include him in the XI because he hadn't played at the WACA before, and young quicks who don't have prior experience of its pace and bounce can sometimes go a bit crazy the first time they play there.

Another quick one from Brett Lee during the second Test against India at the MCG.

I must admit that I still wasn't completely convinced about Brett when I watched him play in a Pura Milk Cup game 10 days later: he got wickets but Daniel Marsh and Mark Atkinson of Tasmania seemed pretty comfortable against him. But when he then blitzed the Warriors a week or so after that, the circumstances were right for his selection in the Boxing Day Test in Melbourne: we were 1–0 up against India, and Brett had enjoyed the confidence boost of a few wickets against the tourists in the Prime Minister's XI match.

It's history now that he more than did the job. Steve, who'd been such an advocate for Brett, cleverly slipped him in for an over before lunch on the third day just to settle his nerves and he bowled

Sadogoppan Ramesh with his fourth ball. He then claimed three wickets in his 14th over, and ended up with 5 for 47 and 2 for 31 on debut. In the five Tests and 17 one-day internationals he's now played, he's broken the 150kmh barrier so routinely that we've almost become blasé about it.

What I like about Brett particularly is that he's got such a good head on his shoulders. He's such a quick learner, and there's more to his bowling than pure pace; being of average height, he has the trajectory for natural outswing, and he understands the importance of variety. He's worked really hard on his physical conditioning, especially in building up his stomach muscles as support for his back, and is prepared to slip into the special ice baths that our physiotherapists recommend at the end of every day's play to improve their recovery rates...squealing like a stuck pig as he does so!

I also like the fact that there are things in Brett's life apart from cricket. He's kept his job selling suits in Sydney, which is really healthy, because it means he keeps a foot in the real world. He's also very keen on his music, playing in a band called Six and Out with his brother Shane and other New South Wales teammates Richard Chee Quee, Brad McNamara and Gavin Robertson. They're not bad either. My view has generally been that cricketers should confine their singing to the dressing room, so I was a bit wary of what they might be like when they played at the waterfront wedding of our physio, Errol Alcott, in January. But they were actually really good. Apparently when they play in pubs they get bigger crowds than come to some Pura Milk Cup matches!

One other impact that Brett might have is on his older brother. Shane, who is three years older than Brett, has been playing for the Blues for eight years, and earned 41 one-day international caps, but you sometimes get the impression that he's in cruise mode. I saw him quoted recently as saying: 'A few months ago I was Shane Lee. Now I'm Brett Lee's older brother.' Perhaps the fact that his little brother's come so far so fast will spur Shane to make full use of his potential. A guy with his abilities should be capable of playing Test cricket, and he would be very good for the balance of the side. I think we've already seen signs, and it would be great to have them both firing in the same team.

DAMIEN MARTYN

BORN: 21 October 1971, Darwin, NT
FULL NAME: Damien Richard Martyn
BATTING STYLE: Right Hand Bat
BOWLING STYLE: Right Arm Medium
TEST DEBUT: Australia v. West Indies at Brisbane, 1st Test, 1992/93

Damien Martyn

Some years ago, about the time he turned 21 in late 1992, Damien Martyn would probably have been voted the young Australian cricketer most likely to succeed. Not only was he clearly blessed with enormous natural batting talent, but it seemed he had the temperament and the mental toughness to make it at the top. Nobody was too surprised, therefore, when Martyn was chosen to make his Test debut against the West Indians in 1992–93, only his second season in first-class cricket. He showed his calibre in the second Test, when Australia's batting collapsed around him, by top-scoring with 67 not out; an innings which enabled Australia to go on to win.

Martyn's future then could hardly have seemed brighter, but Test cricket was to prove an unexpectedly tough arena. For whatever reason, he seemed unable to reproduce there the wonderful batting form which had made him a star of the Western Australian side (and which earned him the state captaincy at the age of 23, the youngest-ever in that state). His budding Test career hit a low at the Sydney Cricket Ground in January 1994. Needing just 117 to win, Australia's batting went to pieces under pressure in the second innings. Martyn tried hard to hold out, but his defensive approach seemed to allow the South Africans to take the offensive, and they went on to win by five runs. Martyn survived for 106

RIGHT: Shane Warne hits one for six during the first Test v. India at the Adelaide Oval.

BELOW: A general view of the Adelaide Oval, one of the most popular venues for Australian Test cricketers.

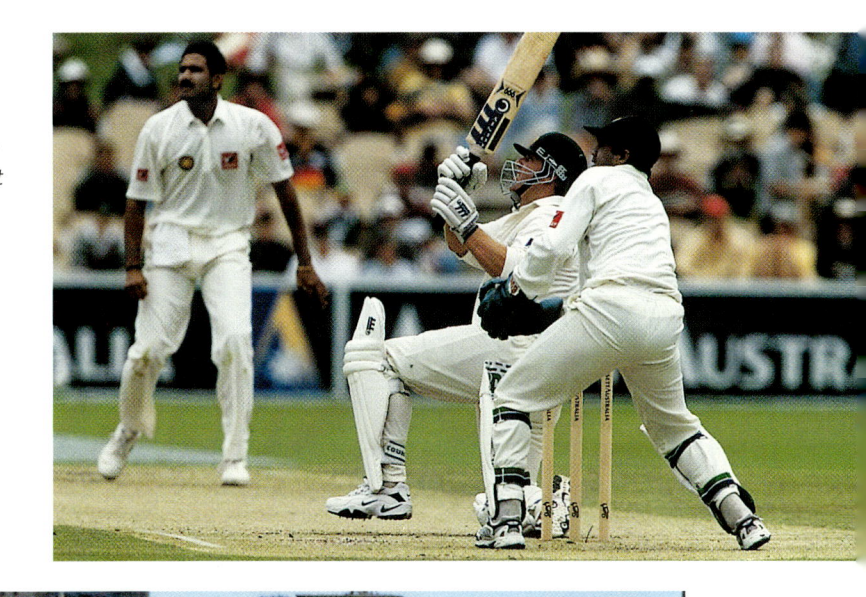

RIGHT: Steve Waugh makes the coin toss for choice of play at the MCG while Sachin Tendulkar, the Indian captain, looks on.

BELOW: The popular Ian Healy takes a lap of honour at the MCG on his retirement from first class cricket.

ABOVE: Brett Lee proudly displays his baggy green cap, awarded to him before the second Test v. India at the MCG.

ABOVE RIGHT: The new quick bowler in the Australian team, Brett Lee, sends down his first ball against India in the second Test at the MCG.

RIGHT: Lunging to his right, Brett Lee fields a ball off his own bowling on day three of his first Test

BELOW: Brett Lee dismisses Javagal Srinath, to reach seven wickets on his Test debut for Australia.

ABOVE: Sachin Tendulkar is dismissed by Shane Warne in the second Test v. India at the MCG.

LEFT: Shane Warne gives some silent advice to noisy Indian fans.

BELOW: Greg Blewett slashes a ball in the second innings against India at the MCG.

ABOVE: The team celebrates after its victory over India at the MCG.

LEFT: Shane Warne has ice packs attached to his shoulder to reduce the pain at the end of the Test match against India in Melbourne.

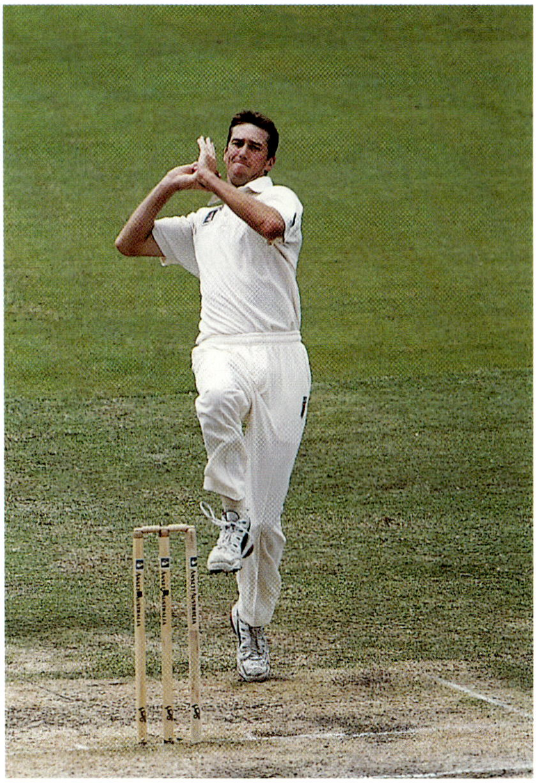
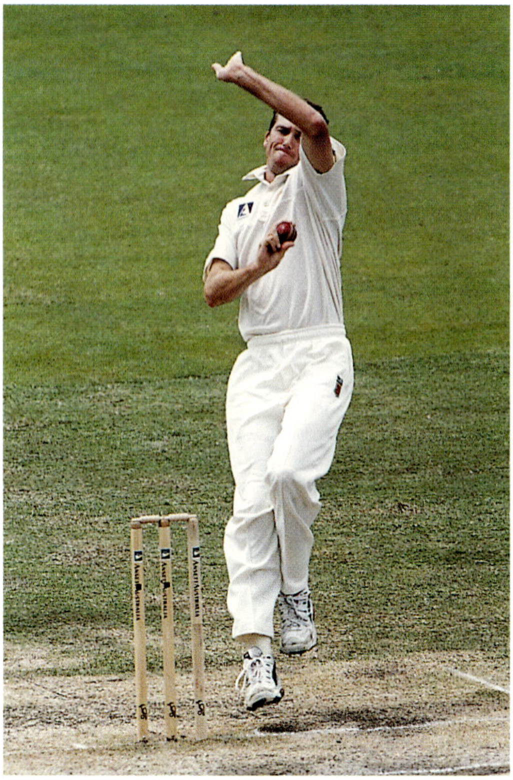
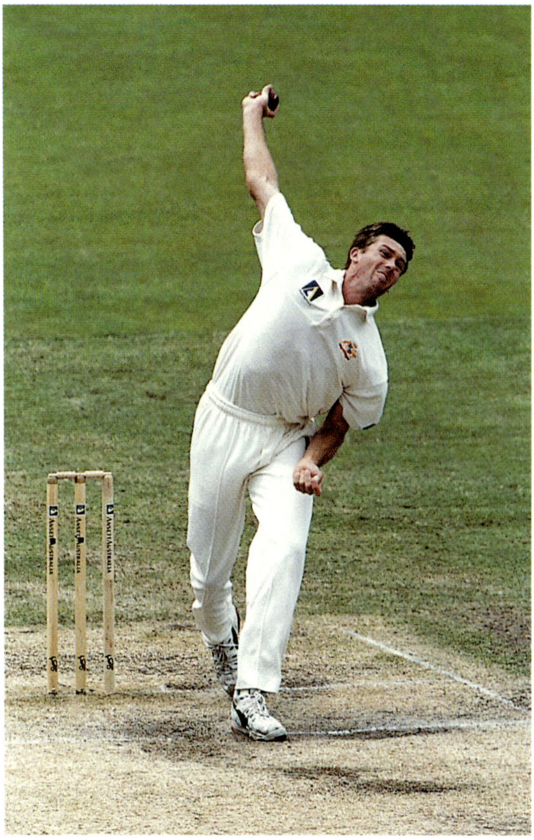
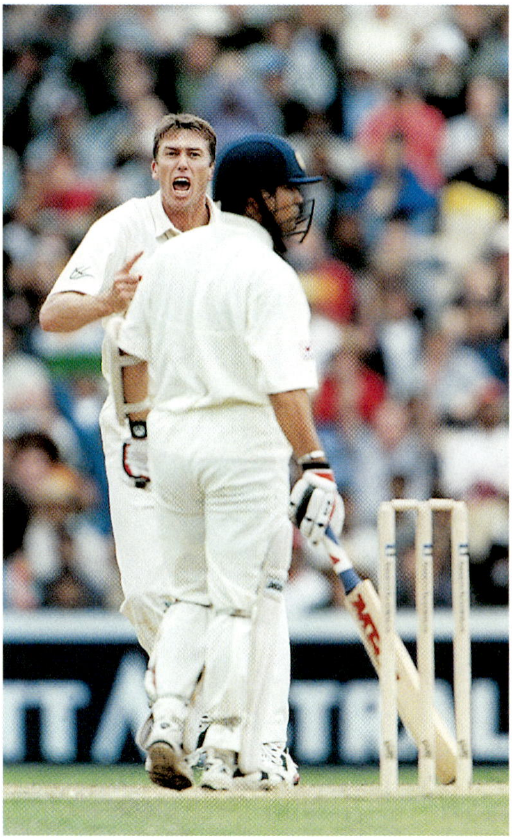

OPPOSITE PAGE: Glenn McGrath bowls and fields with such an incredible intensity that on occasion it boils over as when (in the picture bottom right) he screams at Sachin Tendulkar, the Indian captain, after taking his wicket. In this second Test v. India, McGrath captured 10 wickets.

ABOVE: Justin Langer drives for another four runs on his way to making 223 against India at the Sydney Cricket Ground. This is the highest individual Australian score in a Test match against India. At top right he is seen acknowledging the applause of the crowd when he reaches his double century.

RIGHT: Ricky Ponting and Justin Langer who together made 364 runs out of Australia's 552 for 5 wickets declared.

RIGHT: Steve Waugh holds the Border-Gavaskar trophy and a cheque from a sponsor, after Australia won the Test series against India.

BELOW: Mark Waugh and Steve Waugh enjoy a moment with the Prime Minister, John Howard, in the dressing rooms at the Sydney Cricket Ground.

minutes, but in that time he scored just six singles. It was the slowest innings of six in the history of Test cricket.

Martyn was barely 22 years old at the time, so he could hardly be blamed for what happened that day, yet somehow that Test marked a downturn in his career. He was not merely dropped but, it seemed, he was now on the outer. In the years that followed he kept playing for Western Australia, but he was no longer looked upon as a contender for national selection.

Martyn himself, though, had not given up. He set about changing his attitude and approach to the game, believing this was essential if he were to revive his career. It took time, but eventually in 1998 his hard work and application were rewarded by a recall to the Australian one-day side. His success there suggested he might yet regain his place in the Australian Test side. His chance finally came in New Zealand in 2000 when he was chosen to replace the injured Ricky Ponting. It was Martyn's first Test in six years, and he celebrated the news of his selection by carrying his bat in the final one-day international against New Zealand, scoring 116.

Martyn played in all three Tests in New Zealand and topped the Australian batting averages in the series, scoring 241 runs at an average of 60.25. 'It's been a long, hard slog back,' he was quoted as saying. 'My game's pretty complete now. I'm looking after myself, preparing myself. Hopefully, it will be better second time around.'

Damien Martyn counter-attacks in the first Test against New Zealand.

GLENN McGRATH

BORN: 9 February 1970, Dubbo, NSW
FULL NAME: Glenn Donald McGrath
BATTING STYLE: Right Hand Bat
BOWLING STYLE: Right Arm Fast Medium
TEST DEBUT: Australia v. New Zealand at Perth, 1st Test, 1993/94

Australian Cricket Academy 1992–93
Wisden Cricketer of the Year 1998
Allan Border Medal 2000

Glenn McGrath

People who see Glenn McGrath on the field, dishing it out with ball and banter, know only the half of it. He's almost a split personality. Off the field, Australia's number one strike bowler is actually a nice guy, generally pretty quiet and unassuming. It's just that there's a side of him which comes out when he has the five and a quarter ounces of red leather in his hand. He's ultra competitive, ultra serious, and sometimes crosses the line, but you always know you're in a contest.

Funnily enough, he wasn't always that way. When I played against Glenn for the first time during November 1993, in Queensland's Sheffield Shield match against New South Wales, he was as quiet as a church mouse. He had us in a bit of strife early, and I thought: 'Here's this new young quick. I'll see if I can bait him'. He was wearing these pants that were far too short for him, finishing half way up his calves; he'd obviously found it hard to get trousers that fitted him. So as he was walking past me to the end of his mark, I started calling him 'big dumb country okey' and 'Jethro'. He didn't say boo. I thought: 'That's interesting. He's holding together pretty well. Doesn't seem to affect his bowling either.' But he obviously cottoned on to the verbals pretty quick smart. I don't think anyone would get away with saying that to him today!

That first time I saw him, Glenn was basically a tearaway quick from

The Team

the bush. When he came into the Australian side a week later, he'd only played six first-class games and he was obviously very raw. He tells a story in one of Steve Waugh's books about how I'd get stuck into him for not paying attention when he was down at deep fine leg. Well, captains do expect perfection! But he was actually very good to captain, because he was obviously really keen to learn, and we were on the lookout for a quickie at that point to complement Craig McDermott. It's history now that he's blossomed into something special since. I wouldn't call him an unsung hero, but Warney still probably gets most of the limelight, and there are times when Glenn has carried the attack just brilliantly, especially in the West Indies in 1995.

At the outset of his career, we didn't see Glenn as the kind of bowler who would rocket towards 300 Test wickets. In fact, he got mucked around a bit, because there were people who wanted to turn him into a classic old-time outswing bowler. If you look at it over history, though, the guys who make great swing bowlers tend to be a bit shorter. When you're as tall as Glenn, the natural trajectory seems to stop you doing much with the ball in the air; Glenn basically comes over the top and bowls a shade shorter. To his credit, Glenn sorted everything out, and worked on his strengths: unwavering accuracy—dot ball after dot ball, building up the pressure—and that ability to hit the seam over and over again.

Glenn is also a real thinking bowler. He's taken 288 wickets in his first 62 Tests at 22.9 each, not to mention 179 wickets at 23.2 in one-day internationals, and he could tell you about every one of them: how it was out (whether it was lbw or caught Healy or whatever) and what kind of delivery it was (nipbacker hitting off stump or short one taken in the gully). I don't know whether he's kept his own records and pores over them, or whether it's in his head, but he's completely fastidious about his craft.

Probably my only concern with Glenn is that he always wants to bowl. Though he's been lucky with injuries, he's sometimes bowled when not fully fit. He's one of those guys who, whenever you see him and ask how he's going, he'll always say: 'Fine'. It's almost like you have to tie him down and give him truth serum to find out how he's really feeling! As selectors, we want to encourage our blokes to report the niggles. It's better for them and us, because it's courting disaster to take someone who's a bit crook into a five-day game. But Glenn's so determined that he wouldn't tell you if he had a broken leg.

Another area in which Glenn's determination is evident is his batting. When he started, he was totally unco-ordinated, but he never treated it as a joke. He was always shattered to get out, and he's one of those guys who can't understand why he isn't able to bat like Sir Donald Bradman. Over the past few years, Glenn's gone from hopeless to hopeful, and can really hang in there, which is probably due to the influence of his batting coach, Steve Waugh.

In the dressing room, Glenn's taken over from Merv Hughes as the resident 'fruit fly': the Great Australian Pest. He's one of the guys who's always initiating those little dressing room dramas, throwing ring pulls or bottle tops. He's also fond of showing off his latest commando hold by grabbing you in a headlock. In short, when Glenn's bored, it's time to look out!

Away from cricket, he's got very simple pleasures. He loves getting back to his property with his wife Jane and new son James, and going off after rabbits, shooting and skinning 'em. You see the guys getting on planes with magazines to read, and it's generally the ones to do with sports and fishing. With Glenn, it's usually *Guns & Ammo*, which is a bit of a worry! But like I said, Glenn's really a man of peace. Except when he's got the ball in his hand.

Glenn McGrath starts his run-up at Bellerive Oval, Hobart.

COLIN MILLER

BORN: 6 February 1964, Footscray, VIC
FULL NAME: Colin Reid Miller
BATTING STYLE: Right Hand Bat
BOWLING STYLE: Right Arm Off Break,
Right Arm Fast Medium
TEST DEBUT: Australia v. Pakistan at Rawalpindi,
1st Test, 1998/99

Colin Miller

If Colin Miller had not emerged at the international level when he did, Australian cricket might have wanted to invent a player just like him, for he filled a specific need to perfection. As a bowler, Miller was of a type that had not been seen for years: one who could come on at first change and bowl fastish seam or swing, then drop his pace later and bowl spinners off a short run. The Australian Bill Johnston, a member of Don Bradman's all-conquering 1948 team, was just such a bowler. So was the great West Indian all-rounder Garfield Sobers.

Bowlers of this kind are immensely useful, especially in a four-man attack, and it is surprising that Australia had to wait so long for another to arrive. In fact, Funky Miller chose to reinvent himself as a bowler of this type almost as an after-thought. It happened during the 1996–97 season. Miller was then 32 years old and apparently nearing the end of a moderately successful career as an interstate pace bowler, which had begun as far back as 1985. Born in Victoria, he had played variously for Victoria, South Australia and Tasmania. He had also played as a professional in England and in Holland. It might have seemed he had already done everything in cricket that he would ever do, but he still had one card to play.

About the middle of that 1996–97 season Miller decided to have a go at bowling spin. He took it up seriously in the following season and, almost at once, wickets fell to him in abundance. He took 70 first-class wickets that season, including 12 against South Australia at Hobart; a Tasmanian record. He was still getting a majority of his wickets with his pace, but the addition of off spin to his repertoire had virtually doubled his effectiveness. As a bowler of off spin he proved to be a natural, displaying from the outset the kind of control that other bowlers take a lifetime to develop.

Suddenly, Miller seemed like a new bowler with a new career. The Australian selectors certainly viewed him that way. He was chosen for the tour of Pakistan late in 1998 and there, aged 34, he made his Test debut. To play even one Test was an extraordinary achievement for a bowler of his age and background, but for Miller it was merely the start. He has remained a semi-regular of the Australian Test side. By the end of the tour of New Zealand in 2000, where he played in all three Tests, Miller had taken 43 wickets in 14 Tests at an impressive average of 28.81.

His Test bowling average, it is worth noting, is better than his overall first-class average, which shows where his career has been heading.

That career is not yet over. The indications are that Miller intends to press on and, provided his form holds, he is likely to be a strong contender for the Ashes tour of England in 2001. His second life as a cricketer has, perhaps, only just begun.

A jubilant Funky in New Zealand.

Scott Muller

SCOTT MULLER

BORN: 11 July 1971, Herston, QLD
FULL NAME: Scott Andrew Muller
BATTING STYLE: Right Hand Bat
BOWLING STYLE: Right Arm Fast Medium
TEST DEBUT: Australia v. Pakistan at Brisbane, 1st Test, 1999/2000

Scott Muller

Most fast bowlers who make it to the international scene do so in their early twenties, when they are at the peak of their strength and fitness. Scott Muller was an exception. He was 28 years old when, unexpectedly, the national selectors decided in late 1999 to elevate him to the Australian side. Jason Gillespie had been injured when he collided on the field with Steve Waugh in Sri Lanka, and Muller was rushed there to replace him. He made his first appearance for Australia in the next tour match, and he celebrated the occasion by taking a wicket with his first ball; the first of five wickets in the innings.

For Muller, it was the latest twist to a career which had already taken several unusual turns. He was a product of the Gold Coast, having grown up there and gone to school at Southport School; one of Queensland's GPS schools. He shone at cricket as a teenager and played for Queensland under-17s in 1987–88. Then, aged 19, he was given a startling promotion: he was picked to play for Queensland in a Sheffield Shield match in Melbourne, Queensland's last match of the 1990–91 season. He performed modestly, but he clearly had put a foot in the door of interstate cricket.

So Muller's first-class career had got off to an early start, but it proved a false start. He failed to make the Queensland side in the following season and for several seasons after that. At one stage, in fact, he was relegated to second grade in the Brisbane competition. But he persevered and finally, in 1996–97, almost six years after that initial appearance, he fought his way back into the Queensland side, playing eight Shield matches and taking 21 wickets. But having achieved that, he then decided his playing days were over and announced his retirement.

Before the next season, however, he was persuaded to keep playing. It was fortunate he did, for his bowling had by now moved up a class. Tall and blessed with 'an iron man's physique', as one newspaper described it, Muller bowled at sharp pace, was able to make the ball lift and could swing it dangerously away from the right-handers. When he was 'on song', there were few more potent pace bowlers in Australia. A foot injury restricted him to three matches in 1997–98, yet he managed to take 13 wickets at 17.3. In 1998–99, he played six matches and took 22 at 18.5. It was this bowling which earned him the trip to Sri Lanka.

Scotty Muller is as enthusiastic in training as he is during a Test match.

Muller was still in the selectors' favour when the Test series against Pakistan began in November 1999. He played in the first two Tests with modest results. He took seven wickets, but even his admirers felt he had not performed at his best. To make matters worse, he became the centre of a controversy over the 'can't bowl, can't throw' remark picked up on television. Dropped from the Australian team, he had another strong season with Queensland, taking 22 wickets in seven matches at 22.31. Nobody should rule him out of future contention for the Australian side.

RICKY PONTING

BORN: 19 December 1974, Launceston, TAS
FULL NAME: Ricky Thomas Ponting
BATTING STYLE: Right Hand Bat
BOWLING STYLE: Right Arm Medium
TEST DEBUT: Australia v. Sri Lanka at Perth, 1st Test, 1995/96

Australian Cricket Academy 1992–1993

Ricky Ponting

It's about seven years since Rod Marsh, the guru of the AIS Cricket Academy, confided to me: 'I've got a kid here who's the best I've ever seen. It's only a matter of time before you pick him.' Rod's judgement is so impeccable that I wasn't at all surprised to see that kid blossom into a guy who today is certainly among the very best batsmen in the world.

Ricky Ponting has always been a bloke with big wraps on him. I'm told that he was signed up by Gray-Nicholls in Tasmania as a 12-year-old, and it doesn't surprise me in the least. Those high expectations must have placed a good deal of pressure on the lad, and his career has not been without controversy; Ricky's the kind of guy who doesn't take a backward step whatever he's doing, which sometimes gets him into trouble in the public domain, but the dramas he's been through have only strengthened and matured him. We made him vice-captain of Australia's one-day side last summer when Shane Warne was injured, which attests to our faith in him.

I first played against Ricky in a Sheffield Shield match at the Gabba in October 1994. Queensland had a pretty useful attack, including Carl Rackemann, Dirk Tazelaar and Greg Rowell, but Ricky made an aggressive 119, and put on 208 with Shaun Young. He was difficult to bowl to because he was technically so strong and played so well off both feet: he was a fearless puller and hooker, and he drove anything that was overpitched.

At that stage, Ricky was also developing almost by the day. A year later when Queensland went to Bellerive Oval with our attack strengthened by Craig McDermott and Michael Kasprowicz, he made unbeaten hundreds in both innings; the second of them from 97 balls. Not long afterwards, the selectors picked Ricky for his first Test, replacing Greg Blewett against Sri Lanka in Perth, and only a pretty ordinary lbw decision stopped him four short of yet another century.

He's now just about the complete cricketer, and shaping as the guy most likely to succeed Mark Waugh at number four. He has such faith in his abilities that even the few setbacks he's experienced have made no difference. Last season he started the Test matches with an amazing sequence of three consecutive ducks against Pakistan. But Ricky never became dispirited. I remember him telling me just before the third Test in Perth: 'I'm hitting the ball so well in the nets that I'm sure I'm not out of form. It just seems like I'm out before I can blink. But it's not like I'm struggling for half an hour then getting a really ugly duck. I think I'm in good nick. It's just not happening at the moment.' I knew then that he was liable to explode sooner rather than later, and so he did: he smashed 197 off 288 balls at the WACA, then followed it up against India with 125 from 198 deliveries in Adelaide and 141 not out from 183 deliveries in Sydney. That's an amazing rate of scoring at Test level, but par for the course when Ricky's running hot.

Ricky had the misfortune to suffer a bad ankle injury when he crashed into the SCG fence during the second of the one-day finals on 4 February, but I think the circumstances tell you a lot about him as a cricketer. For a start, he sustained the injury because he was chasing so hard, because he wasn't going to let that bloody ball beat him into the boundary. When it came to undergoing a fitness test shortly afterwards to determine whether he went on the New Zealand tour, he was then honest enough to admit that he wasn't quite right. He was doing fine in the training drills, and he probably would have been passed fit if he'd told us he was OK. But he knew that he wasn't, made himself available and went back to the doctors. It turned out that he needed six months off! Only someone as determined as Ricky would have even tried the fitness test in the first place. Only someone as honest would have admitted he wasn't up to the strain of the tour.

As it is, Ricky has plenty of things to occupy him away from cricket. He's probably the best golfer in the current Australian side, playing off two. He's also crazy about his greyhounds—thus the nickname of Punter that Shane Warne awarded him five years ago—and owns and trains a kennel full. I know that he's got his eye on an allotment outside Launceston which he wants to turn into a dog run.

Ricky is also among the Australian team's most avid pranksters. He started early, too. Sitting in business class with the usual bag of goodies on his first tour to the West Indies in 1995, he suggested that Steve Waugh try out some of the excellent breath freshener he'd just found. Except it wasn't breath freshener. The result was shaving cream all over Tuggas spanking new IBM laptop! I don't think I'd have been game to pull anything like that on my first tour!

Probably Ricky's best Test knock was at Leeds in 1997, where he walked in at 4 for 50 and blasted 127. His stand of 268 with Matthew Elliott in 263 minutes turned the tide of that series, pushing Australia into the lead for the first time from which point we never looked back. Ricky was also Australia's outstanding batsman in Sri Lanka a year ago when the rest of his teammates were really struggling against their brilliant off-spinner Muttiah Muralitharan. You have to be very confident of your abilities when you advance on Murali—he bowls that straight one so well—but confidence is not something Ricky's short of.

The most remarkable aspect of Ricky's career is that he doesn't turn 26 until 19 December 2000. He's already hit a total of 5844 runs in Test matches and one-day internationals and, while he's matured all the way, he may not peak for another three years. That's a bit frightening... for opposition bowlers.

Another ton for Punter.

MICHAEL SLATER

BORN: 21 February 1970, Wagga Wagga, NSW
FULL NAME: Michael Jonathon Slater
BATTING STYLE: Right Hand Bat
BOWLING STYLE: Right Arm Medium
TEST DEBUT: Australia v. England at Manchester, 1st Test, 1993

Australian Cricket Academy 1989

Michael Slater

What you see with Michael Slater is pretty much what you get. Whether he's opening the batting for Australia, or behind the wheel of his Mazda RX7, or joining in the fun after a Test victory, he gives it the kitchen sink. He has a list of 10 commandments which he calls 'The Slater Creed', at the top of which is: 'Above all, enjoy your cricket.' It shows in everything he does.

The first time I saw Slats was on the plane to go to England in 1993. I'd never seen him play, but the selectors liked what they'd seen of him in his dozen first-class games, and from memory he was one of those 'speckies' in which John Benaud used to specialise. I initially thought that Matt Hayden would be Mark Taylor's opening partner for the Tests, and we picked him for the Texaco Trophy matches at the start of the tour. But when Matt struggled, the tour selectors had second thoughts, and in the end it came down to the tour match against Leicestershire before the first Test: Matt got knocked over for 2 and 16, while Slats made 91 and 50 not out. It was still no more than a gut decision to go with Slats, influenced by the fact that he was a right-handed foil to the left-handed Taylor, and that they were New South Wales teammates.

In hindsight, it was a great move. Michael has made 4603 Test runs at almost 44, which is fantastic for an opening batsman, and his

The Team

conversion rate is outstanding: he's passed 50 thirty times in Tests and turned 14 of those into centuries. He's also a brilliant character who lives life at a million miles an hour, and whom we quickly nicknamed Sybil. Like the woman in the movie who had 25 personalities, Slats changes character in post-match celebrations and by the end of the party, he can be very funny.

Although he made a lot of runs in England, the first time he really impressed me was in the second Test against South Africa at Sydney in January 1994. The Proteas bowled really well in that match—Donald, de Villiers, Matthews and Symcox were a really hot attack—and maintained the pressure all the way. Slats made 92 and the pair of us took more than four hours to grind out 104 for the fourth wicket. I remember him coming down the wicket and saying: 'Gee, how hard is this? Where are you meant to score a run?' I replied: 'Welcome to Test cricket. This is what it's like.' We ended up losing that Test, but through no fault of Michael's, and he certainly gained a lot from the experience.

Like many guys who wear their hearts on their sleeves, Michael can get down on himself, and being dropped in November 1996 was a huge ordeal for him. Understandably, he found it very hard to comprehend how he could be left out after 34 consecutive Tests and 2655 runs at 47.4. Steve Bernard had the job of telling Slats, and he got a bit of a lashing. Some guys take it well when they're omitted, even though you can tell they're burning inside, but Michael went off his nut.

In hindsight, the decision had a mixed result. The guy who probably suffered as much as Michael from his absence was Mark Taylor. Mark had always combined really well with Slats: Slats always took it up to the bowlers and the way he disrupted their line and length meant that Mark was able to score with more freedom. In Michael's absence, Mark's form suffered, which hurt the side despite his continuing excellence as skipper.

From Michael's viewpoint, however, I think that being dropped was a good wake-up call for him. Like Steve Waugh, he had the character to come back, and to do so a better player: he topped 1000 runs in calendar 1999, his first full year back, and made them without any cost to his natural flair.

It's great for the team to have him back, too, because he's a terrific influence on the dressing room. He loves his cars and drives like a madman. He also genuinely rates himself as the new Elvis Presley. At Errol Alcott's wedding in January, he did several spots as guest vocalist with the Lee brothers' band Six and Out and was a real hit. In a similar situation, most guys will just stand behind the mike happy enough to remember the words, but Slats had all the moves and the gestures down pat, even the gyrating hips!

Michael's wife Stephanie, whom he married after getting home from the Ashes tour in 1993, is a brilliant girl, a really effervescent personality. She and Michael are probably as mad as each other! I can see Michael having a future on television when he's through playing, on a lifestyle show or hosting a quiz, because he's got the sort of personality that lights up a room.

The only thing that really bugs Michael these days is why he hasn't made the transition into Australia's one-day side. He's not shy about saying so either! Most guys when they have a selection problem will seek you out for a quiet word. Not Michael. He's in your face. He wants to know why. Which I actually don't mind at all; it's always best being honest about these things. The best answer I can give him is that his record in the one-day games he's played isn't the best (987 runs in 42 games at an average of 24) and also that he is a better player than his record for NSW in the Mercantile Mutual Cup (averaging 25 in 25 games). We all know that he has the game to succeed in the one-day form. But, unlike Matthew Hayden, he hasn't given us much ammunition. I'm sure in the not too distant future he will.

Michael Slater is a picture of concentration as he prepares to attack the Sri Lankan bowling.

SHANE WARNE

BORN:	13 September 1969, Ferntree Gully, Melbourne, VIC
FULL NAME:	Shane Keith Warne
BATTING STYLE:	Right Hand Bat
BOWLING STYLE:	Leg Break, Googly
TEST DEBUT:	Australia v. India at Sydney, 3rd Test, 1991/92

Wisden Cricketer of the Year 1994
Australian Cricket Academy 1990
Selected as one of five Wisden cricketers of the century, 2000

Shane Warne

For Shane Warne, life is a competition. Go round the golf course with him, and he can't help it; he has to have a few side bets. Go to the casino, and he has to try his luck; he believes in the magical properties of 23 Red (his old number when he was an Australian rules footballer for St Kilda). Get him on a cricket field, of course, and he'll back himself to do anything. Which, much more often than not, he can.

Unlike his bowling, Warney as a bloke is entirely straightforward. He lives life at breakneck pace, and he can charm anyone. Whether he's talking to James Packer, or the battler bloke in the pub, he's exactly the same guy. There's a public perception that he's a bit of a big-head, a lair, and he certainly is a confident and exuberant character. But he's an open book. He just wears his heart on his sleeve.

His cricket, of course, is something special. He's added so much to the game. Warney might just be the best bowler of all time, and he must be the best leg-spinner in history. He was great for me personally; it enlarged my captaincy enormously to suddenly be able to call on a match-winning slow bowler in terms of the fields we were able to set and the alternatives we could explore.

Shane had a pretty ordinary introduction to Test cricket. On his debut against India in January 1992, after only seven first-class matches, he took 1 for 150 off 45 overs. But, while it's easy to say so after the fact, I never had any doubts that he would succeed. I liked Shane straight away, and there was something about his bowling from the very start. Nobody could have predicted that he'd achieve what he has, but you could tell that his raw potential was enormous.

He wasn't the fittest bloke going round in those days. He liked a good time, and he was a bit overweight. But once Warney had gotten a taste of the big time, he made a huge effort to measure up to its requirements and improved his fitness enormously. I remember clapping eyes on him when we got together before his first tour to Sri Lanka about eight months after his Test debut; he'd lost so much weight that we hardly recognised him.

The first Test of that series in Colombo was a real turning point for Shane. In the first innings, Arjuna Ranatunga hit us everywhere, Romesh Kaluwitharana looked like a reincarnation of Don Bradman, and Warney got belted. The pitch was turning, but Shane came up to me and said: 'AB, I don't know what to do.' I told him that there wasn't much he could do; it was just two guys on a real hot streak.

Happy days for Warney in Zimbabwe.

Then when we were really up against it on the last day—they were 2 for 127 needing another 54 to win—it was Greg Matthews who came up and said: 'You've got to use Warney. It's turning square.' My initial thought had been to bring Craig McDermott back, but I thought: 'Yeah, OK. He's accurate. He won't bowl rubbish.' At that stage, Shane's Test figures were 1 for 335. But he took three wickets for none and we won a Test that we had no right to.

The Team

To recite all Shane's feats in international cricket would need a whole book. He's taken more wickets (356 in Tests and 228 in one-day internationals) and bowled more balls (31,551 altogether) than anyone in Australian cricket history. Nearly as important has been his economy rate. Once upon a time, it was said that leg-spinners were an expensive luxury. But Warney gives away only 2.4 runs per Test over, which means that he can perform the roles of both shock and stock bowler according to the conditions.

To cover all the controversies that Shane's been sucked into would probably need another book. He certainly doesn't have to do much to get on the front page. Probably the worst one of all was his involvement with that Indian bookmaker six years ago, for which he was fined at the time, then absolutely hammered by the media when the story came out four years later. As far as I'm concerned, however, he was absolutely frank. He didn't know at the time he accepted the money from the guy in the casino in Sri Lanka that he was a bookie; he just thought it was a gift. It only emerged what he'd been dragged into when this bloke started ringing Shane seeking pitch and weather information in Australia. To Warney's credit, he accepted his wrongdoing and copped the fine.

As for the Scott Muller business last season, that was simply ridiculous. As Shane said afterwards, if he had said 'Can't bowl, can't throw', he would have been man enough to confess it. After all, many worse things have been said on a cricket field. But the fact was that he hadn't said it, as all the available evidence proved. I must say I thought Shane showed a lot of guts sticking to his guns the way he did.

Only one thing worries me a bit about Shane, and that's his diet. Not only is he a smoker, but I've never seen an international cricketer with poorer eating habits. Fruit and vegetables have never been known to pass his lips, and he even turns up his nose at steak. He sticks to toasted cheese sandwiches, Twisties, pizzas and strawberry milkshakes. He's even fond of the old tomato sauce roll! Basically, he eats the way we all ate as teenagers, except that he's now a 31-year-old with a wife and two gorgeous kids. I'm not one to lecture him on diet, though I wonder when he's going to start making a few concessions to being a sportsman. But I guess that's Shane in a nutshell. He does things his way.

MARK WAUGH

BORN: 2 June 1965, Canterbury, Sydney, NSW
FULL NAME: Mark Edward Waugh
BATTING STYLE: Right Hand Bat
BOWLING STYLE: Right Arm Medium, Right Arm Off Break
TEST DEBUT: Australia v. England at Adelaide, 4th Test, 1990/91

Wisden Cricketer of the Year 1991

Mark Waugh

Mark Waugh may have played 103 Test matches, but to me he remains an enigma. I look at the really great players of the modern era—Sachin Tendulkar, Brian Lara, Steve Waugh—and find it hard to believe that Mark with all his talent isn't up there. I wonder whether 6593 runs at 41.7 is the right sort of Test record for him, or whether he hasn't really been underachieving for the last decade.

Perhaps I'm not being fair, because Mark has given so many people so much pleasure over the years. When he's in full flow with the bat, there is nobody you'd rather watch. He's also one of very few players who can turn a match in the field, by latching on to some impossible catch, and lifting his teammates as a result. All the same, Junior's a bit of a puzzle. He says that he's tougher than people think, but he seems to lack ruthlessness.

I could tell Mark was special the first time I saw him. I was playing as an overseas professional for Essex at the time and, conscious I'd be unavailable for the 1989 season when the Ashes series was on, recommended him to the club. I said: 'I know you don't know him but, take it from me, he's a class act.' They took the gamble, and I stood down from a Sunday League game at Colchester in August 1988 to let them have a look at him. He got 103 and took 2 for 16 against Nottinghamshire. I gave myself a pat on the back for that!

The result was that Mark had played 100 first-class matches by the time he made his Test debut and scored 25 centuries; I'd only made two hundreds when I played my first Test, by way of contrast, while Steve hadn't made any. And that experience was obviously of great benefit to him. He came in at 4 for 104 on the first day of that Adelaide Test in January 1991 and peeled off a hundred in less than three hours, as easy as you like. I remember when we were congratulating him after he came in. While most guys in that situation are pretty quiet and humble, Junior said: 'Well, you should've picked me ages ago.' Not a lot we could say to that; maybe he was right.

Occasionally, though, Mark might be too confident for his own good. Sometimes before going in, he seems almost sleepy. He must be nervous but he never shows it (maybe he's thinking about the horses he's got running at the weekend!) and he can be vulnerable when he gets a good one early. In fact, he must be among the worst starters ever: there's a lot of ducks and scores of less than 10 between those 17 Test hundreds and 38 half-centuries.

Junior's got such faith in his abilities that he also rarely seems bothered by a poor score. He might say 'Gee, that was a good one' or 'What a shocking shot', but five minutes later he'll be fine. I remember him coming in after his fourth duck in a row in Sri Lanka eight years ago, when most guys would have been totally traumatised and taking it out on his teammates or his bag, but Mark didn't seem unusually depressed or worried.

Perhaps it would do Mark good to struggle a bit more. He can certainly apply himself when he needs to. His match-winning 116 at Port Elizabeth in March 1997 was made under incredible pressure: nobody else could have played that knock. And Mark's 153 not out against India in Bangalore a year later, still his highest Test score, came when he was crook. Maybe we should slip him a dodgy vindaloo before every innings, because he played as well as you can imagine anyone playing.

But things come so easily to Mark at other times that his guard can drop. Sometimes he seems to say: 'I don't rate this bowler. I'll take him down.' Which is something Steve would never do; he respects all his opponents, and knows that any bowler has the ability to get you out.

On the field, Mark is a very good influence on the team. He's competitive but relaxed, which is what you want players to be. He also has a pretty dry sense of humour. When the team played New Zealand earlier this year, one of our blokes was getting stuck into their Australian-born number three Matthew Sinclair, saying that he'd come to New Zealand because he wasn't good enough to get a game in the country of his birth; in fact 'Skippy' Sinclair's family emigrated when he was five. This went on for a while until Junior interjected: 'Yeah, he really struggled to get a game in the under-6s.'

In the team's off-field sporting challenges between the cool Julios and the uncool Nerds, Junior is a leading Julio. He's a smart dresser who prides himself on his style. He loves his rugby league, supporting the Canterbury Bulldogs in the NRL, and lives for his punting; in fact, one of the many telegrams that arrived after Mark scored that hundred on his Test debut was from the Revesby TAB! He leased his first horse, a trotter, with his dad Rodger, and has since invested in many more. The only sad part about Mark's love of the turf is that he's allergic to horsehair, which means that he breaks out in a rash the moment he comes into contact with any of his stable!

Mark's 35 now, which means he has more cricket behind him than in front. But when his name has come up at selection meetings, we've always felt that he still has value left in him. In one-day cricket especially, he's proved of immense value to the side, consistently getting the team off to good starts and scoring his 7,492 runs at an excellent average of 38.2. Perhaps this coming season will be the one where he resolves that enigma once and for all.

A typically poised stroke by Mark Waugh as he glides the ball away during a tour match in Zimbabwe.

STEVE WAUGH

BORN:	2 June 1965, Canterbury, Sydney, NSW
FULL NAME:	Stephen Rodger Waugh
BATTING STYLE:	Right Hand Bat
BOWLING STYLE:	Right Arm Medium
TEST DEBUT:	Australia v. India at Melbourne, 2nd Test, 1985/86

Steve Waugh

Australia's 40th Test skipper is not only one of the toughest men I've ever played cricket with, and the outstanding Australian batsman of his era, but an important link with the past. Steve Waugh has lasted so long that he's our last remaining link with the bad old days, when we had a habit of butchering more games than I care to remember. I'm sure it's the fact that Steve has played in losing sides, and survived so many disappointments, that's made him such an effective leader.

The first time I saw Steve play was way back in the 1984–85 Sheffield Shield final. A last-minute replacement for Geoff Lawson in the New South Wales team, he proved one of the main reasons why we Queenslanders had to wait another decade before winning the coveted trophy. His quick-fire 71 in a low-scoring match cost us a lot of momentum, and you could tell straight away: 'This kid's pretty special.' It was no surprise when he was awarded his baggy green the following season; although, by his own admission, Steve probably wasn't quite ready at that point, especially against India with their very accurate spin attack.

Steve's first few Tests were a hard initiation for him. He was hot and cold with the bat—probably trying to live up to the hype about his being some sort of excitement machine—and it was really his useful medium-pace bowling which kept him in the side. In fact, it was as a bowler that he made his first real impact at the top level, turning into our 'iceman' who closed out every innings. He and Simon O'Donnell were the first guys in the game who really cottoned on to the slower ball, bowled out of the back of the hand, as an important part of a limited-overs bowler's armoury. Steve also had a really competitive nature, so you could count on him not to get the wobbles under pressure.

Although Steve played a crucial role in our 1987 World Cup victory with the ball, I think he always considered himself a batsman first and foremost. He had to wait 27 Tests to get a three-figure score, and when he made the breakthrough in the 1989 Ashes series he really made it count: 177 not out at Headingley followed by 152 not out at Lord's.

I think the real turning point in Steve's career, however, was 18 months later, when the selectors dropped him in favour of his brother Mark. Until then, Steve'd been a bit of a thrashing machine with the bat, and he really had to rethink his game. The guy who came back is pretty much the guy we have now: tough, amazingly positive, and self-confident. One of the first things he did when we got to England for the 1993 Ashes series was bet £25 at 8/1 on himself to be our top scorer. That was typical Tugga. He probably thought: 'There'll only be six of us in the hunt, so the odds are in my favour.'

Steve and I put on 322 at Headingly together in that series, and he was kind enough to write: 'Batting with Border makes you concentrate that little bit extra because you can see how much it means to him to give his wicket away'. But I wouldn't want to take any credit for Steve's success because, while we were playing together, we really didn't spend that much time talking to each other. Frankly, from the very start of his career, he always looked as though he could look after himself.

Steve is now a very worldly character. He's very interested in the latest technologies, but brings to the side a tremendous sense of history; his knowledge of the game is extensive. His work on behalf of charities is fantastic, particularly his sponsorship since 1998 of the Udayan Boys Home in Calcutta. You can get very insular playing cricket. If you're in India or Pakistan, most guys will tend to just hang around the hotel watching TV and ordering room service. But Steve really likes to get out and about, likes to meet the people, and will photograph anything that moves.

The Team

By the same token, there are some things about Steve I still don't understand. He looks like someone who's the master of every situation, but he's actually pretty superstitious. He never bats without this old red rag in his pocket. I don't know where the custom started but, if I was one of Steve's opponents the first thing I'd try to do is pinch it! Perhaps under all that certainty there's still a tiny seed of doubt.

For a guy who's renowned for his meticulous preparation, Steve is also incredibly untidy. I've never seen anyone with a messier kit. Packing is complete chaos: you could put a sandwich in Steve's coffin and he wouldn't find it for two years! It's nothing to see him bouncing on top of his bags trying to shut them. Maybe it's a bit of a release for him, that his corner of the dressing room is the place he can let it all hang out.

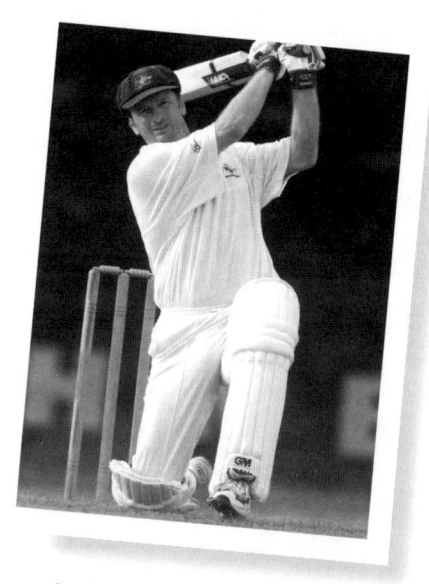

Confident and determined as ever, Steve Waugh hits a four against Sri Lanka in Colombo.

While Steve tends to keep his emotions in check, he can lose his temper. I remember a BNZ Trophy match against New Zealand in Hamilton in March 1993. We had the Kiwis 4 for 94 chasing 7 for 247, and it was really just about applying the finishing touches. But this 19-year-old called Jeff Wilson—later picked as a winger for the All Blacks—got stuck into Steve towards the end and they won with a couple of balls to spare. When the crowd ran on, they really let us know about it, Steve especially, and he was absolutely wild when he came off. He hurled his cap down and aimed a colossal kick at his coffin but, wearing spikes on the concrete floor, he fell flat on his arse. Then he got up and tried to do it again with the same result. The other boys laughed themselves sick to see The Iceman melting, but it tells you quite a lot about Steve: under that cool exterior beats the heart of a very passionate cricketer.

Adam Gilchrist celebrates his century
with Justin Langer at Hobart.

Shane Warne's Story

3

*'If a single game epitomises why
Australia has become
the superpower of world cricket it is
the Test against Pakistan in Hobart
in late 1999.'*

When Adam Gilchrist strode out to join Justin Langer and helped construct that magnificent sixth-wicket partnership which took us to within spitting distance of a remarkable victory, all of us back in the dressing room believed they would do it. Even though we were 5 for 126 chasing 369 to win, the thought of defeat did not enter our minds. And I write as the bloke who was padded up ready to go in next.

There can be no better example of the self-belief within the team that helps to make us The Dominators. We think we can win from any situation, no matter how tricky it looks, because so many of us have come through demanding challenges in the past. The Aussies have been at the top for a few years now, but the process of getting to the present stage, where we managed to win ten Tests back-to-back last summer, stretches back a lot further. It has been a gradual process, an evolution rather than a revolution.

You can go all the way back to the days when Allan Border took over the captaincy to see when Australia's fortunes first began to alter. Mark Taylor took us on a very enjoyable journey at a period when the side changed quite substantially yet managed to retain the strong team ethic forged by Border. Steve Waugh then accepted the baton. Meanwhile, our backroom team has kept up to date with the latest methods to give us the best back-up in the game. When you think of the strength of our domestic cricket and the depth of talent available to the selectors it is easy to see why we have become one of the strongest teams in the world.

Sometimes it takes a defeat to jerk a side into top gear and truly bring it together. Our World Cup bid in England really started when we lost to Pakistan at Headingley because we knew we had made such a strong effort when everything was going against us, and never looked back from that day. By the same token, our brilliant run in 1999–2000 can be traced to a rare occasion when we lost. I am thinking about our defeat to Sri Lanka at Kandy.

The game will be remembered for the horrible collision between Steve Waugh and Jason Gillespie. That was a sickening moment, the worst I've ever seen on a cricket field and we had to drag ourselves off the floor. We had been dismissed for 188 and their batsmen were cruising, but we pulled ourselves round with a magnificent display in the field and although there was too much to do, we realised we were close to achieving something worthwhile. I am convinced we would have won that series if the second and third Tests had not been savaged by rain.

By the end of the summer, after the successful one-off Test against Zimbabwe in Harare and the convincing wins over Pakistan, India and New Zealand, it was easy to forget those games in Sri Lanka. We needed to bounce back, and we responded with a combination of pride, passion and determination. The Pakistan series in particular was tighter than the 3–0 scoreline suggests, but when something needed doing, at the crucial moments in the Tests, we dug deep and always reacted ruthlessly.

Again, Hobart springs to mind. But you can also look at the first Test at Brisbane, a happy hunting ground for Australia of late. Pakistan were

Damien Fleming becomes living sculpture as the afternoon sun
outlines his bowling action at Bellerive Oval, Hobart.

3 for 265 close to stumps when Damien Fleming ripped out a couple of their batsmen with the second new ball to drag us back in. The Pakistanis slept that night knowing a big chance had passed them by and from then on it was a matter of us simply concentrating and playing efficiently to capitalise. We derive great inner strength from knowing that somebody will come along and pull us out of trouble from any position, not that we want to leave it to someone else, and the great thing is that we do not have to rely on the same people all the time.

In the second Test against New Zealand at Wellington, when we were 4 for 51 after Chris Cairns had raised their hopes with a fiery hundred, it was Michael Slater who dragged us around in partnership with Steve Waugh. Then, in the final match at Hamilton, the Kiwis pushed us to an even worse position 5 for 29. This time Adam Gilchrist and the in-form and rejuvenated Damien Martyn got us out of jail. On both occasions we went on to win. We grew and grew as a unit through the summer.

Any successful side needs the right balance, not simply between batsmen and bowlers. It requires a combination that can adjust quickly to all situations. One factor that set us apart last summer was the speed at which we scored our runs. Michael Slater can set up a game by hitting 60 or 70 before the other side has time to think. Mark and Steve Waugh have played more than 100 Tests each and have become superbly adaptable. The one thing everybody knows about Steve is that he pushes back when he is up against a wall. Mark is known as one of the best stroke-makers in the world, and rightly so, but I remember his innings against South Africa in Adelaide in 1997–98 which even Steve could not have bettered for sheer grit. On the outside he is laid back, but deep down he has a lot of passion and determination.

Clearly you pick your best side, but over the years our selectors have been clever in ensuring the right mix between senior and younger players. We all love to pick teams on the back of an envelope or a beer coaster. Constructing a real-life XI is much more difficult. Where our people have got it bang on is by choosing a player when he is in form. I've been on tours and seen other countries go for a bloke who has scored, say, three hundreds earlier in the season but started to fail a few times yet still get picked—the right man at the wrong time. You have to be confident in your own game going in to a Test match.

Allan Border really showed the Australian team how to play on the Ashes tour in 1989. I spent that summer in a city called Bristol in England and watching those games on the television really kindled my ambition to play for Australia. He gave the Poms absolutely nothing. From when I made my debut in 1991–92 until 1994–95 there was a gradual changing of the guard. We lost Merv Hughes, Dean Jones, Bruce Reid, Mike Whitney, Geoff Marsh, David Boon, Greg Matthews and Tim May in a relatively short period of time.

What the team has now is a good balance between young players and senior players which I think works extremely well. For example Justin Langer has developed into a really high-class left-handed number-three batsman who is tough and adaptable, from once being thought of as a block artist. His 122 from as many balls against New Zealand in Hamilton was one of the quickest hundreds ever made by an Aussie.

Barring injuries there should not be any need to chop and change, to bring in four or five new players at any one go. Continuity is vital to success and has contributed to our present well-being. Without talented players it is a struggle to succeed. But those players need to be honed and directed. This is why our back-up deserves to share some of the credit for our domination. John Buchanan has made a big impact since he succeeded Geoff Marsh as coach after the World Cup. Unlike Geoff, he did not have a reputation as a player, but we all had enormous respect for his achievements as a coach at Queensland. He appreciates the way technology can be used to highlight strengths and weaknesses in the opposition and to improve our own games. You can have your own gut feeling about a player, but it is always reassuring to have that supported by the evidence of cameras or video recordings. He has also helped to gel the side together. I remember the first team meeting John ran and it was a very interesting one. He wanted to improve us as people first, then as cricketers. It was all coming from a different and new angle most of us hadn't experienced before but we all went in with our eyes wide open and we all embraced it.

Absolutely nothing is left to chance. There is a purpose behind every minute of our practice and every exercise in the warm-up routines. We do not go out there to be seen to be practising. There is a reason for everything and I think our net sessions must be the toughest of any national side. We hate getting out to each other and the verbals have been known to fly. But one of our biggest strengths is that we do the basics well. Cricket is a simple game—if the ball is pitched up you go forward, if it's short you go back, you bowl a tight line outside off stump on a good length, hold your catches. Buchanan has not tried to complicate things.

David Misson has been fantastic as the fitness trainer. The fact that his old man played Test cricket gives him an appreciation of the requirements of playing at the highest level. His recovery sessions are particularly good. There are times when we can relax and share a beer or two, but there are also times for stretches and sessions in the swimming pool. He realises that we are human beings and need to switch off now and then. The best word to describe him is professional. Errol Alcott is a great physio who has the trust of the players and Brian Murgatroyd has taken care of the public relations side with real efficiency. Having previously worked for the England and Wales Cricket Board it's a new experience being part of a winning team and 'Murgers' seems to be enjoying himself with us.

I have gone on record before in my admiration of Steve Waugh as captain. Contrary to certain reports there is no problem between us. I think we complemented each other well and I did enjoy being his vice-captain. He has a strong, clear mind, and has plenty of ideas. We are different characters, but we have been friends for a long time and have come through some tough periods together. We have also had great times off the field and taking the good with the bad is what life is all about. Steve does not need to prove anything to anybody, including himself.

We all strive to improve and our strong work ethic is another reason

A mighty strike by Justin Langer helps the score along in the
first Test against New Zealand at Auckland.

for our success. At no time when we were putting together that run of wins did we think of resting on our laurels. We are very honest and open with each other. If we have a bad day we do not hide from the facts by making excuses. Our belief in each other is strong enough for us to know that between us any problem can be overcome.

We do not want to end our careers with regrets. We want to make sure that when our time comes we don't wonder what might have been if we'd put in a bit more work, spent a few minutes longer working on our fielding or running that extra lap to get into better condition. We play as a team rather than a collection of individuals. As long as everybody gives it all for the good of the team there are never any complaints.

If you watch us carefully there are small examples of the way we play for each other. We pay particularly close attention to what may seem like little things. But as we know, that's what life is all about. By looking after the little things the rest takes care of itself. With every throw, from fine leg all the way around to third man, our aim is to throw the ball over the top of the stumps. This is a pride thing. At the start of an over, somebody will run to the bowler to take his sweater and the baggy green cap to the umpire. When Steve Waugh and Jason Gillespie suffered that dreadful collision our first thought was to run over to Stephen to cover his nose so that his wife and daughter back home didn't have to see how much damage had been inflicted. Poor Jason was in great pain as well but got a bit overlooked at first. He has been really unlucky with injuries—we didn't know until later that he had broken an arm as well as a leg in the accident. Dizzy is a guy who works so hard at his game that he deserves a good run. Hopefully he can now stay injury free because if so he will be a very useful performer for Australia.

We are also a team away from the grounds. When the luggage van arrives somebody will always jump in and get the bags for everyone, not just his own. If somebody has missed the alarm we don't sit there on the bus waiting, looking forward to a bloke having to stew. Somebody will go to knock him up.

A few of the things we do behind the scenes might sound a bit unorthodox, some might say a load of rubbish. But it is something different. One of them is the daily poetry session, introduced at the start of last summer by Dave Misson. The idea is that one bloke every day has to compose a poem related to cricket and read it out in front of the team after our warm-up on the field. Some of the efforts have been fantastic, others like Mark Waugh's have been, shall we say, short and to the point. Often the guys have stopped in their rooms to produce something really special. One by Ricky Ponting sticks in my mind from the start of the World Cup. I've never seen Michael Slater as nervous as when he had to read his poem. The guy was physically shaking, but he still managed to punch it out somehow and it wasn't the worst poem by any stretch of the imagination. I've done a couple up to now—let's just say that I won't be remembered as another William Wordsworth.

Then, every couple of weeks or so, we have to speak to the rest of the team on three different topics: the history of Australia, the history of Australian cricket and a subject of our choice. The sessions are supposed to last for 15 or 20 minutes but usually they go well beyond an hour. I'm amazed at the little pockets of knowledge within the dressing room. Mike Kasprowicz gave a talk on the World Wrestling Federation and Hulk Hogan. Michael Slater did Bon Jovi, his favourite band, and Greg Blewett gave us some golfing tips. Brian Murgatroyd, our media relations officer, gave one of the most memorable. His speech about The Bee Gees was fascinating. My session was about World Series Cricket and I also spoke about casinos as my free topic, and how to improve the chances of winning at blackjack and roulette. The boys kept their paper but judging by some of the results they don't seem to have listened.

The free section is a bit of fun, but there is a serious point behind the idea. The sessions give us an appreciation of where we have come from, about what it means to be representing Australia and the sacrifices the players of yesterday made for our generation. There is a strong sense of patriotism within the side and enormous pride every time we step over the boundary rope. We are not just playing a game of cricket, we are playing for Australia. One of the biggest motivating factors has been to ensure that our Test players of the future can reflect upon our contribution with the same respect we have for Don Bradman, Keith Miller, Richie Benaud, Ian Chappell and Dennis Lillee, to name just a few.

All the players feel at ease in the dressing room. We enjoy each other's company on and off the field. I remember my own introduction to the side in 1991–92 season. It was New Year's Eve and we were in a hotel in Sydney watching the traditional fireworks bring in the New Year. Allan Border, who was the captain then and one of my big heroes, came over with Geoff Marsh to share a few stubbies and make sure I felt part of what was happening. I didn't really know Geoff Marsh at the time, I had only recently met David Boon and Bruce Reid I had not met at all until that night.

Back in the early 90s there was still a bit of the old school theory. You had to earn your stripes and although there is still a bit of that around, it is nowhere as much as it used to be. I sensed that Allan Border in particular, made me think I was there on merit, because he thought I could do a job rather than just fill in for somebody else. I took some time to get started and when I was being clouted around in the early days I did begin to wonder whether I deserved to be playing in such company, but all the time Border gave me the reassurance I needed. I was in and out of the team, but came back into the side on Boxing Day 1992, took 7 for 52 against the West Indies and felt part of the team. Everybody was genuinely happy for me and I was pleased that I had contributed to the win.

Of course, there are different personalities in the side. That is inevitable, but when we go to a function or out for dinner we go together. Travelling with each other every day, especially on tour can be quite difficult. We get to know the different characters and we also understand what makes each of us tick. We know when somebody wants to be left alone and respect how far to take a joke. Equally, anybody who becomes too big for his boots is quickly cut down to size.

There is a balance between coming into the team and earning your stripes, and then becoming part of the furniture. Everybody who joins the side recognises that performances in the middle count for more than

Glenn McGrath's bowling action is caught perfectly in this picture
taken during the second Test against Sri Lanka at Galle.

words. Anybody can talk a good game, but that has to be backed up. What has impressed me over the last few years is the way the newcomers are so keen to learn. As a team we do not nip off back to the hotel immediately after play. We stay in the dressing room to talk about the game and share our experiences sometimes for an hour or so before starting to get changed.

In Test matches we were able to put a lot of pressure on the opposition last summer by notching so many runs on the board. As a spin bowler it makes an enormous difference to be able to set a field with men around the bat waiting for nicks if I want, rather than a run-saving ring. It also has a big effect on the state of mind of the batsmen. Our batting is the envy of every other country, but I sometimes think the depth of our bowling is our strength. The four main pacemen—Glenn McGrath, Brett Lee, Damien Fleming and Jason Gillespie are all high class, wicket-taking performers. Lee came from nowhere last winter and made a huge impact, bringing genuine out-and-out pace to the team. Behind the shop window there is quality, too. In Shield cricket you have good quality back up bowlers, who could easily earn a place in a lot of other Test teams.

There were times in the 90s when I felt the pressure of being expected to run through a side, to get four, five or six wickets and bowl out a side on the final day. These days there is much more emphasis on bowling in partnerships. It isn't often now that a single bowler wins a Test. If you look at the scorecards people bag twos and threes together. Besides, when somebody does come away with a hatful it owes much to the bloke who is keeping it tight and tidy at the other end. If one bowler is cramping up the batsman then he is more likely to take chances against the rest. One reason for our recent success was the way we bowled as a team.

Apart from giving the selectors a broad pool, this depth of bowling talent means that young batsmen coming in to Shield cricket are really tested from the word go. Their techniques are placed under great scrutiny and they are also challenged mentally. Anybody who scores runs consistently at this level has to be a very good player. Everything is geared to the best interest of the national side.

Every innings counts, every minute of every game. When a batsman knows he might be having his only hit for a month it is bound to concentrate his mind. I also think that our practice facilities are the best in the world. We are very lucky to have a good climate in which to play the game, but there has also been investment to give kids the best chance of making the grade. Our structure starts from a young age and the pyramid, with the Test team at the peak, is distinct all the way through. When you move up from third to second grade you feel you have made progress, but you have the grounding to be able to cope. In some countries every step seems to be a giant leap.

Spending the summer in England with Hampshire was something of an eye-opener. One question I was asked day after day was how Australia could afford to leave out players like Darren Lehmann, Jamie Cox and Stuart Law to name but three. These players were scoring runs for fun, but when I asked who we should leave out to make way I tended to see blank faces staring back. You can assess the strength of a side by the players left out, and I honestly believe that an Australia 2nd XI would be very competitive.

I wonder what we must be like to play against. There have been some very kind words from other sides lately. We try to be intimidating, and use the aura surrounding the team at the moment. We want to apply pressure from the first ball and take the initiative straight away. We are favourites going into every game and when we begin well it is possible to sense the opposition thinking 'Here we go again'. Alternatively, as I have said before, if we fall behind the pace we know that somebody will pull us back.

Cricket forges friendships that ought to last for the rest of your life. But the field is not the place to make those buddies. We play as hard as we can and I will admit we try to get under the skin of certain players if we think they are vulnerable. We don't mind having a word with a batsman if we reckon it will unsettle him. But I think some people have exaggerated the way we go about this. It is not always a matter of snarling abuse. In fact I can think of one incident that was little more than a bit of a chat.

It happened during a game against Pakistan in Sydney, when Basit Ali had really started to annoy us. He was actually quite a nice bloke, but on this occasion he was driving us all to distraction. He was never ready when we were about to bowl and kept pulling away when I had begun my run up. Because of this we were already in overtime and late with our overs. Before the last ball of the day I called Ian Healy over for a chat in the middle. 'Heals,' I said, 'this so-and-so has held us up, we'll make him wait for a bit now.'

With all the pointing going on and the knowing grins on our faces poor old Basit thought we had suddenly spotted a flaw in his technique and were plotting his imminent downfall. Actually, we were discussing whether to go for an Italian or Mexican meal that evening. At the end of the conversation I asked Heals in passing what I ought to bowl. 'Oh, just do what you like, mate,' he said. By this time Basit was beginning to twitch and worry. I dropped a leg-break outside leg stump, he thrust his pad out and it bowled him through his legs. I'm convinced he had lost his concentration.

I don't know much about psychology, but I recognise the importance of knowing you can win from any position. We have had some great games against South Africa down the years. There is no doubt we have the wood over them. More important, they know it, too. In tight situations in the big matches we tend to come through. They can intimidate other teams—especially at places like the so-called Bull Ring in Johannesburg with 30,000 spectators screaming for them—but we don't let it happen. We use it to our advantage and derive motivation from these sort of things.

South Africa are the closest to matching us all-round at the moment. I am looking forward to our series over there in 2001–02, which I am sure will receive a lot of attention in every cricket-playing country in the world. It will be billed as a heavyweight title decider, but I think we have the edge in every department, even if their fielding pushes us close. I think our main advantage is in the variety of our attack.

Thinking back, the best Test match I ever played in was against Sri

Lanka in 92. However while this book is concentrating on our recent Test performances, I have to think back to that wonderful World Cup semi-final in 1999 as the best game of cricket I have ever played in. I am convinced that Allan Donald and Lance Klusener would have scored the final, winning run against any other side but Australia. They just wanted to beat us so badly that I think they lost concentration at that final moment and became caught up with the occasion. They must have been under so much pressure because they knew we had beaten them so many times from what appeared to be worse positions before—not least in the Super Six game at Headingley a few days earlier. Those two copped a lot of criticism, but we didn't really get the praise we deserved for applying the pressure when it mattered. Our body language was not that of a side that expected to lose. Sometimes I think that players contrive to intimidate themselves against us.

We are a very brave side. We do not shirk challenges and do not take the easy route if it reduces our chances. The best example of this was when we toured the West Indies in 95. This was a ground-breaking Test series and by winning in the Caribbean—the first side to do so for 15 years—we laid claim to being the best team in the world. In my opinion we have been up there ever since. It was a real credit to Mark Taylor that he got the team into the way of winning.

At the start of the tour we decided that if their fast bowlers were going to intimidate us by bowling bouncers at our lower-order batsmen, then we would do the same to theirs. This also came from Mark Taylor and we all owe him and Allan border a lot for the tactics we learned when playing under their leadership. We knew it would fire them up, but we wanted to stand up to them and let them know we were unafraid. It surprised them in the early stages because they were not used to sides retaliating in kind. In that series they had Brian Lara on top of his game, Richie Richardson and the pace pair of Curtly Ambrose and Courtney Walsh probably at their peak. With no quarter given by either side this was one of the fiercest series I have been involved in and we won it through sheer guts as much any anything else.

The reactions we get from the crowds provide an indication of the way we are perceived. In some parts of the West Indies we were booed. In the final Test of that series the Waughs hit boundaries that went unapplauded. We looked upon that as a compliment. The people were effectively acknowledging that we were on top, which in turn spurred us on even more.

There is no reason why we cannot continue to dominate, as long as we do not become complacent and think that the job is done. To continue along the present winning path we must remember not just what we have achieved, especially last summer, but the reasons for our success. This is a rich time for Australian cricket with so many fine players available. But I hope we have shown that talent is merely the starting point. Without dedication, self-belief, the right attitude, confidence in each other and a strong work and team ethic we would not have emerged through so many close games to win 10 on the trot. In finishing I would like to say that in my opinion the journey of life is something to be enjoyed. Enjoy the ups and downs, the good times and the bad, the mistakes we make and learn by them, and if we all do that no matter what we do in life, we will become better people. I hope you enjoy the book and enjoy the cricket. Keep spinning!

Steve Waugh's Story

4

*'Many individuals never get the chance
to experience it
and those who do never forget it.'*

Winning a Test match is something that can never be taken away from you and this is the aspiration of every international cricketer.

Victory is so special to an Australian side that we join arm in arm and rejoice in our team song for hours afterwards in the dressing rooms to further strengthen our bond and to celebrate.

Put simply, to win a Test match for your country is as good as it gets.

To have won 10 consecutive Tests is therefore a feat thought to be almost unattainable in cricket lore and to be a part of it is a delight I never thought I'd experience in my playing days.

To be the captain of such a great unit gives me immense pleasure and satisfaction, filling me with a sense of pride and patriotism. Now we must make sure we forge ahead to the world record, which is only two wins away.

Coming on top of our recent world one day record of 13 consecutive victories, this would cap off one of the great periods of Australian cricket and ensure our place in history as an era of sustained excellence.

Test match cricket is exactly what the title suggests.

It is a test of many skills and attributes that can be exposed or eroded if you are not up to the challenge.

Many people think it's a test of just your natural talent, which of course, forms a piece of the overall jigsaw. But to me Test cricket also entails dedication, sacrifice, commitment, unselfishness, camaraderie, courage, pride, passion and much more. To win you must have all these attributes. You have to be able to handle pressure better than your adversary over a sustained period. You have to be able to seize the moment when a game is in the balance, but more importantly know when this moment is nigh. You have to pull together 11 different personalities and characters and get them all going in the one direction. You have to believe in each other when there are doubts from others outside of the team. You have to strive to continually improve your own game, both mentally and physically, while at the same time suppress any egos that may cause problems to the 'karma' of the team.

These factors, plus the indefinable ones, make this such a great and unique game, and one that can very often expose or bring to the surface your very essence.

Cricket to me can in many ways be much more than a game. It can teach you a lot about yourself and it gives you the opportunity to continually improve and grow as a person.

The game exposes you to many different scenarios and situations that not only have an effect on the match, or your career, but also later on in life, which may lead you in a certain direction.

To me a winning cricket side is not all about talent, but rather a collection of people who are mature enough to take responsibility for their actions and decisions and live by them. Having said this, no one is perfect and we all make our fair share of mistakes, but I believe this current Test squad is full of good people as well as talented cricketers and

Jason Gillespie is carried off the ground by security manager
Reg Dickason and Dave Misson after a
horrific collision with Steve Waugh at Kandy, Sri lanka.

this has contributed enormously to our success.

This winning streak of ours began in the unlikely venue of Harare, Zimbabwe, where the two nations met for the first time in a Test match. Coming into this historic game we weren't exactly setting the cricket world ablaze.

From my point of view as captain I felt we were missing a couple of key ingredients—enjoyment and hunger.

When a team isn't going as well as everyone wants or expects it's hard to pinpoint the problem and for me this was a source of frustration. The previous tour to Sri Lanka was an enormously trying tour. We contended with constant rain, poor practice facilities, lack of options away from the game, the announcement that Swampy (Geoff Marsh) our coach was retiring, injuries and indiscipline off the field, all of which led to a one nil loss over the three Tests.

Personally it was the toughest tour I'd ever been on, both physically and mentally.

The horrific collision in Kandy with Jason Gillespie left me with a compound fracture of the nose, accompanied by four other broken bones, a sternum bent at a 30-degree angle and a deep gash. Dizzy ended up in a much worse situation with a broken tibia, and was later diagnosed with a fractured wrist; two injuries serious enough to see him miss the entire Australian season. My injury, of course, was painful but the time away from the team while recovering left me feeling helpless and distant. I could see not only my strength as a leader fading by my absence, but also a team that was losing focus and direction.

The laid back atmosphere of Zimbabwe was a much needed destination for the Aussie team and because of this our enjoyment seemed to resurface.

Our new stop-gap coach, Allan Border, was the perfect man for the job during this mini tour, with an approach that was in many ways old-fashioned, but it also livened us up and got us going. Our training sessions were good old hard work; social activities, such as having a beer

Mark Waugh lines up a ball he will send to the boundary during the one-off Test match against Zimbabwe.

together after the tour games, were encouraged and suddenly our hunger began to resurface.

One particular 'team bonding' exercise that will stay with me forever was the Bulawayo to Victoria Falls railway journey. Rarely on tour these days do we get a couple of days off and even less do we get an opportunity to travel the country via a different mode of transport.

An Ashes tour is always a great tour because we spend so many hours hurtling down those motorways together on the team bus, watching videos, playing cards, reliving old memories and just plain old getting to know each other. On this occasion we had just completed a comprehensive win against a Zimbabwe Board XI and were given a choice of three ways to get to Harare in time for the Test match; a chartered plane, a hired coach or a detour via Victoria Falls by rail, then a plane trip.

Being an avid 'Tommy Tourist' and inquisitive by nature, I joined fellow squad members Ponting, Blewett, McGrath, Langer, Nicholson, Miller, Hayden, Katich, MacGill and Misson, to experience African rail travel and to see one of the seven wonders of the world. Our unofficial tour leader Stuey MacGill had earlier gone out shopping and his supply of food, and more importantly beverages, was excellent and more than adequate. Together with our music box we had the time of our lives.

It was like being on a school excursion where you let your hair down and experience life. Stories were exchanged, drinks were downed, and even cigars were lit as we meandered through the African scrub under skies full of stars that literally sparkled like diamonds. The trek was a 15-hour marathon with 36 stops, but to us all time was standing still and we couldn't get enough of it. Many moments will stay with me forever, one of which was the wearing of ridiculous hats that we all had to buy from the locals, then wear for the remainder of the trip. I lost my hat and sunnies when I stuck my hangover head out the window to take a snap of some leaping gazelle as the early morning sunrise lit up the cloudless horizon.

Seeing the falls was almost an anti-climax, but this whole episode galvanised us as a group and made the bond between us stronger than it was before we hopped on board.

Needless to say, the much anticipated clash between the two teams was an enjoyable and successful encounter, especially for us as it got us back on the rails and re-established our confidence for the testing times that lay ahead.

Winning the toss, I believed, would be important to us as the wicket was nicely covered in grass, and as such would assist our pacemen of McGrath and Fleming, and to a lesser extent Miller. Amazingly, the local captain, Alistair Campbell, decided to bat first after calling correctly, obviously more worried about the prospect of batting last against Warney.

But he'd clearly forgotten about what might happen on day one to his exposed batsmen. Bowling Zimbabwe out for 194 was, to me as a captain, definitely a positive result, and even more so in the knowledge that we bowled better the longer the innings went. The bowlers shared the wickets equally except for Miller whose 19 overs for 36 runs went unrewarded, but from a team point of view he did a great job as it allowed me as a captain to attack from the other end when the Zimbabweans needed to break the shackles imposed upon them.

Our reply was just what we had talked about. To have a lead of over 200 was the game plan, as it would leave Zimbabwe in an almost impossible position to squeeze out of.

Brother Mark caught my ailment by getting out in the 90s and had the double blow inflicted when he was told that a century would have made him the first player ever to post a century against each Test-playing country. Getting out to Grant Flower was further misery, but it wasn't all bad news for the Waugh family because my 151 not out enabled me to have the next chance at this unique record, as India was now the only team I hadn't reached triple figures against.

Our final total of 422 was helped by the 'photographer's delight' Damien Fleming, whose flourishing blade carved an exquisite 65 as I looked on in awe.

To score a century is always a good feeling as they are all different and scored under many variable conditions. This particular one wasn't my best but I was pleased with my concentration and desire to 'hang tough' and get through the shaky periods, which is essential to consistency. This was also the first time I had been given a chance in the 90s, after previously falling at the last hurdle nine times. I must buy Grant Flower a beer in the future because it was a straight-forward chance that would have added to my dubiously held record of the most 90s in Test cricket. After working so hard in the early part of the Zimbabwean second innings we got the rewards later on when the last eight wickets fell for 32 runs, leaving Slats and Blewy to score the five needed for victory.

For me the highlight and most encouraging sign for us was the way we kept on believing in ourselves during the second innings when Zimbabwe were 2 for 200 and looking to set us a big score to win. Never once did our heads drop and our work ethic was great all the way through. If we can keep working on these aspects, nothing can stop us from achieving what we want to.

These days, the norm is for the teams to disappear after the match and head separate ways, but not this time, with both sides enjoying a beer and each other's company for three or four hours, a welcome change to us all, and a reminder that after all it is still only a game.

Back in Australia the real test for the team and myself awaited in the form of Pakistan, who in their own words, were out to prove they were the best Test team in the world and India, a team that provided us with our last losing series in Test cricket. These six Tests would be a measuring stick for us to see whether or not we were falling behind, stagnating, or on the way to improvement as a unit.

Coming into a series or, more significantly, a home season, planning ahead is a crucial element to the whole process and to how the team is going to approach the coming challenge.

Having a new coach is a major change, especially so when most of the guys had only met John Buchannan a couple of times previously before his appointment.

RIGHT: Brett Lee demonstrates his underwater form in Quay West Hotel, Sydney before the third Test against India.

CENTRE: The Australian team including fitness adviser, stand-in physio, manager, coach and scorer before the first Test against New Zealand at Eden Park, Auckland.

BELOW: Adam Gilchrist surfaces during a water work-out at the Australian team base at Napier, New Zealand.

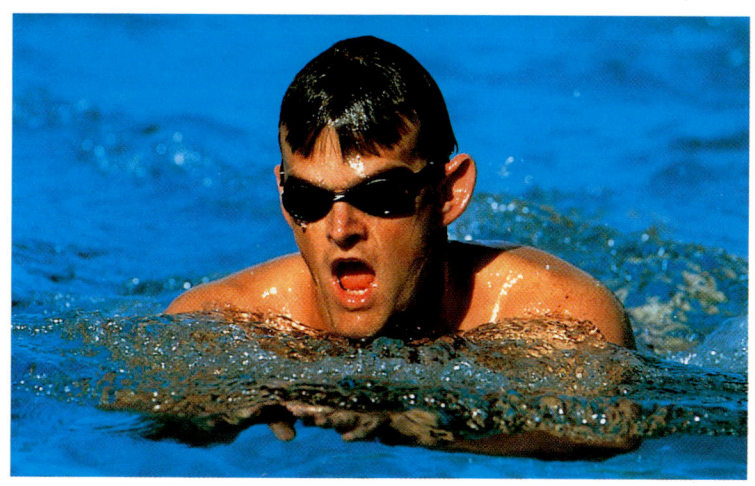

RIGHT: Jubilant Australian players rush to congratulate Shane Warne after he takes his 356th Test wicket.

BELOW: A confident Adam Gilchrist drives a ball to the boundary during the second innings of the first Test against New Zealand at Eden Park, Auckland.

TOP: Shane Warne is applauded by members of the Australian team as he leaves the field at Eden Park, Auckland after taking his 356th Test wicket to pass the record previously held by Dennis Lillee.

ABOVE: Joined by his father and brother after the match, Shane Warne celebrates his record number of Test wickets.

TOP: A group photo of the Australian and New Zealand teams at the start of the third Test at Hamilton, New Zealand.

ABOVE: General view of Westpac Trust Park during play in the last match of the series again New Zealand.

RIGHT: Matthew Hayden and Shane Warne make some positive fielding decisions at Hamilton, during the third Test v. New Zealand.

FAR RIGHT: Shane Warne runs up to deliver yet another leggie, or is it something else?

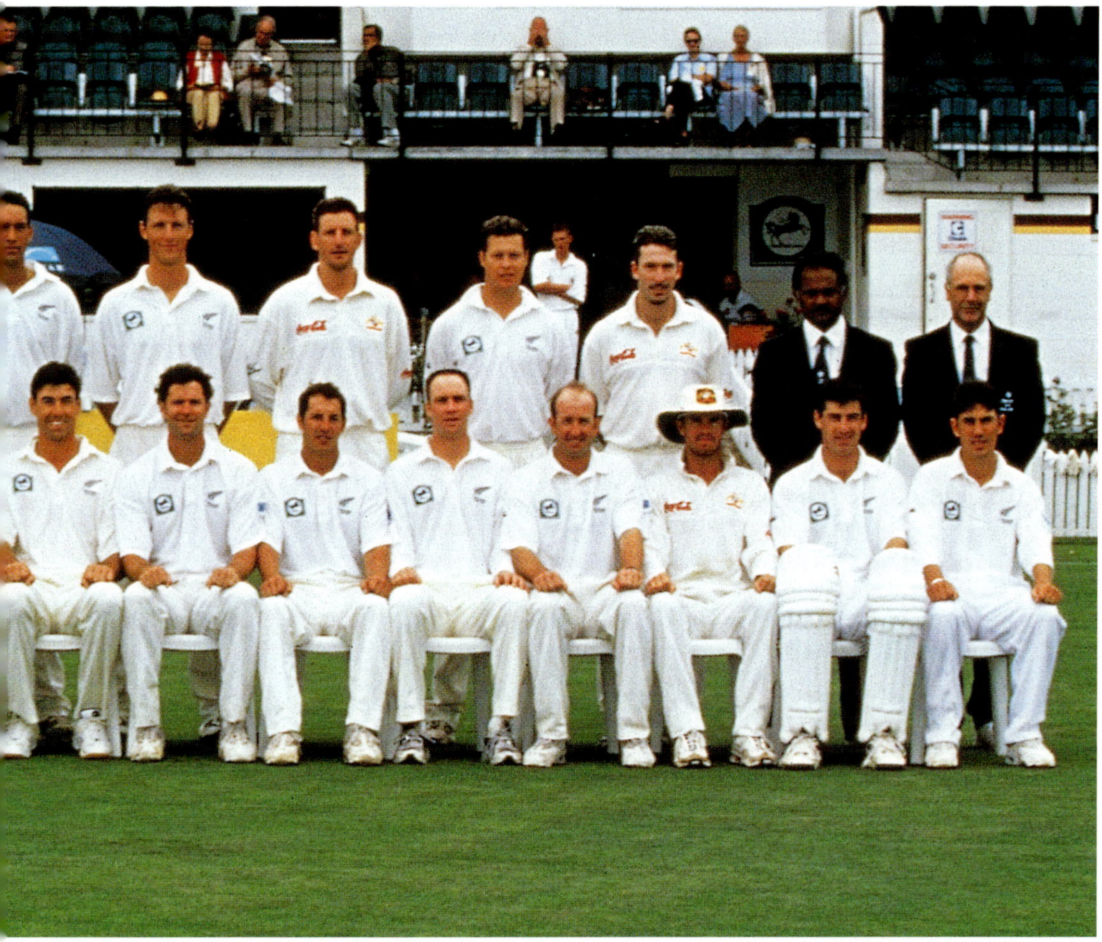

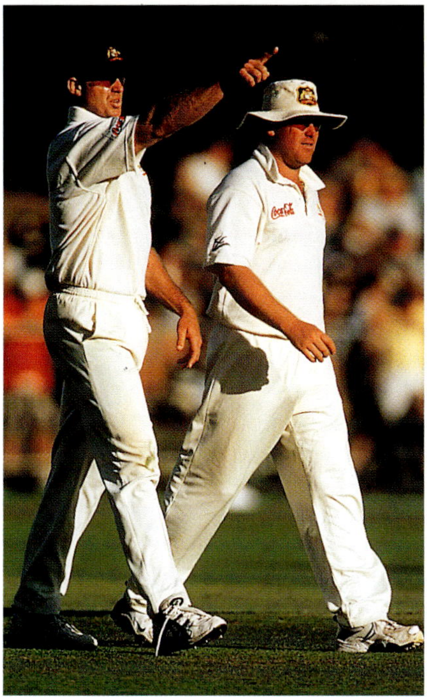

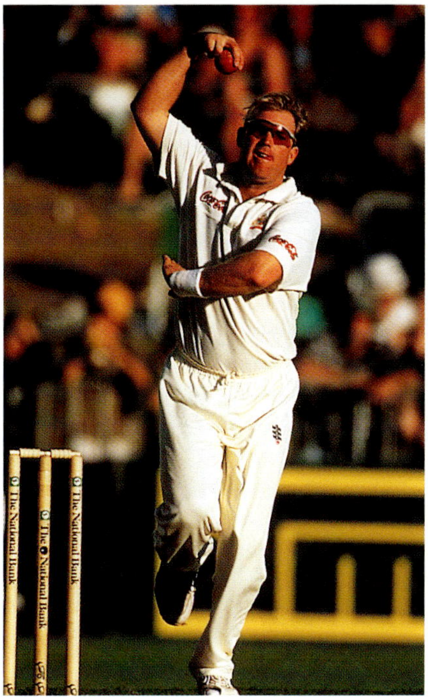
The National Bank
The National Bank
The National Bank

ABOVE: Funky Miller takes a new ball in training at the Grumpy Mole Saloon, Napier, New Zealand.

OPPOSITE TOP LEFT: Writing a book about the Dominators and the current success of the Australian cricket team wouldn't seem right without a picture of the Australian baggy green cap.

OPPOSITE TOP RIGHT: Not just an exciting fast bowler and pretty face. Brett Lee also oozes talent on the guitar as he showed in Hamilton, New Zealand, during his third test match.

OPPOSITE BOTTOM: Another celebration well earned after the first Test match in Auckland, New Zealand.

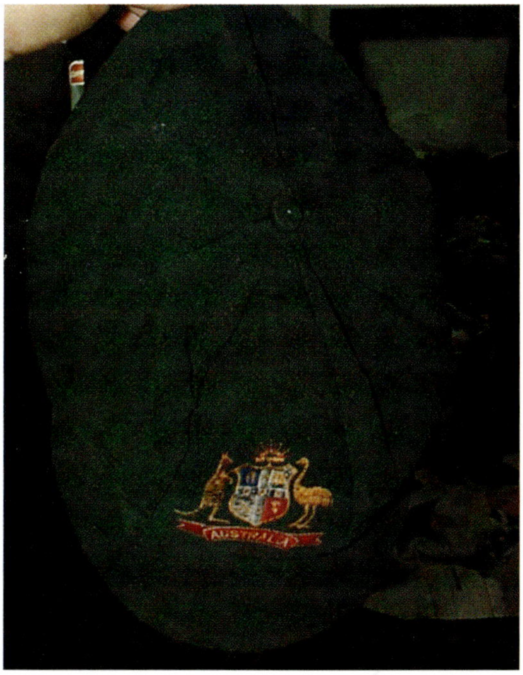
AUSTRALIA

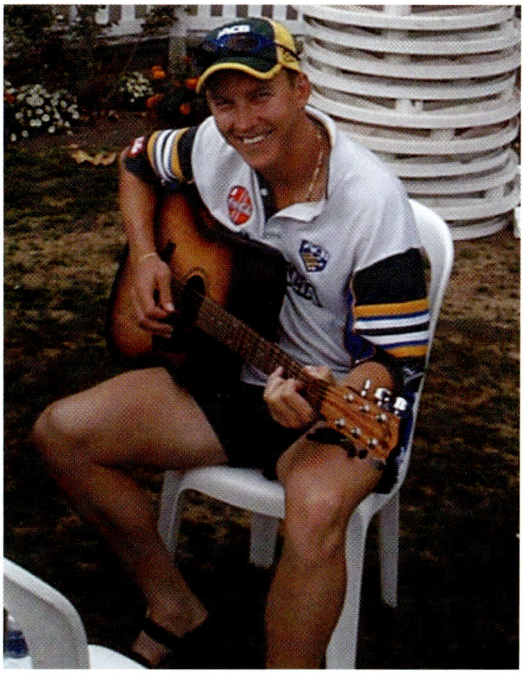

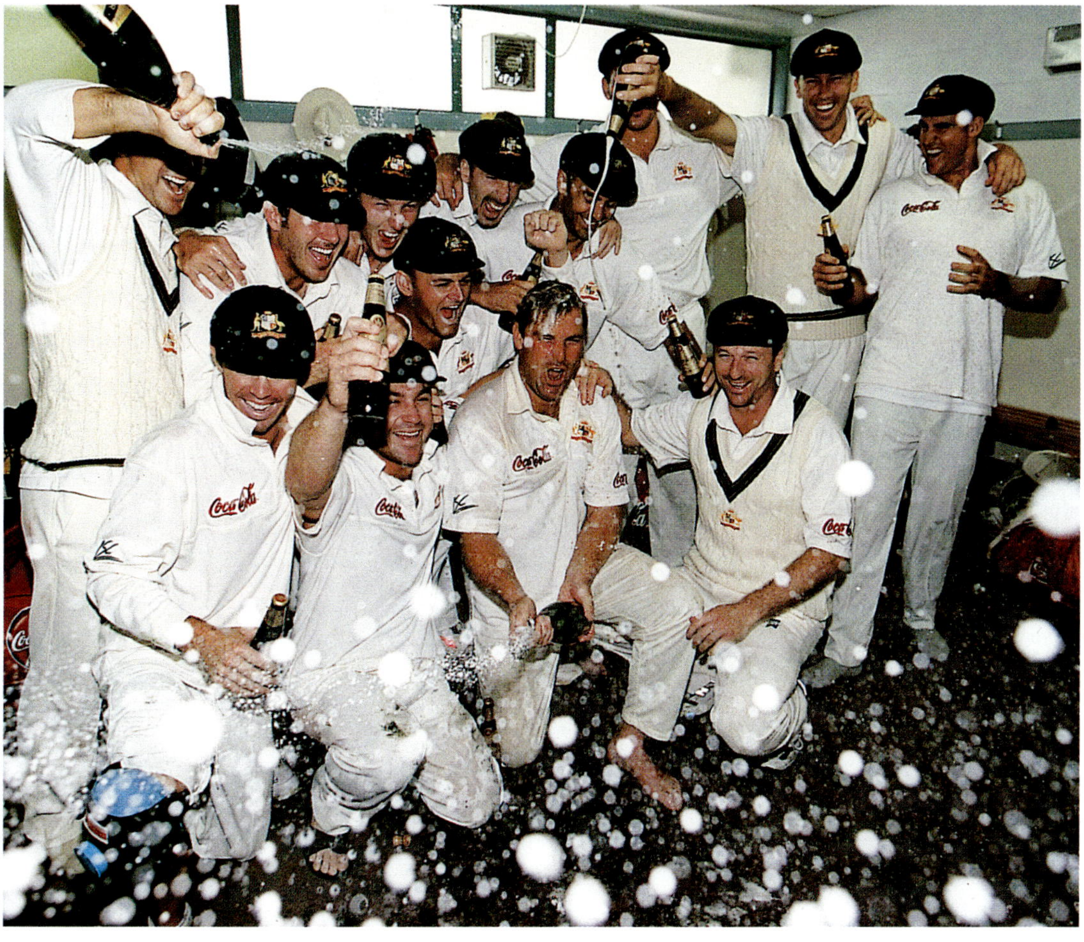
Coca-Cola

ABOVE: The amount of baggage taken along by a touring Test team can weigh tonnes, particularly when valuable cricketing memorabilia is included. Careful checking before departure is essential.

Linking up with the team only three days before the first Test wasn't an ideal situation, especially for myself, as I also had to contend with a huge press contingent wanting interviews and comments about this game and the season, while at the same time make sure my own game was in order.

The moment the first team meeting was over, we knew we had the right man on board. Buck delivered an initial talk, backed up by his notes on his beloved butcher's paper, addressing what he thought were our concerns, but most impressively what we were going to get from him and what he expected from us in return.

The overwhelming message that came through was that we had a coach who was going to give his all to make sure we all fulfilled our potential. He was going to do this by being honest, fair, loyal, hardworking, committed and dedicated to the team. Perhaps crucially, he wanted to get to know us as human beings firstly, and cricketers secondly, as well as trying to make all of us more responsible for our own actions and grow as people.

It was a meeting that certainly made me feel at ease and confident about the future, as many of his ideas and goals were similar to mine.

As captain, I must give the players an idea of what I want and the things I expect to happen, as well as act as a guide as to how we should be

Adam Gilchrist reveals his inner gloves as he gives his hands a rest during the second Test against Pakistan at Hobart.

playing our cricket. Looking around at the talent and potential in our squad it made sense for us to be aggressive and positive in our outlook and for each player to back himself and have faith in his abilities. This I believe is the key because everyone has talent at international level. It's just a matter of how we can reproduce our skills often enough to be winners.

Players can sense if people doubt their ability and as captain I believe it's my responsibility to make them feel wanted, relaxed and confident about their chances of success. It's also critical for players to put the team ahead of themselves—a quality which is a trademark of great teams.

After going through the opposition player by player, assessing their strengths and weaknesses, I listed what I thought were the dangers for the season ahead. Preparation, I think, has sometimes caused us problems in the past and in Brisbane this was my main worry and concern, for ours had been very rushed with too many functions, a new coach and the enormous media attention that had been focused on Adam Gilchrist replacing the great Ian Healy on his home turf. Complacency has sometimes caused us problems, too, and I wanted to make it clear that this was not going to be tolerated and neither was it to be discussed again. Thirdly, nobody's ego would be allowed to cause any problems as it could lead to division and cliques appearing, which is certainly not what we're about.

These three potential problems I didn't really envisage appearing, but it's better to let everyone know what to expect.

To finish off, I told the lads that a drawn Test was no good to anyone unless it was back-to-the-wall stuff and defeat was upon us. Rather, we were good enough to try to win all six home Tests and this should be our goal. On top of this Buck started his reign by saying on the morning of his first Test, 'Today is the first Test of our journey to the 'Invincibles'. Let's make the ride enjoyable and attainable.' I must admit when I first saw the words hanging from the dressing room wall, I thought they were a little ambitious and tempting fate a little as there was, and will only ever

Greg Blewett and Michael Slater come off the ground after hitting the winning runs in the Test match against Zimbabwe at Harare.

be one 'Invincibles', the great '48 side.

The three Tests against Pakistan ended very favourably from our point of view with a 3–0 victory, but in reality, the series was keenly contested and evenly balanced. The distinguishing feature, or attribute, that enabled us to win was our identifying the crucial moments during the course of the match and winning the battle at each of them.

Rather than go into the deeds and feats of individual players, it would perhaps be more relevant to list the turning points, or defining moments, in each Test. Day one of the Brisbane Test saw us under pressure and no one was feeling it more than me, when with less than half an hour to go Pakistan had cruised to 3 for 265 after I'd put them in on a greenish looking pitch. I could see the headlines already 'Waugh Blunder at the Toss'. But true to our beliefs in hard work paying off we took two very important late wickets to square the ledger on day one at 6 for 280. This may not sound that great but to take 2 for 15 in the last half an hour after five and a half hours in the hot sun gave us tremendous confidence for the following day.

Our general strategy against Pakistan was to be consistent, persistent, relentless and positive, primarily because we saw them as a team full of individual stars. At separate times they had their moments, but as a team they lacked the cohesiveness to battle through the tough periods, which also affected their consistency. To us this meant that if we were consistent and patient we would eventually get chances to gain the ascendancy. This fits in nicely with the three Ps we trust in—Patience, Pressure and Partnerships.

After finishing off the Pakistani batting in grand style we batted like a team possessed with Slater, Blewett, M Waugh, Warne and Gilchrist being aggressive and uninhibited in their method and stroke play.

In fact our 575 total was scored at more than four runs per over, something that was especially pleasing, because as players we want people to come and watch us play and be entertained at the same time.

Adam Gilchrist lines up with Bill Brown, a member of the 1948 Australian Test team known as the 'Invincibles'.

The importance of our excellent comeback on day one was further evident in our continuing improvement in the second innings which set us up for a great 10-wicket win when the rampaging duo of Blewett and Slater enabled Ricky Ponting to get up on the table to lead us into our winning team song. For me it also meant a quick dash to the airport to be present when Lynette gave birth to our second child.

The Hobart Test was a memorable one for anyone associated with the squad, firstly because we had dinner with four of the members from the great '48 Australian side prior to the match, Doug Ring, Bill Johnston, Arthur Morris and Bill Brown. This really put us in the mood for the battle ahead. Past stories, memories and works of inspiration were soaked up by the boys of the modern era.

I believe tradition and culture are vital ingredients in sporting success. They link all the events together and show you where you've come from and where you're going. The Langer-Gilchrist partnership will rightly go down as one of Test cricket's great partnerships. But even more substantially is the fact that it gave us all tangible proof that 'anything is possible' and that the game is never lost if you don't want it to be.

As players we always talk about coming from behind, or near impossible situations, but until you actually achieve this, it remains an unknown factor which you hope you can confront. Seeing the lads put on 238 to reach the third highest total in Test history against an attack of Akram, Younis, Akhtar and Mushtaq was indeed inspirational. Going into day five we all believed we could win, but if we had lost an early wicket the pendulum certainly would have swung towards Pakistan, but in our corner we could see our boys were focused and ready for the battle ahead.

A feeling of total solidarity and belief began to engulf the side, and being among the boys in the change rooms as the runs came tumbling down will always be a career highlight. Cricketers are very superstitious, and none of the lads changed seats on that final day so as not to tempt fate. Magazines and papers were re-read and crossword puzzles agonised over for hours. It worked and the sheer joy and excitement was overwhelming when Gilly smashed the winning runs in a century that showed he is a player of rare class and skill.

The third Test in Perth presented us with a chance to get rid of the tag for being a team that performed poorly in so called 'dead rubber' Tests. This was partly justified, but as captain I was very determined to put an end to it at the first opportunity. Being 2–0 in the best of three was as good a place as any to start and the boys responded in magnificent fashion.

A result in our favour in under three days was exactly the ruthless, professional performance we were all looking for and it was achieved by focusing on our jobs and, very importantly, enjoying ourselves.

Ricky Ponting best exhibited what we were all about by coming off a run of three ducks in a row to thrash an exhilarating 197, full of fearless stroke making and exquisite timing, when many thought his position was under threat. Being able to back yourself no matter what has become a 'silent' motto among the team, and here the courage and conviction of

Shoaib Akhtar, the Pakistani fast bowler was a source of controversy for his unique bowling action.

Steve Waugh and the Indian captain Sachin Tendulkar walk out for the toss at the start of the second Test against India at the MCG.

'Punter' shone through and further extolled the virtues of the team.

Our next challenge ahead was a further three Tests in quick succession against an Indian team led by the batting maestro Sachin Tendulkar along with many other world-class performers.

My initial thinking about the Indian team was that if we could plan to dominate them early then they would fall apart, particularly if we could get to Tendulkar. I see him as a reluctant leader in charge of a mentally fragile team with a disastrous away tour record.

On the other hand the Indians are a dangerous foe because they are very good front runners with a batting line-up consisting of four players with a 50-plus Test average.

The battle began at the world's most picturesque venue, the Adelaide Oval, and at lunch we had collapsed to be at one stage 5 for 52 against an enthusiastic attack, on what dangerously for us was a batting paradise. The partnership between myself and Ponting of 239 set us up to win the match and gave yours truly the honour of scoring 100 against each Test playing country, a record Mark should have held. Scoring over 400 in the first innings always puts immense pressure on the opposition. To win the game they realistically have to score more than that as they will have to bat last on a crumbling wicket against the spinners. One point we also discussed about the Indians was their extremely heavy bats, which are great on low slow wickets where you generally play vertical bat shots, hitting through the line. However, on fast, bouncy wickets, where the need for horizontal bat shots is far greater, the extra weight may cause a problem in timing and technique. With this in mind we employed a fair bit of short stuff, which finally unsettled their top order players.

Not surprisingly Tendulkar stood out and without doubt his two dismissals proved to be the turning points of the game. He was probably unlucky to be given out in the first innings at bat pad just when he looked very comfortable, but his second innings duck was a crazy dismissal. Ducking a McGrath bouncer he was struck in the ribs when it didn't get up to the height it should have reached, and he was adjudged to be LBW. This was a fair and correct decision, but such is Tendulkar's importance to the outcome of the game that many people refused to accept that he was out and that he had not been robbed.

If you duck a short ball which fails to bounce up you can still be given out lbw as Sachin Tendulkar discovers to his cost.

Sachin Tendulkar, the Indian captain, drives a ball to the boundary at the MCG as wicketkeeper Adam Gilchrist looks on.

Winning this match comfortably was the tonic we needed to plough on and accomplish something no other Aussie team had done by winning all six home Tests. The boys felt good about themselves and the unit was growing closer and tougher by the minute, and nothing seemed too big a challenge to stop us.

Team meetings were now pretty short but sweet with the message being, 'Keep an eye on your own game and be diligent in your preparation and professionalism.'

The inclusion of the thrilling talent of Brett Lee added spark to the squad for the Boxing Day Test match. Having only played with Brett the previous week for New South Wales against Western Australia, it was

Steve Waugh's Story

obvious this kid was special and ready for his Test match debut. Only once in a career do you see someone as exciting as this and I believe he will do to quick bowling what Shane Warne did for spin bowling. Kids will want to be tearaways in Brett's mould and this is great news for the game.

A great team effort in the batting, with consistent scores right through, set us up again to put pressure on the Indians. Tendulkar shone like a beacon, blazing a brilliant hundred while Lee dazzled, too, starting his career with a five-wicket haul.

The manner in which we played the remaining part of this Test best summed up our cricket for the summer. With bad weather affecting the time left to push for victory, we threw caution to the wind, upping our tempo in the second innings, sending Gilchrist in at number four and batting through bad light, making it clear that we were playing for a win at all costs. This attitude definitely forced the pressure back on India and I think it unsettled them to a certain extent. They were intimidated by our body language and assurance.

Victory wasn't easy and only came in the last session of the match for us, as we toiled away looking for any sign of weakness to exploit. Perhaps the last-ball wicket, of Ganguly by Blewett, and the Mark Waugh double strike in one over just before tea, turned things in our favour. But overall I was extremely pleased because this was a real team effort with every player contributing towards the end result.

The prospect of a clean sweep certainly kept us on edge and focused on to the task ahead in Sydney. Being something of a historian of the game I wanted this team to have a link with the past. This match was the first of the year 2000, and with the help of the ACB we as a team wore replicas of the caps donned by the Aussie team in 1900. We did it as a sign of respect and also to join hands with the past. This sentimental move inspired the passionate Langer to a career best 223, which was also helped by some words by the inspirational Pat Farmer, who joined us in the dressing rooms during a rain delay.

Ponting showed his mind power and skill again to post three hundreds on the trot, an exceptional effort considering his three previous scores were all ducks. McGrath and Lee ran amok in India's first innings, tearing the heart of the innings out after their captain strangely elected to bat on a green, moist surface. The team goal for this match was to bat only once and we achieved this when India capitulated in their second dig. Laxman played an astounding lone hand but was aided by the very aggressive field placements I employed. We all had two reasons to try to win in four days. Firstly, the game might get washed out on day five and we didn't want to risk it, and secondly, we all wanted an extra day's rest before our imminent New Zealand tour. Our win was achieved in the last over of the extra 30 minutes we had claimed with a farcical run. We erupted as one at our great win and historic home season.

The journey across the Tasman was seen as a major challenge. The Kiwis had just come off a highly rewarding series in which they whitewashed the West Indies.

Also, a feeling of tiredness and of being jaded had swept over the team. We had been playing for 20 of the previous 22 months and we were definitely starting to feel the effects. As a result we backed off on our training sessions and had some days completely away from the game, visiting wineries and golf courses to chill out and get recharged. Once again our game plan was to be aggressive but also patient, and to continually make the opposition feel the pressure. We identified their top order as suspect and their bowling to centre on Cairns and Vettori. With this in mind we knew there would be moments in the game that

Brett Lee puts that last ounce of effort into his bowling against India at the MCG.

would need to be identified as being key times to go on the offensive and to capitalise.

Eden Park was always going to be our greatest challenge with a pitch suited to their team, low and slow with some turn. This was also a 'hoodoo' ground for Australians not having won here in over 20 years. If ever there was a team to break the hoodoo this was it, because statistics like these are certainly treated now as a challenge rather than an obstacle. Victory here was sweet, especially so for Mark Waugh who salvaged our first innings with a class knock and to the 'born again spinner' Colin Miller who claimed his first 'five for' in the baggy green. Warney, to everyone's delight, overtook the great D K Lillee as our top wicket-taker with the last ball of the Test to further enhance his already legendary status. It was a gutsy, ugly win, but one that teams need to be able to pull off if they aspire to greatness and it couldn't have happened in a tougher environment.

Wellington was another emphatic win, although the brilliance of Cairns was memorable to watch. His hundred rekindled memories of Botham as he manhandled both our greats, Warne and McGrath, in an awesome display of clean hitting power. Slats and myself dug in after we came together at 4 for 51 to add 299 and set the match up for another win. It was exhilarating stuff watching Slats 'lay into them' like William Wallace of *Braveheart* fame, in the face of adversity and uncertainty. But, this is where attack is the best form of defence. As a captain I love it when we have to get our hands dirty and then come out on top and not only did we do it with our batting but our second innings bowling was a real workmanlike performance with everyone digging deep in the cold blustery conditions. The 177 runs to win were achieved in trademark fashion, aggressively and quickly with the almost re-invented Langer rising to the occasion again.

The last hurdle was one that we almost came to grief over as we again wrestled with the fatigue factor. Each player was asked at the team meeting leading up to the match, 'What is going to excite you over the course of the match?'

Another classic drive by Michael Slater at Eden Park, Auckland during the first Test against New Zealand.

This was a move to ensure everyone was focused and switched on for the battle ahead. Another fine effort was produced in the field, with McGrath and Lee taking the bit between their teeth in some heroic spells.

Disaster appeared on the horizon when we had slumped to 5 for 29 in our reply but again our resolve and self-belief saved the day through a brilliant counter attack from Gilchrist and Martyn. A slender first-innings lead put the game in the balance and from here we had to summon up one last effort in the field. For the first time all season I felt we were slipping in our intensity and desire and consequently I gave the lads a bit of a rocket to get things fired up. Responding as I thought they would with pride and passion we hung on for dear life which eventually allowed us to chase 212 for victory. Langer again shone, tearing into the Kiwis with such intensity that it looked like he held a personal grudge against them. The target was achieved and the team sang songs with one very proud Aussie atop the table. With Punter injured the honour had to be passed on and he generously let me do the ritual.

What a feeling it was seeing the boys arm in arm after such a long haul, stringing together 10 wins in a row. It doesn't get any better than this and the good news is 'the journey has only just begun!'

In Zimbabwe, another rousing chorus of
Under the Southern Cross I Stand led by Ian Healy with
stump in hand and all the usual suspects including
scorer, Mike Walsh (grey hair) and stand-in physio,
Patrick Farhart (no hair).

Poems from the Pitch

5

As Shane Warne said earlier in this book, many of the things the team does behind the scenes may sound a bit unorthodox. One of them is the daily poetry session, introduced by Dave Misson. The idea is that every day one of the players has to compose a poem and read it out in the dressing room before the morning warm-ups. Some of the offerings have shown definite literary talent but none can compete with Australian team manager Steve 'Brute' Bernard, who went one step further and wrote poems in praise of team members. We publish them here by kind permission of the author.

An inspirational moment as Adam Gilchrist and Shane Warne leave the field after one of the greatest Test match comebacks in cricketing history in the second Test v. Pakistan at Hobart.

The Leggie

There was a fear not long ago, about the art of spin,
Could it survive, or even thrive, its numbers were so thin,
While young boys bowled off fearsome runs,
    hoping to bowl with pace,
They didn't want to spin the ball, it was a dying race.

Then on the scene, out of left field, appeared the cavalry,
To save the cause, and lift the hearts, of the spin fraternity,
A Melbourne boy, St Kilda born, a spinner worth a mention,
He soon became to one and all, world cricket's new dimension.

A flashing smile, and shock of hair, coloured strawberry blonde,
With fingers strong, his supple wrist, became a wonder to gaze on,
Despite a start, to his career, which crawled to say the least,
The wickets came, and on the way, turned famine into feast.

The gatting ball, the flipper too, were in his box of tricks,
His over spin, just one more way, he has to get his kicks,
No matter what conditions were, he always had the answers,
Possessing skill to overcome, any circumstances.

With teasing flight and vicious turn, hardly run of the mill,

A favourite with the Aussie crowds, who love his unique skill,
But English crowds and Kiwis too, are somewhat less amused,

They hate the way their players seem, constantly confused.

I see him in the dressing room, a grin upon his lips,
Amusing mates with stories tall, asides and funny quips,
He's never been the fittest man, I'm sure he would confess,
But Shane remains, to everyone, a legend nonetheless.

Bloodbath McGrath

He shuffles back to his distant mark,
In an angry mood, decidedly dark,
A man out of luck, not known for his smile
And equipped with a bite as bad as his bark.

The gods conspire to mock his toil,
And his blood begins slowly to boil
He charges in all grace and style,
Aching all over as muscles uncoil.

There's nothing easy about bowling fast,
As only the strongest will ever last,
Sprinting and toiling month after mile,
With a short term future and lengthening past.

The hammies are tight, there's an aching hip,
And nothing gets caught when snuck to slip
The burden of the quick can be a trial
'Cause there's always the worry that form might dip,

He's all washed up, the papers say,
In their morning pars nearly every day,
An ex, a former, a man in denial,
They say no longer worth their pay.

But cream will always rise to the top,
And the man called Pigeon will never stop
While batsmen exist to churn his bile,
The man the selectors would never drop.
He'll always have a dip, no ifs or buts,
A champion bowler with tons of guts,
But even his mates will say with a smile
He bats like a gate that's open, not shut.

The Crowd Favourite

There's a buzzing hum round the SCG,
Coming in is the boy from Wagga'
On a dashing, smashing, slashing spree,
Don't dare believe he's just a slogger.

An eye like a hawk, with time to spare,
Once described as a reckless chancer,
Seemingly nerveless without a care,
As light of foot as a ballet dancer.

He's carved attacks around the globe,
Thrilling fans who've come to look,
Dazzling all like a flashing strobe,
With a delicate cut or a vicious hook.

His deeds have gained him cricketing fame,
As word has spread about his feats,
Attack and offense his signature game,
The favourite son putting bums on seats.

A sight to make a hard heart soft,
Is a century in another test,
With arms outstretched, helmet held aloft,
And planting a kiss on the Aussie crest.

Flem, the Sultan of Swing

With a prominent nose and a permanent grin,
An angular frame that's decidedly thin,
And a thatch of hair that's turning grey,
He is the king of swing and sway.

Swing bowling is such a difficult art,
Demanding skill and plenty of heart,
'Cause if the ball forgets to swing,
You become a slave, no longer king.

But when the ball decides to swing,
It's like he's got it on a string,
The ball curves late towards the slips,
To hungry hands, waiting for nicks.

Yet I'll always think of that fateful day,
When he had the Indians in disarray,
Probably some time mid December,
A day the Flem will always remember.

It was Adelaide on a hat trick ball,
And with cricket history about to call,
Lady luck became his mistress of whim,
The catch went down, yet he still raised a grin.

Punter, Man for all Seasons

You always notice the impish grin,
When Rick walks through the door,
A body lithe, and youthfully slim,
As he effortlessly glides across the floor.

He's tough as teak and hard as nails,
And moves on the field like a scalded cat,
Making all others look like snails,
It's a joy to watch his flashing bat.

His fielding feats are just sublime,
As good as this author has seen,
Throwing down stumps time after time,
With an arm as straight as a laser beam.

He's just as good with a club in hand,
With a handicap that's nearing scratch,
Plays like a pro out of the sand,
No one in cricket is near his match.

He has been known to have a bet,
And loves a day at the track,
The form guide causes worry and fret,
Deciding whom he's going to back.

The Kangaroos are his favourite team,
About whom he loves to enthuse,
The greatest team there's ever been,
He's disconsolate whenever they lose.

And when the Aussies have had a win,
Rick's on the table, beer in hand,
Leading the team in a noisy din,
Of Underneath The Southern Cross I Stand.

The Skipper

There's a roaring hush around the ground
The seagulls' cries are the only sound
Australia's backs are to the wall
In a heap of trouble if another one falls.

In the middle there's a raging fight
With the batsmen trying to last till night
And that won't be an easy chore
But at the crease is the captain Waugh.

If he loves one thing, it is the fight
When the game is poised and the bowling tight
And the bowling attack is sensing blood
If they get his wicket, there'll be a flood

An hour to stumps by the umpire's watch
And the bowlers lift their efforts a notch
Sensing the game is theirs to take
With destiny at hand and history to make.

He glares at the enemy, defying them all
Repelling their best and standing tall
A man more of substance than pretty style
When stumps are called, he allows a grin.

The battle is over, at least for the day
But tomorrow again, he'll resume the fray
And guts and courage will come to the fore
To him it is no game, he's off to war.

Twiggy Blewett

He's been described as a pole in creams
A description I'd say is hardly extreme
When I've heard it said by some of the lads,
Look at Blewey, he's a matchstick in pads.

When he does the body fat test
Five of him equals one of the rest
And Dave Misson says, 'Have a gander at him
My caliphers can't find any spare skin.'

But send him out to the middle to bat
And no one thinks of his lack of fat
As he hooks and cuts and pulls with ease
A beautiful striker guaranteed to please.

He's tall and elegant and will surprise
With the power belying his lack of size
And moves in the field like a startled gazelle
With fielding skills that more than excel.

Kaspa

*You know the name is not true blue
And cricketing Kasprowiczs are rather few,
The boys call him names meant to annoy,
Like Kaspa and crabby and salami boy.*

*A pleasant nature, he's always up
Like a gentle giant or playful pup,
A strapping lad with a generous smile
And an arse as big as a country mile.*

*But you wouldn't want to take for granted,
That playfulness can't be supplanted
By a roaring mass of energy
Who will compete to the nth degree.*

*He took the field in Bangalore
A depleted attack, all hot and sore,
Two nil down to an Indian team
Playing like the cat who swallowed the cream.*

*Kaspa led the way that day,
Pumped and fierce he entered the fray
Went through their team to Aussie cheers,
First time we'd won in 23 years.*

*We drank some beers to toast our win,
His face engulfed in a dopey grin
Kaspa was lauded our bowling sensation,
As we sat in our room in celebration.*

Alfie Langer, Scrapper Extrordinaire

He's been called a garden gnome, who hasn't got a shot,
But by the end of summer, he showed he had the lot
And if a journo muses, does Alf deserve his place?
He quietly scores another ton, and puts him in his place.

He may be small of stature, I see him as a giant,
And in the heat of battle, he'll always be defiant,
Competitive by nature, a fight won't make him hide,
You'd have him in your corner, you'd want him on your side.

Coming down to push and shove, when playing on the ground,
Forget the opposition, I'll back him pound for pound,
A never-give-up battler, blue collar to the end,
He's a bad enemy, you want him as a friend.

A passionate team member, he loves the baggy green,
He's won his right to wear it, and does with pride extreme,
When beating the West Indies, he got himself a tattoo,
Of kicking down some palms by a boxing kangaroo.

When fielding at short leg, he will not give an inch,
When they smash him in the shins, he will not even flinch,
And bowlers get a shock if they hit him in the head,
He'll grin and burst out laughing, and ask the ump for leg.

Gilly—Talent to Burn

He's a very nice young bloke, rather tall and slim
And though his hair is neatly cut, his ears could use a trim,
He's always nicely groomed, looking neat and clean,
The Richie Cunningham of the current Aussie team.

He struggled in the east, to make his cricket name,
Then headed off to Perth, where finally he found fame,
Was eventually picked for Aussie, in the one-day team,
Where he demonstrated class, with a talent rarely seen.

He's a devastating batsman, blessed with power and strength,
With a talent to straight drive, or pull from any length,
He terrifies the bowlers, with an attitude of scorn,
Try bowling him a maiden, try climbing the Matterhorn.

He's quick behind the stumps, with all its tough demands,
Taking horizontal catches, in the tips of sticky hands,
He's got a reputation, for getting the difficult take,
Making leg-side stumpings, quick as a cobra snake.

The crowds get quite excited, when he's walking through the gate,
He even stops the Mexican wave, as they sit and concentrate,
'Cause if he gets a hundred, they know he will enthral,
As the scoreboard tumbles over, at more than a run a ball.

He's broken many records since he played his debut test,
And he's more than likely pleased as he strives to match the best
He only started playing tests, sometime late last year,
And after playing nine he's yet, to taste a losing beer.

Brett (Bing) Lee—
Fastest Gun in the West

Remember the time when Dennis Lillee burst upon the scene,
Charging in from near the fence, with fiery pace extreme,
Fast forward now some thirty years, to Christmas ninety-nine,
The crowd's excitement's just the same, except it's Brett this time.

There's nothing matches searing pace to fire up the crowd,
And when that guy's an Aussie boy, the roar becomes so loud,
They shout and scream from bay 13, and from the Sydney Hill,
Baying for the batsman's blood, to see the claret spill.

The batsman's edgy at the crease, he takes his guard and waits,
Despite the noise around the ground, he's got to concentrate,
'Cause when the ball's delivered, a missile's on its way,
He has only got a nanosecond, to play or duck or sway.

Now, Brett's just started on the scene, a smiling country boy,
Being picked for the Aussie team has been his greatest joy,
He bowls with great enthusiasm, and boundless energy,
His leaping appeal when he gets a nick is a lasting memory.

I look forward to the future, and dream of days ahead,
When Bing will bowl with speed to kill, and fill the bats with dread,
And when a batsman feels the pain, and goes weak at the knee,
I'll shake my head and think aloud, I'm glad it's him not me.

The Statistics

CONSECUTIVE TEST VICTORIES

11	West Indies	1983-84	to	1984-85
10*	Australia	1999-2000		
8	Australia	1920-21	to	1921
7	England	1884-85	to	1887-88
7	England	1928	to	1928-29
7	West Indies	1984-85	to	1985-86
7	West Indies	1988	to	1988-89

(* unbroken)

1999-2000 AUSTRALIAN TEST MATCHES

Venue	Australia		Opponent			Winning Margin
Harare	422	0-5	Zimbabwe	194*	232	10 wickets
Brisbane	575	0-74	Pakistan	367*	281	10 wickets
Hobart	246	6-369	Pakistan	222*	392	4 wickets
Perth	451	–	Pakistan	155*	276	inns & 20 runs
Adelaide	441*	8d-239	India	285	110	285 runs
Melbourne	405	5d-208	India	238	195	180 runs
Sydney	5d-552	–	India	150*	261	inns & 141 runs
Auckland	214*	229	New Zealand	163	218	62 runs
Wellington	419	4-177	New Zealand	298*	294	6 wickets
Hamilton	252	4-212	New Zealand	232*	229	6 wickets

(* denotes batted first)

1999-2000 AUSTRALIAN TEST AVERAGES

BATTING	M	I	NO	R	HS	50s	100s	Avrge	Ct/St
Ricky Ponting	7	10	2	603	197	3	1	75.38	10
Justin Langer	10	16	1	952	223	4	2	63.47	10
Damien Martyn	3	6	2	241	89*	0	2	60.25	2
Adam Gilchrist	9	14	3	629	149*	1	5	57.18	38/3
Steve Waugh	10	16	3	699	151*	1	3	53.77	12
Mark Waugh	10	16	3	522	100	3	1	40.15	24
Michael Slater	10	18	2	629	169	2	2	39.31	8
Michael Kasprowicz	2	3	2	34	21*	0	0	34.00	1
Greg Blewett	9	16	2	403	89	0	2	28.79	6
Damien Fleming	7	6	2	108	65	0	1	27.00	2
Shane Warne	10	12	1	229	86	0	2	20.82	11

Matthew Hayden	1	2	0	39	37	0	0	19.50	0
Brett Lee	5	5	1	47	27	0	0	11.75	1
Glenn McGrath	10	10	0	56	14	0	0	5.60	5
Ian Healy	1	1	0	5	5	0	0	5.00	2
Colin Miller	4	5	0	16	8	0	0	3.20	1
Scott Muller	2	2	2	6	6*	0	0	–	2

BOWLING	M	O	Mdns	R	W	BB	5W/i	10W/m	Avge
Mark Waugh	10	7	1	23	2	2/12	0	0	11.50
Brett Lee	5	169.4	45	499	31	5/47	2	0	16.10
Glenn McGrath	10	416.2	130	1000	50	5/48	2	1	20.00
Damien Fleming	7	270	66	733	32	5/30	2	0	22.91
Colin Miller	4	165	45	413	15	5/55	1	0	27.53
Shane Warne	10	439.3	117	1256	41	5/110	1	0	30.63
Michael Kasprowicz	2	45	7	217	7	4/53	0	0	31.00
Scott Muller	2	58	8	258	7	3/68	0	0	36.86
Greg Blewett	9	39	8	130	3	1/5	0	0	43.33
Michael Slater	10	1	0	2	0	–	0	0	–
Steve Waugh	10	16	2	57	0	–	0	0	–
Damien Martyn	3	7	4	12	0	–	0	0	–
Ricky Ponting	7	14	4	39	0	–	0	0	–

ZIMBABWE v. AUSTRALIA

Only Test Match

At Harare Sports Club Ground, Harare, October 14, 15, 16, 17, 1999. Australia won by 10 wickets. Toss: Zimbabwe. Test debut: T.R. Gripper.

Man of the Match: S.R. Waugh.

Close of play: First day, Australia (1) 0-6 (Slater 4, Blewett 1); Second day, Australia (1) 5-275 (S.R. Waugh 90, Healy 5); Third day, Zimbabwe (2) 1-80 (Gripper 25, Goodwin 11).

Zimbabwe

G.J. Rennie c Ponting b McGrath	18	–	(4) c McGrath b Miller	23
G.W. Flower c Ponting b Fleming	1	–	lbw b McGrath	32
M.W. Goodwin run out (Blewett/Langer)	0	–	c S.R. Waugh b Warne	91
*A.D.R. Campbell c Slater b Fleming	5	–	(5) run out (Slater/Healy)	1
+A. Flower c M.E. Waugh b McGrath	28	–	(6) c Healy b McGrath	0
N.C. Johnson c M.E. Waugh b McGrath	75	–	(7) c M.E. Waugh b McGrath	5
T.R. Gripper lbw b Warne	4	–	(1) lbw b Miller	60
H.H. Streak c M.E. Waugh b Warne	3	–	(9) lbw b Warne	0
G.J. Whittall c Healy b Warne	27	–	(8) c M.E. Waugh b Warne	2

B.C. Strang run out (Blewett/Langer) 17 — c Langer b Miller 0
H.K. Olonga not out 0 — not out 0
    B 2, l-b 4, n-b 10 16 B 9, l-b 2, w 1, n-b 6 18
                                            ****   ****
(85 overs, 341 mins) 194 (122.1 overs, 456 mins) 232
Fall: 6 6 22 37 107 119 125 165 190 194 Fall: 56 154 200 208 211 220 227 227 232 232

Bowling: *First Innings* – McGrath 23-7-44-3; Fleming 15-6-22-2; Miller 19-6-36-0; Warne 23-2-69-3; Ponting 1-1-0-0; S.R. Waugh 4-1-17-0. *Second Innings* – McGrath 31-12-46-3; Fleming 21-6-31-0; Miller 34-10-66-3; Ponting 1-1-0-0; Warne 30.1-11-68-3; Blewett 5-1-10-0.

Australia

M.J. Slater c A. Flower b Strang 4 — (2) not out 0
G.S. Blewett c Campbell b Streak 1 — (1) not out 4
J.L. Langer run out (Olonga/A. Flower) 44
M.E. Waugh c and b G.W. Flower 90
*S.R. Waugh not out 151
R.T. Ponting c Johnson b Streak 31
+I.A. Healy c A. Flower b Strang 5
S.K. Warne c A. Flower b Streak 6
D.W. Fleming lbw b Streak 65
C.R. Miller c Johnson b Streak 2
G.D. McGrath c Johnson b G.J. Whittall 13
    L-b 5, w 4, n-b 1 10 w 1 1
                              ****   ****
(139.4 overs, 563 mins) 422 (0.3 overs, 3 mins) (0 wkt) 5
Fall: 6 8 96 174 253 275 282 396 398 422 Fall:

Bowling: *First Innings* – Olonga 17-1-83-0; Streak 34-8-93-5; Strang 44-14-96-2; Johnson 2-0-14-0; G.J. Whittall 21.4-3-74-1; G.W. Flower 18-3-38-1; Gripper 3-0-19-0. *Second Innings* – Strang 0.3-0-5-0.

Umpires: G. Sharp (England) and I.D. Robinson.
TV Umpire: K.C. Barbour.
Referee: G.R. Viswanath (India).

First Test between Australia and Zimbabwe. Steve Waugh scored his 20th Test century.

ZIMBABWE v. AUSTRALIA AVERAGES

Zimbabwe

BATTING	M	I	NO	R	HS	100s	50s	Avge	Ct
M.W. Goodwin	1	2	0	91	91	0	1	45.50	0
N.C. Johnson	1	2	0	80	75	0	1	40.00	3

Scoreboard

T.R. Gripper	1	2	0	64	60	0	1	32.00	0
G.J. Rennie	1	2	0	41	23	0	0	20.50	0
G.W. Flower	1	2	0	33	32	0	0	16.50	1
G.J. Whittall	1	2	0	29	27	0	0	14.50	0
A. Flower	1	2	0	28	28	0	0	14.00	3
B.C. Strang	1	2	0	17	17	0	0	8.50	0
A.D.R. Campbell	1	2	0	6	5	0	0	3.00	1
H.H. Streak	1	2	0	3	3	0	0	1.50	0
H.K. Olonga	1	2	2	0	0*	0	0	–	0

Signifies not out.

BOWLING	O	M	R	W	BB	5W/i	10W/m	Avge
H.H. Streak	34	8	93	5	5/93	1	0	18.60
G.W. Flower	18	3	38	1	1/38	0	0	38.00
B.C. Strang	44.3	14	101	2	2/96	0	0	50.50
G.J. Whittall	21.4	3	74	1	1/74	0	0	74.00
T.R. Gripper	3	0	19	0	–	0	0	–
N.C. Johnson	2	0	14	0	–	0	0	–
H.K. Olonga	17	1	83	0	–	0	0	–

Australia

BATTING	M	I	NO	R	HS	100s	50s	Avge	Ct
M.E. Waugh	1	1	0	90	90	0	1	90.00	5
D.W. Fleming	1	1	0	65	65	0	1	65.00	0
J.L. Langer	1	1	0	44	44	0	0	44.00	1
R.T. Ponting	1	1	0	31	31	0	0	31.00	2
G.D. McGrath	1	1	0	13	13	0	0	13.00	1
S.K. Warne	1	1	0	6	6	0	0	6.00	0
G.S. Blewett	1	2	1	5	4*	0	0	5.00	0
I.A. Healy	1	1	0	5	5	0	0	5.00	2
M.J. Slater	1	2	1	4	4	0	0	4.00	1
C.R. Miller	1	1	0	2	2	0	0	2.00	0
S.R. Waugh	1	1	1	151	151*	1	0	–	1

Signifies not out.

BOWLING	O	M	R	W	BB	5W/i	10W/m	Avge
G.D. McGrath	54	19	90	6	3/44	0	0	15.00
S.K. Warne	53.1	13	137	6	3/68	0	0	22.83
D.W. Fleming	36	12	53	2	2/22	0	0	26.50
C.R. Miller	53	16	102	3	3/66	0	0	34.00
G.S. Blewett	5	1	10	0	–	0	0	–
R.T. Ponting	2	2	0	0	–	0	0	–
S.R. Waugh	4	1	17	0	–	0	0	–

AUSTRALIA v. PAKISTAN

First Test Match

At Brisbane Cricket Ground, Brisbane, November 5, 6, 7, 8, 9, 1999. Australia won by 10 wickets. Toss: Australia. Test debut: A.C. Gilchrist and S.A. Muller (Australia), Abdur Razzaq (Pakistan).

Man of the Match: M.J. Slater. *Attendance:* 41,639.

Close of play: First day, Pakistan (1) 6-280 (Azhar Mahmood 7, Abdur Razzaq 9); Second day, Australia (1) 0-233 (Slater 134, Blewett 77); Third day, Australia (1) 9-515 (Warne 34, Muller 1); Fourth day, Pakistan (2) 4-223 (Saeed Anwar 118, Abdur Razzaq 2).

Pakistan

Saeed Anwar c M.E. Waugh b Warne	61	–	c Gilchrist b McGrath	119
Mohammad Wasim c Gilchrist b Fleming	18	–	lbw b Fleming	0
Ijaz Ahmed c Warne b Fleming	0	–	c Gilchrist b McGrath	5
Inzamam-ul-Haq lbw b McGrath	88	–	c Ponting b Fleming	12
Yousuf Youhana c Gilchrist b Fleming	95	–	c M.E. Waugh b Muller	75
Azhar Mahmood c Slater b McGrath	13	–	(8) st Gilchrist b Warne	0
Mushtaq Ahmed c Gilchrist b Fleming	0	–	(10) not out	1
Abdur Razzaq c M.E. Waugh b Muller	11	–	(6) c Ponting b Warne	2
+Moin Khan run out (Ponting/Gilchrist)	61	–	(7) c Muller b Fleming	17
*Wasim Akram c and b Muller	9	–	(9) b Fleming	28
Shoaib Akhtar not out	0	–	b Fleming	5
B 4, l-b 2, n-b 5	11		B 6, l-b 6, n-b 5	17
(117.1 overs, 464 mins)	367		(74.1 overs, 315 mins)	281

Fall: 42 42 113 265 280 280 288 334 356 367

Fall: 3 8 37 214 223 225 227 273 276 281

Bowling: *First Innings* – McGrath 28-4-116-2; Fleming 31-5-65-4; Muller 19-4-72-2; Warne 28.1-11-73-1; Blewett 5-1-22-0; Ponting 5-1-12-0; S.R. Waugh 1-0-1-0. *Second Innings* – McGrath 21-9-63-2; Fleming 14.1-2-59-5; Muller 10-1-55-1; Warne 25-8-80-2; Ponting 4-0-12-0.

Australia

M.J. Slater c Yousuf Youhana b Azhar Mahmood	169	–	(2) not out	32
G.S. Blewett lbw b Mushtaq Ahmed	89	–	(1) not out	40
J.L. Langer c Abdur Razzaq b Mushtaq Ahmed	1			
M.E. Waugh c Wasim Akram b Mushtaq Ahmed	100			
*S.R. Waugh c Moin Khan b Shoaib Akhtar	1			
R.T. Ponting lbw b Shoaib Akhtar	0			
+A.C. Gilchrist b Shoaib Akhtar	81			
S.K. Warne c Mushtaq Ahmed b Wasim Akram	86			
D.W. Fleming lbw b Shoaib Akhtar	0			
G.D. McGrath c Yousuf Youhana b Wasim Akram	1			
S.A. Muller not out	6			

B 3, l-b 12, n-b 26	41	L-b 2	2

(139.1 overs, 607 mins)   575   (14.2 overs, 56 mins) (0 wkt)   74

Fall: 269 272 311 328 342 465 485 486 489 575

Bowling: *First Innings* – Wasim Akram 31.1-6-87-2; Shoaib Akhtar 32-2-153-4; Abdur Razzaq 17-3-66-0; Azhar Mahmood 19-2-52-1; Mushtaq Ahmed 38-3-194-3; Ijaz Ahmed 2-0-8-0. *Second Innings* – Wasim Akram 4-0-14-0; Shoaib Akhtar 5-0-25-0; Azhar Mahmood 3.2-0-13-0; Mushtaq Ahmed 2-0-20-0.

Umpires: E.A. Nicholls (West Indies) and D.J. Harper.
TV Umpire: P.D. Parker.
Referee: J.R. Reid (New Zealand).

Australian Test Debuts: Adam Gilchrist (# 381), Scott Muller (# 382). Michael Slater/Greg Blewett record opening partnership of 269 at the Gabba in all Tests and the highest by Australia against Pakistan. Shane Warne/Scott Muller record 10th wicket partnership of 86 at the Gabba in all Tests and the highest by Australia against Pakistan. Michael Slater/Greg Blewett 2nd highest wicket partnership of 269 at the Gabba in all Tests for all wickets. (Highest 276 DG Bradman/AL Hassett Australia v. England, 1946-47). Michael Slater (169) scored his 13th Test century. Michael Slater when 22 reached 4,000 Test Runs. Mark Waugh (100) scored his 17th Test century. Shane Warne Highest Test and first class Score of 96. Damien Fleming (5/59) took five wickets in an innings for the second time. Saeed Anwar (119) scored his 9th Test century. Adam Gilchrist (81) scored the second highest score on debut by an Australian wicket-keeper. The highest was Arthur Jarvis (82) v. England in Melbourne in 1884-85.

AUSTRALIA v. PAKISTAN

Second Test Match

At Bellerive Oval, Hobart, November 18, 19, 20, 21, 22, 1999. Australia won by four wickets.
Toss: Australia.

Man of the Match: J.L. Langer. *Attendance:* 20,730.

Close of play: First day, Australia (1) 0-29 (Slater 16, Blewett 9); Second day, Pakistan (2) 1-61 (Saeed Anwar 36, Saqlain Mushtaq 0); Third day, Pakistan (2) 7-351 (Inzamam-ul-Haq 116, Wasim Akram 1); Fourth day, Australia (2) 5-188 (Langer 52, Gilchrist 45).

Pakistan

Saeed Anwar c Warne b McGrath	0	–	b Warne	78
Mohammad Wasim c Gilchrist b Muller	91	–	c McGrath b Muller	20
Ijaz Ahmed c Slater b McGrath	6	–	(4) c S.R. Waugh b McGrath	82
Inzamam-ul-Haq b Muller	12	–	(5) c M.E. Waugh b Warne	118
Yousuf Youhana c M.E. Waugh b Fleming	17	–	(6) c Ponting b Fleming	2
Azhar Mahmood b Warne	27	–	(7) lbw b Warne	28
+Moin Khan c McGrath b Muller	1	–	(8) c Gilchrist b Fleming	6
*Wasim Akram c Gilchrist b Warne	29	–	(9) c Blewett b Warne	31

Saqlain Mushtaq lbw b Warne	3	–	(3) lbw b Warne	8
Waqar Younis not out	12	–	run out (Gilchrist)	0
Shoaib Akhtar c Gilchrist b Fleming	5	–	not out	5
B 10, l-b 6, w 3	19		L-b 6, w 1, n-b 7	14

****

(72.5 overs, 283 mins) 222   (128.5 overs, 521 mins) 392

Fall: 4 18 71 120 148 153 188 198 217 222   Fall: 50 100 122 258 263 320 345 357 358 392

Bowling: *First Innings* – McGrath 18-8-34-2; Fleming 24.5-7-54-2; Muller 12-0-68-3; Warne 16-6-45-3; Blewett 2-1-5-0. *Second Innings* – McGrath 27-8-87-1; Fleming 29-5-89-2; Warne 45.5-11-110-5; Muller 17-3-63-1; S.R. Waugh 4-1-19-0; M.E. Waugh 2-0-6-0; Ponting 2-1-7-0; Blewett 2-0-5-0.

Australia

M.J. Slater c Ijaz Ahmed b Saqlain Mushtaq	97	–	(2) c Azhar Mahmood b Shoaib Akhtar	27
G.S. Blewett c Moin Khan b Azhar Mahmood	35	–	(1) c Moin Khan b Azhar Mahmood	29
J.L. Langer c Mohammad Wasim b Saqlain Mushtaq	59	–	c Inzamam-ul-Haq b Saqlain Mushtaq	127
M.E. Waugh lbw b Waqar Younis	5	–	lbw b Azhar Mahmood	0
*S.R. Waugh c Ijaz Ahmed b Wasim Akram	24	–	c and b Saqlain Mushtaq	28
R.T. Ponting b Waqar Younis	0	–	lbw b Wasim Akram	0
+A.C. Gilchrist st Moin Khan b Saqlain Mushtaq	6	–	not out	149
S.K. Warne b Saqlain Mushtaq	0	–	not out	0
D.W. Fleming lbw b Saqlain Mushtaq	0			
G.D. McGrath st Moin Khan b Saqlain Mushtaq	7			
S.A. Muller not out	0			
B 2, l-b 6, n-b 5	13		B 1, l-b 4, n-b 4	9

****

(80 overs, 355 mins) 246   (113.5 overs, 503 mins) (6 wkts) 369

Fall: 76 191 206 206 213 236 236 236 246 246   Fall: 39 81 81 125 126 364

Bowling: *First Innings* – Wasim Akram 20-4-51-1; Shoaib Akhtar 17-2-69-0; Waqar Younis 12-1-42-2; Saqlain Mushtaq 24-8-46-6; Azhar Mahmood 7-1-30-1. *Second Innings* – Wasim Akram 18-1-68-1; Waqar Younis 11-2-38-0; Shoaib Akhtar 23-5-85-1; Saqlain Mushtaq 44.5-9-130-2; Azhar Mahmood 17-3-43-2.

Umpires: P. Willey (England) and P.D. Parker.
TV Umpire: S.J. Davis.
Referee: J.R. Reid (England).

Michael Slater dismissed in the nineties for the seventh time. Inzamam-ul-Haq (118) scored his 8th Test century. Justin Langer/Adam Gilchrist 10th highest sixth wicket partnership in Test cricket (238). Glenn McGrath captured his 250th Test wicket. Australia's fourth innings total of 6-369 was the third highest score to win a Test. Justin Langer (127) scored his 4th Test century. Adam Gilchrist (149*) scored his debut Test century. Saqlain Mushtaq captured his 100th Test wicket.

AUSTRALIA v. PAKISTAN

Third Test Match

At WACA. Ground, Perth, November 26, 27, 28, 1999. Australia won by an innings and 20 runs. Toss: Pakistan.

Man of the Match: R.T. Ponting. *Man of Series:* J.L. Langer. **Attendance:** 42,166.

Close of play: First day, Australia (1) 4-171 (Langer 63, Ponting 62); Second day, Pakistan (2) 2-40 (Ijaz Ahmed 19, Saqlain Mushtaq 4).

Pakistan

Saeed Anwar c Ponting b McGrath	18	c Gilchrist b Fleming	6
Wajahatullah Wasti c Ponting b McGrath	5	c Fleming b McGrath	7
Ijaz Ahmed b Fleming	1	c Slater b Kasprowicz	115
Inzamam-ul-Haq c S.R. Waugh b Kasprowicz	22	(5) c M.E. Waugh b McGrath	8
Yousuf Youhana c Gilchrist b McGrath	18	(6) c S.R. Waugh b McGrath	0
Azhar Mahmood c Warne b Fleming	39	(7) b Warne	17
+Moin Khan c and b Fleming	28	(8) c Gilchrist b McGrath	26
*Wasim Akram not out	5	(9) c McGrath b Kasprowicz	52
Saqlain Mushtaq c Blewett b Kasprowicz	7	(4) lbw b Kasprowicz	12
Shoaib Akhtar b Kasprowicz	0	c Warne b Fleming	8
Mohammad Akram c M.E. Waugh b Kasprowicz	0	not out	10
L-b 4, n-b 8	12	L-b 6, n-b 9	15
(52 overs, 224 mins)	155	(69.4 overs, 295 mins)	276

Fall: 18 26 26 51 83 135 142 155 155 155
Fall: 15 25 53 56 114 168 230 256 261 276

Bowling: *First Innings* – McGrath 19-3-44-3; Fleming 19-7-48-3; Kasprowicz 12-2-53-4; Warne 2-0-6-0.
Second Innings – McGrath 21-5-49-4; Fleming 19.4-3-86-2; Kasprowicz 16-3-79-3; Warne 13-1-56-1.

Australia

M.J. Slater lbw b Wasim Akram	0
G.S. Blewett c Inzamam-ul-Haq b Mohammad Akram	11
J.L. Langer c Moin Khan b Shoaib Akhtar	144
M.E. Waugh c (sub) Ghulam Ali b Mohammad Akram	0
*S.R. Waugh c Yousuf Youhana b Mohammad Akram	5
R.T. Ponting c Ijaz Ahmed b Azhar Mahmood	197
+A.C. Gilchrist b Mohammad Akram	28
S.K. Warne c Moin Khan b Saqlain Mushtaq	13
M.S. Kasprowicz not out	9
D.W. Fleming lbw b Saqlain Mushtaq	0
G.D. McGrath c Azhar Mahmood b Mohammad Akram	0
B 9, l-b 9, n-b 26	44
(110.5 overs, 517 mins)	451

Fall: 0 28 48 54 381 424 424 448 450 451

Bowling: Wasim Akram 17-2-55-1; Mohammad Akram 27.5-1-138-5; Shoaib Akhtar 16-2-74-1; Azhar Mahmood 23-2-91-1; Saqlain Mushtaq 26-7-75-2; Wajahatullah Wasti 1-1-0-0.

Umpires: P. Willey (England) and D.B. Hair.
TV Umpire: T.A. Prue.
Referee: J.R. Reid (New Zealand).

Justin Langer (144) scored his 5th Test century. Ricky Ponting (197) scored his 5th Test century. Justin Langer/Ricky Ponting 3rd highest 5th wicket partnership in Test cricket (327). Ijaz Ahmed (115) scored his 12th Test century. The match ended inside 3 days for the 5th time in 27 Tests.

AUSTRALIA v PAKISTAN AVERAGES

Australia

BATTING	M	I	NO	R	HS	100s	50s	Avge	Ct/St
A.C. Gilchrist	3	4	1	264	149*	1	1	88.00	12/1
J.L. Langer	3	4	0	331	144	2	1	82.75	0
M.J. Slater	3	5	1	325	169	1	1	81.25	3
G.S. Blewett	3	5	1	204	89	0	1	51.00	2
R.T. Ponting	3	4	0	197	197	1	0	49.25	5
S.K. Warne	3	4	1	99	86	0	1	33.00	4
M.E. Waugh	3	4	0	105	100	1	0	26.25	7
S.R. Waugh	3	4	0	58	28	0	0	14.50	3
G.D. McGrath	3	3	0	8	7	0	0	2.67	3
D.W. Fleming	3	3	0	0	0	0	0	0.00	2
M.S. Kasprowicz	1	1	1	9	9*	0	0	–	0
S.A. Muller	2	2	2	6	6*	0	0	–	2

Signifies not out.

BOWLING	O	M	R	W	BB	5W/i	Avge
M.S. Kasprowicz	28	5	132	7	4/53	0	18.86
D.W. Fleming	137.4	29	401	18	5/59	1	22.28
G.D. McGrath	134	38	393	14	4/49	0	28.07
S.K. Warne	130	37	370	12	5/110	1	30.83
S.A. Muller	58	8	258	7	3/68	0	36.86
G.S. Blewett	9	2	32	0	–	0	–
R.T. Ponting	11	2	31	0	–	0	–
M.E. Waugh	2	0	6	0	–	0	–
S.R. Waugh	5	1	20	0	–	0	–

Pakistan

BATTING	M	I	NO	R	HS	100s	50s	Avge	Ct/St
Saeed Anwar	3	6	0	282	119	1	2	47.00	0
Inzamam-ul-Haq	3	6	0	260	118	1	1	43.33	2
Ijaz Ahmed	3	6	0	209	115	1	1	34.83	3
Yousuf Youhana	3	6	0	207	95	0	2	34.50	3
Mohammad Wasim	2	4	0	129	91	0	1	32.25	1
Wasim Akram	3	6	1	154	52	0	1	30.80	1
Moin Khan	3	6	0	139	61	0	1	23.17	5/2

Azhar Mahmood	3	6	0	124	39	0	0	20.67	2
Waqar Younis	1	2	1	12	12*	0	0	12.00	0
Mohammad Akram	1	2	1	10	10*	0	0	10.00	0
Saqlain Mushtaq	2	4	0	30	12	0	0	7.50	1
Abdur Razzaq	1	2	0	13	11	0	0	6.50	1
Wajahatullah Wasti	1	2	0	12	7	0	0	6.00	0
Shoaib Akhtar	3	6	2	23	8	0	0	5.75	0
Mushtaq Ahmed	1	2	1	1	1*	0	0	1.00	1

*Signifies not out.

BOWLING	O	M	R	W	BB	5W/i	Avge
Saqlain Mushtaq	94.5	23	251	10	6/46	1	25.10
Mohammad Akram	27.5	1	138	5	5/138	1	27.60
Waqar Younis	23	3	80	2	2/42	0	40.00
Azhar Mahmood	69.2	8	229	5	2/43	0	45.80
Wasim Akram	90.1	13	275	5	2/87	0	55.00
Shoaib Akhtar	93	11	406	6	4/153	0	67.67
Mushtaq Ahmed	40	3	214	3	3/194	0	71.33
Abdur Razzaq	17	3	66	0	–	0	–
Ijaz Ahmed	2	0	8	0	–	0	–
Wajahatullah Wasti	1	1	0	0	–	0	–

AUSTRALIA v. INDIA

First Test Match

At Adelaide Oval, Adelaide, December 10, 11, 12, 13, 14, 1999. Australia won by 285 runs. Toss: Australia.

Man of the Match: S.R. Waugh. *Attendance:* 65,610.

Close of play: First day, Australia (1) 5-298 (S.R. Waugh 117, Gilchrist 0); Second day, India (1) 4-123 (Tendulkar 12, Ganguly 12); Third day, Australia 2-71 (Blewett 26, M.E. Waugh 0); Fourth day, India (2) 5-76 (Ganguly 31, M.S.K. Prasad 6).

Australia

G.S. Blewett c Prasad b Srinath	4	–	(2) b Agarkar	88
M.J. Slater c Ramesh b Ganguly	28	–	(1) c Ganguly b Srinath	0
J.L. Langer lbw b Venkatesh Prasad	11	–	c Gandhi b Kumble	38
M.E. Waugh c Prasad b Venkatesh Prasad	5	–	c Laxman b Agarkar	8
*S.R. Waugh c Prasad b Agarkar	150	–	c Prasad b Agarkar	5
R.T. Ponting run out (Agarkar/M.S.K. Prasad)	125	–	c Prasad b Venkatesh Prasad	21
+A.C. Gilchrist c and b Agarkar	0	–	c Laxman b Srinath	43
S.K. Warne lbw b Kumble	86	–	c Dravid b Srinath	0

M.S. Kasprowicz b Kumble	4	–	not out		21
D.W. Fleming not out	12				
G.D. McGrath c Prasad b Venkatesh Prasad	4				
B 1, l-b 5, n-b 6	12		B 3, l-b 8, w 2, n-b 2		15
	****				****
(125.3 overs, 512 mins)	441		(89.5 overs, 386 mins) (8 wkts dec)		239
Fall: 8 29 45 52 291 298 406 417 424 441			Fall: 1 65 95 113 153 204 205 239		

Bowling: *First Innings* – Srinath 29-3-117-1; Agarkar 26-5-86-2; Venkatesh Prasad 24.3-4-83-3; Ganguly 7-1-34-1; Kumble 34-1-101-2; Tendulkar 2-0-12-0; Laxman 3-1-2-0. *Second Innings* – Srinath 21.5-4-64-3; Agarkar 18-6-43-3; Venkatesh Prasad 18-5-48-1; Kumble 32-9-73-1.

India

D.J. Gandhi c Kasprowicz b McGrath	4	–	c Gilchrist b McGrath		0
S. Ramesh run out (Blewett)	2	–	lbw b Warne		28
V.V.S. Laxman c S.R. Waugh b McGrath	41	–	b Fleming		0
R.S. Dravid c Langer b Warne	35	–	c Gilchrist b Warne		6
*S.R. Tendulkar c Langer b Warne	61	–	lbw b McGrath		0
S.C. Ganguly st Gilchrist b Warne	60	–	c Gilchrist b Fleming		43
+M.S.K. Prasad b Warne	14	–	c Langer b Fleming		11
A.B. Agarkar b Fleming	19	–	c S.R. Waugh b Fleming		0
J. Srinath c S.R. Waugh b Fleming	11	–	c Slater b McGrath		11
A.R. Kumble not out	17	–	b Fleming		3
B.K. Venkatesh Prasad lbw b Fleming	0	–	not out		2
L-b 1, w 1, n-b 19	21		L-b 1, n-b 5		6
	****				****
(113.4 overs, 464 mins)	285		(38.1 overs, 177 mins)		110
Fall: 7 9 90 107 215 229 240 266 275 285			Fall: 0 3 24 27 48 93 93 102 108 110		

Bowling: *First Innings* – McGrath 30-13-49-2; Fleming 24.4-7-70-3; Kasprowicz 11-2-62-0; Warne 42-12-92-4; Blewett 6-1-11-0. *Second Innings* – McGrath 12-2-35-3; Fleming 9.1-2-30-5; Warne 10-6-21-2; Kasprowicz 6-0-23-0; Waugh 1-1-0-0.

Umpires: R.S. Dunne (New Zealand) and D.J. Harper.
TV Umpire: S.J. Davis.
Referee: R.S. Madugalle (Sri Lanka).

Steve Waugh (150) scored his 21st Test century. Steve Waugh the only Test cricketer to score a century against all Test opponents. Steve Waugh's 117 runs became his 8,000th Test run. Ricky Ponting (125) scored his 6th Test century. Steve Waugh/Ricky Ponting 239 was the 14th highest fifth wicket partnership in Test cricket and the highest at the Adelaide oval for the same wicket. Damien Fleming captured his third five wickets in an innings. He missed the hat-trick when Shane Warne dropped the chance. Shane Warne (86) equaled his highest score. Anil Kumble took his 50th Test wicket for the calendar year.

Scoreboard

AUSTRALIA v. INDIA

Second Test Match

At Melbourne Cricket Ground, Melbourne, December 26, 27, 28, 29, 30, 1999. Australia won by 180 runs. Toss: India. Test debut: B. Lee (#383), H.H. Kanitkar (India).

Man of the Match: S.R. Tendulkar. *Attendance:* 134,554.

Close of play: First day, Australia (1) 3-138 (Slater 64, S.R. Waugh 5); Second day, Australia (1) 5-332 (Ponting 59, Gilchrist 77); Third day, India (1) 9-235 (Kumble 26, Venkatesh Prasad 10); Fourth day, India (2) 1-40 (Ramesh 26, Dravid 10).

Australia

G.S. Blewett b Srinath	2	–	(2) c Ganguly b Kumble	31
M.J. Slater c Srinath b Venkatesh Prasad	91	–	(1) lbw b Agarkar	3
J.L. Langer lbw b Srinath	8	–	c Prasad b Agarkar	9
M.E. Waugh lbw b Agarkar	41	–	(5) not out	51
*S.R. Waugh c Prasad b Venkatesh Prasad	32	–	(6) lbw b Agarkar	32
R.T. Ponting lbw b Srinath	67	–	(7) not out	21
+A.C. Gilchrist c Ganguly b Agarkar	78	–	(4) c Srinath b Kumble	55
S.K. Warne c Prasad b Agarkar	2			
D.W. Fleming not out	31			
B. Lee c and b Srinath	27			
G.D. McGrath run out (Kanitkar)	1			
B 1, l-b 9, w 1, n-b 14	25		L-b 2, w 1, n-b 3	6
	****			****
(118.1 overs, 526 mins)	405	(59 overs, 263 mins)	(5 wkts dec)	208

Fall: 4 28 123 192 197 341 343 345 404 405   Fall: 5 32 91 109 167

Bowling: *First Innings* – Srinath 33.1-7-130-4; Agarkar 28-7-76-3; Venkatesh Prasad 26-6-101-2; Ganguly 2-0-10-0; Kumble 29-3-78-0. *Second Innings* – Srinath 14-0-45-0; Agarkar 17-3-51-3; Venkatesh Prasad 10-0-38-0; Kumble 18-3-72-2.

India

V.V.S. Laxman c M.E. Waugh b McGrath	5	–	c McGrath b Fleming	1
S. Ramesh b Lee	4	–	retired hurt	26
R.S. Dravid c Gilchrist b Lee	9	–	c Gilchrist b Lee	14
*S.R. Tendulkar c Langer b Fleming	116	–	lbw b Warne	52
S.C. Ganguly c M.E. Waugh b McGrath	31	–	b Blewett	17
H.H. Kanitkar lbw b Warne	11	–	lbw b Fleming	45
+M.S.K. Prasad b Lee	6	–	c Warne b M.E. Waugh	13
A.B. Agarkar lbw b Lee	0	–	c Blewett b M.E. Waugh	0
J. Srinath c M.E. Waugh b Lee	1	–	(10) c Warne b Lee	1
A.R. Kumble not out	28	–	(9) run out (S.R. Waugh/Fleming)	13

B.K. Venkatesh Prasad c M.E. Waugh b McGrath	10	–	not out	6
L-b 8, n-b 9	17		L-b 4, n-b 3	7
	****			****
(76.1 overs, 346 mins)	238		(89.3 overs, 371 mins) (9 wkts dec)	195
Fall: 11 11 31 108 138 167 167 169 212 238			Fall: 5 72 110 133 162 162 184 185 195	

Bowling: *First Innings* McGrath 18.1-3-39-3; Fleming 15-0-62-1; Lee 18-2-47-5; Warne 24-5-77-1; M.E. Waugh 1-0-5-0. *Second Innings* – McGrath 17-8-22-0; Fleming 21.3-7-46-2; Warne 26-7-63-1; Lee 19-6-31-2; Blewett 3-1-17-1; M.E. Waugh 3-0-12-2.

Umpires: D.R. Shepherd (England) and S.J. Davis.
TV Umpire: W.P. Sheahan.
Referee: R.S. Madugalle (Sri Lanka).

Michael Slater (91) was dismissed for the eighth time in the nineties. Now one innings behind Steve Waugh. Slater scored his 1000th run for the calendar year. Ricky Ponting scored the fastest half-century at the MCG in 49 balls. Sachin Tendulkar (116) scored his 22nd Test century. Shane Warne claims his 350th Test wicket. Mark Waugh claims his 50th Test wicket. Brett Lee on debut became the 13th Australian to take a wicket in his first over (4th ball). Mark Waugh takes his 123rd catch to move into 3rd place on the all time list of catches by fieldsman. Mark Taylor tops the list with 157.

AUSTRALIA v. INDIA

Third Test Match

At Sydney Cricket Ground, Sydney, January 2, 3, 4, 2000. Australia won by an innings and 141 runs. Toss: India.

Man of the Match: G.D. McGrath. *Man of Series:* S.R. Tendulkar. *Attendance:* 106,636.

Close of play: First day, India (1) 8-121 (Kumble 1, Srinath 2); Second day, Australia (1) 4-331 (Langer 167, Ponting 34).

India

+M.S.K. Prasad c M.E. Waugh b McGrath	5	–	(2) c M.E. Waugh b McGrath	3
V.V.S. Laxman c Slater b Lee	7	–	(1) c Gilchrist b Lee	167
R.S. Dravid c Ponting b McGrath	29	–	c Warne b McGrath	0
*S.R. Tendulkar lbw b McGrath	45	–	c Langer b Fleming	4
S.C. Ganguly c S.R. Waugh b Blewett	1	–	c M.E. Waugh b McGrath	25
H.H. Kanitkar c Gilchrist b Lee	10	–	c Slater b Lee	8
V.R. Bharadwaj c Gilchrist b Lee	6			
A.R. Kumble c Langer b McGrath	26	–	(7) c Ponting b McGrath	15
A.B. Agarkar c M.E. Waugh b Lee	0	–	(8) c Gilchrist b McGrath	0
J. Srinath c Ponting b McGrath	3	–	(9) not out	15

B.K. Venkatesh Prasad not out	1	–	(10) run out (Gilchrist)	3
L-b 12, w 1, n-b 4	17		B 4, l-b 2, w 1, n-b 14	21
	****			****
(67.5 overs, 295 mins)	150		(58 overs, 260 mins) (9 wkts dec)	261

Fall: 10 27 68 69 95 118 119 119 126 150   Fall: 22 26 33 101 145 234 234 258 261

Bowling: *First Innings* – McGrath 18.5-7-48-5; Fleming 13-7-24-0; Lee 21-9-39-4; Warne 12-4-22-0; Blewett 3-2-5-1. *Second Innings* – McGrath 17-1-55-5; Fleming 13-2-47-1; Lee 11-2-67-2; Blewett 2-0-16-0; Warne 13-1-60-0; Ponting 1-0-8-0; Slater 1-0-2-0.

Australia

G.S. Blewett b Venkatesh Prasad	19		+A.C. Gilchrist not out	45
M.J. Slater c Prasad b Srinath	1			
J.L. Langer c Venkatesh Prasad b Tendulkar	223		B 2, l-b 21, n-b 11	34
M.E. Waugh b Ganguly	32			****
*S.R. Waugh lbw b Srinath	57		(140.2 overs, 608 mins) (5 wkts dec)	552
R.T. Ponting not out	141		Fall: 9 49 146 267 457	

S.K. Warne, D.W. Fleming, B. Lee, G.D. McGrath did not bat.

Bowling: Srinath 28-4-105-2; Agarkar 19-3-95-0; Venkatesh Prasad 28-10-86-1; Kumble 33.2-6-126-0; Ganguly 12-1-46-1; Bharadwaj 12-1-35-0; Tendulkar 7-0-34-1; Kanitkar 1-0-2-0.

Umpires: I.D. Robinson (Zimbabwe) and D.B. Hair.
TV Umpire: S.J.A. Taufel.
Referee: R.S. Madugalle (Sri Lanka).

Australia win their seventh consecutive Test. One behind the record Australian victories by Warwick Armstrong's 1920-21 team. Justin Langer (223) scored his first Test double century and his 6th Test century overall. Justin Langer (223) scored the highest individual score in a Australian-India Test match. The previous highest was Kim Hughes 213 (Adelaide, 1980-81). Ricky Ponting (141*) scored his seventh Test century. Glenn McGrath captures 10 wickets in a Test for the second time (5/48 & 5/55). Ajit Agarkar became the first batsman to be dismissed first-ball in four consecutive Test innings. He has registered five consecutive ducks equaling Bob Holland in 1985-86. VVS Laxman scored 167 out of the teams 261 (63.98%).
This is the third highest pecentage per innings by one batsman in Test cricket. C Bannerman (Aus) tops the list with 67.34% v. England in 1876-77.

AUSTRALIA v. INDIA AVERAGES

Australia

BATTING	M	I	NO	R	HS	100s	50s	Avge	Ct/St
R.T. Ponting	3	5	2	375	141*	2	1	125.00	3
J.L. Langer	3	5	0	289	223	1	0	57.80	6
A.C. Gilchrist	3	5	1	221	78	0	2	55.25	9/1
S.R. Waugh	3	5	0	276	150	1	1	55.20	4

M.E. Waugh	3	5	1	137	51*	0	1	34.25	8
S.K. Warne	3	3	0	88	86	0	1	29.33	3
G.S. Blewett	3	5	0	144	88	0	1	28.80	1
B. Lee	2	1	0	27	27	0	0	27.00	0
M.S. Kasprowicz	1	2	1	25	21*	0	0	25.00	1
M.J. Slater	3	5	0	123	91	0	1	24.60	3
G.D. McGrath	3	2	0	5	4	0	0	2.50	1
D.W. Fleming	3	2	2	43	31*	0	0		0

*Signifies not out.

BOWLING	O	M	R	W	BB	5W/i	Avge
M.E. Waugh	5	1	17	2	2/12	0	8.50
G.D. McGrath	113	34	248	18	5/48	2	13.78
B. Lee	69	19	184	13	5/47	1	14.15
D.W. Fleming	96.2	25	279	12	5/30	1	23.25
G.S. Blewett	14	4	49	2	1/5	0	24.50
S.K. Warne	127	35	335	8	4/92	0	41.88
M.S. Kasprowicz	17	2	85	0	–	0	–
R.T. Ponting	1	0	8	0	–	0	–
M.J. Slater	1	0	2	0	–	0	–

India

BATTING	M	I	NO	R	HS	100s	50s	Avge	Ctt
S.R. Tendulkar	3	6	0	278	116	1	2	46.33	0
V.V.S. Laxman	3	6	0	221	167	1	0	36.83	2
S.C. Ganguly	3	6	0	177	60	0	1	29.50	3
A.R. Kumble	3	6	2	102	28*	0	0	25.50	0
S. Ramesh	2	4	1	60	28	0	0	20.00	1
H.H. Kanitkar	2	4	0	74	45	0	0	18.50	0
R.S. Dravid	3	6	0	93	35	0	0	15.50	1
M.S.K. Prasad	3	6	0	52	14	0	0	8.67	10
J. Srinath	3	6	1	42	15*	0	0	8.40	3
B.K. Venkatesh Prasad	3	6	3	22	10	0	0	7.33	1
V.R. Bharadwaj	1	1	0	6	6	0	0	6.00	0
A.B. Agarkar	3	6	0	19	19	0	0	3.17	1
D.J. Gandhi	1	2	0	4	4	0	0	2.00	1

*Signifies not out.

BOWLING	O	M	R	W	BB	5W/i	Avge
A.B. Agarkar	108	24	351	11	3/43	0	31.91
S.C. Ganguly	21	2	90	2	1/34	0	45.00
S.R. Tendulkar	9	0	46	1	1/34	0	46.00

J. Srinath	126	18	461	10	4/130	0	46.10
B.K. Venkatesh Prasad	106.3	25	356	7	3/83	0	50.86
A.R. Kumble	146.2	22	450	5	2/72	0	90.00
V.R. Bharadwaj	12	1	35	0	–	0	–
H.H. Kanitkar	1	0	2	0	–	0	–
V.V.S. Laxman	3	1	2	0	–	0	–

NEW ZEALAND v. AUSTRALIA
First Test Match

At Eden Park, Auckland, March 11, 12, 13, 14 (no play), 15, 2000. Australia won by 62 runs. Toss: Australia.

Man of the Match: D.L. Vettori.

Close of play: First day, New Zealand (1) 4-26 (Fleming 0); Second day, Australia (2) 5-114 (Martyn 10, Gilchrist 4); Third day, New Zealand (2) 5-151 (McMillan 58, Cairns 20); Fourth day, No play.

Australia

M.J. Slater b Cairns	5	-	(2) c Horne b Cairns	6
G.S. Blewett c Astle b Wiseman	17	-	(1) c Spearman b Vettori	8
J.L. Langer st Parore b Wiseman	46	-	c Astle b Vettori	47
M.E. Waugh not out	72	-	c Parore b Vettori	25
*S.R. Waugh c Spearman b Vettori	17	-	c and b Wiseman	10
D.R. Martyn c Astle b Vettori	17	-	b Vettori	36
+A.C. Gilchrist lbw b Wiseman	7	-	c Fleming b Vettori	59
S.K. Warne c Fleming b Vettori	7	-	c Wiseman b Vettori	12
B. Lee c Parore b Vettori	6	-	not out	6
C.R. Miller b Cairns	0	-	st Parore b Vettori	8
G.D. McGrath c Spearman b Vettori	8	-	lbw b Wiseman	1
B 7, l-b 4, n-b 1	12		B 7, l-b 4	11
	****			****
(71 overs, 286 mins)	214		(77.5 overs, 292 mins)	229

Fall: 10 77 78 114 138 161 184 192 193 214
Fall: 7 46 67 81 107 174 202 214 226 229

Bowling: *First Innings* – Cairns 18-0-71-2; Doull 14-6-21-0; Vettori 25-8-62-5; Wiseman 14-2-49-3.
Second Innings – Cairns 4-1-13-1; Wiseman 33.5-6-110-2; Vettori 35-11-87-7; Doull 5-1-8-0.

New Zealand

M.J. Horne c Blewett b McGrath	3	-	c Langer b Miller	11
C.M. Spearman c Martyn b Lee	12	-	lbw b McGrath	4
M.S. Sinclair lbw b Warne	8	-	lbw b Miller	6
P.J. Wiseman b Lee	1	-	(11) c Gilchrist b Warne	9
*S.P. Fleming st Gilchrist b Miller	21	-	(4) c Gilchrist b Miller	8

N.J. Astle c M.E. Waugh b Warne	31	–	(5) b Warne	35
C.D. McMillan lbw b Warne	6	–	(6) c Warne b Lee	78
C.L. Cairns c Gilchrist b McGrath	35	–	(7) c S.R. Waugh b Miller	20
+A.C. Parore c Gilchrist b McGrath	11	–	(8) c S.R. Waugh b Lee	26
D.L. Vettori not out	15	–	(9) c Warne b Miller	0
S.B. Doull c Lee b McGrath	12	–	(10) not out	5
B 4, l-b 1, n-b 3	8		B 7, l-b 7, n-b 2	16
	****			****
(62.1 overs, 241 mins)	163		(73.3 overs, 289 mins)	218
Fall: 5 25 25 26 80 80 102 134 143 163			Fall: 15 25 25 43 121 151 195 204 204 218	

Bowling: *First Innings* – McGrath 11.1-2-33-4; Miller 22-8-38-1; Warne 22-4-68-3; Lee 7-4-19-2.
Second Innings – McGrath 23-8-33-1; Lee 12-4-36-2; Miller 18-5-55-5; Warne 20.3-5-80-2.

Umpires: S. Venkataraghavan.(India) and B.F. Bowden.
TV Umpire: D.B. Cowie.
Referee: M.H. Denness (England).

Australia win their eighth successive Test therefore equalling the record set by Warwick Armstrong's team in 1920-21. Lights were used for the first time in New Zealand during a Test match. A helicopter was used to assist in drying the ground on the fourth day. S.P. Fleming passed 3,000 Test runs. J.L. Langer passed 2,000 Test runs. D.L. Vettori took his 100th Test wicket. At 21 years 46 days, Vettori is the third youngest to take 100 Test wickets, behind Kapil Dev and Waqar Younis. Vettori took 12 for 149 in the match, the second best return by a New Zealander in a Test. Shane Warne in taking the wicket of P.J. Wiseman became the highest wicket taker for Australia passing D.K. Lillee's 355 Test wickets. C.R. Miller claimed his best bowling figures in Test cricket, 5/55. Australia's victory at Eden park was their first at this venue since 1976-77.

NEW ZEALAND v. AUSTRALIA

Second Test Match

At Basin Reserve, Wellington, March 24, 25, 26, 27, 2000. Australia won by six wickets.
Toss: New Zealand.

Man of the Match: M.J. Slater.

Close of play: First day, Australia (1) 2-29 (Slater 22); Second day, Australia (1) 5-318 (S.R. Waugh 109, Martyn 41); Third day, New Zealand (2) 5-189 (Fleming 53, Cairns 61).

New Zealand

M.J. Horne c Warne b Lee	4	– b Lee	14
C.M. Spearman c Gilchrist b Lee	4	– c Langer b Miller	38
M.S. Sinclair lbw b Miller	4	– b Lee	0
*S.P. Fleming c Miller b Warne	16	– c Blewett b Miller	60
N.J. Astle c M.E. Waugh b Warne	61	– b Warne	14

C.D. McMillan c Gilchrist b Lee	1	– c M.E. Waugh b Warne	0
C.L. Cairns c Blewett b Miller	109	– lbw b McGrath	69
+A.C. Parore c Gilchrist b Blewett	46	– run out (Blewett)	33
D.L. Vettori c Langer b Warne	27	– c S.R. Waugh b Lee	8
S.B. Doull c Slater b Warne	12	– c S.R. Waugh b Warne	40
S.B. O'Connor not out	2	– not out	4
B 1, l-b 8, n-b 3	12	B 3, l-b 7, n-b 4	14
	****		****
(80.5 overs, 333 mins)	298	(96.2 overs, 401 mins)	294
Fall: 4 8 18 53 66 138 247 282 287 298		Fall: 46 46 69 88 88 198 205 222 276 294	

Bowling: *First Innings* – McGrath 17-4-60-0; Lee 17-2-49-3; Miller 20-2-78-2; Warne 14.5-1-68-4; Blewett 8-1-24-1; S.R. Waugh 4-0-10-0. *Second Innings* – McGrath 22.2-11-35-1; Lee 23-6-88-3; Miller 21-5-54-2; Warne 27-7-92-3; Blewett 3-0-15-0.

Australia

M.J. Slater c Parore b McMillan	143	– (2) st Parore b Vettori	12
G.S. Blewett c Astle b Doull	0	– (1) b Cairns	25
S.K. Warne lbw b Vettori	7		
J.L. Langer c Parore b Cairns	12	– (3) c Spearman b O'Connor	57
M.E. Waugh c Sinclair b Cairns	3	– (4) not out	44
*S.R. Waugh not out	151	– (5) c Fleming b O'Connor	15
D.R. Martyn c Parore b McMillan	78	– (6) not out	17
+A.C. Gilchrist c Parore b O'Connor	3		
B. Lee lbw b O'Connor	0		
C.R. Miller c and b McMillan	4		
G.D. McGrath c and b Cairns	14		
L-b 1, n-b 3	4	B 2, l-b 2, W 3	7
	****		****
(120.3 overs, 479 mins)	419	(54.1 overs, 225 mins) (4 wkts)	177
Fall: 8 29 47 51 250 364 375 375 386 419		Fall: 22 83 110 144	

Bowling: *First Innings* – Cairns 26.3-2-110-3; Doull 19-3-78-1; Vettori 15-1-50-1; O'Connor 26-2-78-2; Astle 11-2-45-0; McMillan 23-10-57-3. *Second Innings* – Cairns 13-2-45-1; O'Connor 11-3-42-2; Vettori 8-1-19-1; Doull 10-2-35-0; McMillan 2-0-13-0; Astle 10.1-4-19-0.

Umpires: Riazuddin (Pakistan) and D.M. Quested.
TV Umpire: E.A. Watkins.
Referee: M.H. Denness (England).

S.R. Waugh became the first Test batsman to score in excess of 150 in a Test against every Test playing opponent.

NEW ZEALAND v. AUSTRALIA

Third Test Match

At Westpac Trust Park, Hamilton, March 31, April 1, 2, 3, 2000. Australia won by six wickets.
Toss: Australia. Test debut: D.R. Tuffey.

Man of the Match: A.C. Gilchrist.

Close of play: First day, Australia (1) 1-4 (Slater 2, Warne 0); Second day, New Zealand (2) 3-58
(Spearman 29, Astle 2); Third day, Australia (2) 3-137 (Langer 71, S.R. Waugh 1).

New Zealand

M.J. Horne c Gilchrist b McGrath	12	–	run out (Miller)	0
C.M. Spearman c Gilchrist b McGrath	12	–	c Gilchrist b Lee	35
M.S. Sinclair c Warne b Lee	19	–	lbw b Miller	24
*S.P. Fleming lbw b Lee	30	–	c Gilchrist b Miller	2
N.J. Astle lbw b Lee	0	–	c Gilchrist b Warne	26
C.D. McMillan c Gilchrist b Lee	79	–	c M.E. Waugh b Warne	30
C.L. Cairns c Martyn b Lee	37	–	b McGrath	71
+A.C. Parore not out	12	–	c Gilchrist b McGrath	16
P.J. Wiseman b Warne	1	–	c Gilchrist b Lee	16
D.R. Tuffey c Gilchrist b McGrath	3	–	not out	1
S.B. O'Connor c Gilchrist b McGrath	0	–	lbw b Lee	0
B 5, l-b 7, w 2, n-b 13	27		L-b 4, n-b 4	8
	****			****
(82.5 overs, 359 mins)	232		(86.4 overs, 340 mins)	229

Fall: 22 42 53 53 131 208 212 224 227 232
Fall: 3 49 53 71 111 130 165 220 228 229

Bowling: *First Innings* –McGrath 21.5-8-58-4; Lee 23-8-77-5; Warne 20-5-45-1; Miller 11-4-28-0;
Martyn 7-4-12-0. *Second Innings* –McGrath 20-7-50-2; Lee 18.4-2-46-3; Miller 20-5-58-2;
Warne 25-11-61-2; S.R. Waugh 3-0-10-0.

Australia

M.L. Hayden c Parore b O'Connor	2	–	(2) c Spearman b Wiseman	37
M.J. Slater lbw b O'Connor	2	–	(1) lbw b O'Connor	9
S.K. Warne lbw b O'Connor	10			
J.L. Langer b Cairns	4	–	(3) not out	122
M.E. Waugh c Sinclair b Wiseman	28	–	(4) c Sinclair b Wiseman	18
*S.R. Waugh c Fleming b Cairns	3	–	(5) retired hurt	18
D.R. Martyn not out	89	–	(6) lbw b O'Connor	4
+A.C. Gilchrist c Horne b Wiseman	75	–	(7) not out	0
B. Lee c McMillan b Cairns	8			
G.D. McGrath b O'Connor	7			
C.R. Miller c Tuffey b O'Connor	2			
B 4, l-b 6, n-b 12	22		L-b 1, n-b 3	4

	****		****
(61.5 overs, 268 mins)	252	(41.3 overs, 180 mins)	(4 wkts) 212

Fall: 3 16 17 25 29 104 223 233 248 252   Fall: 13 96 124 190

Bowling: *First Innings* – Cairns 22-7-80-3; O'Connor 15.5-5-51-5; Tuffey 9-0-75-0; Astle 4-3-5-0; Wiseman 11-3-31-2. *Second Innings* – Cairns 10-1-60-0; O'Connor 11-1-53-2; Wiseman 9-1-42-2; Tuffey 11-1-52-0; McMillan 0.3-0-4-0.

Umpires: A.V. Jayaprakash (India) and R.S. Dunne.
TV Umpire: D.B. Cowie.
Referee: M.H. Denness (England).

NEW ZEALAND v. AUSTRALIA AVERAGES

New Zealand

BATTING	M	I	NO	R	HS	100s	50s	Avge	Ct/St
C.L. Cairns	3	6	0	341	109	1	2	56.83	1
C.D. McMillan	3	6	0	194	79	0	2	32.33	2
A.C. Parore	3	6	1	144	46	0	0	28.80	7/3
N.J. Astle	3	6	0	167	61	0	1	27.83	4
S.B. Doull	2	4	1	69	40	0	0	23.00	0
S.P. Fleming	3	6	0	137	60	0	1	22.83	4
C.M. Spearman	3	6	0	105	38	0	0	17.50	5
D.L. Vettori	2	4	1	50	27	0	0	16.67	0
M.S. Sinclair	3	6	0	61	24	0	0	10.17	3
M.J. Horne	3	6	0	44	14	0	0	7.33	2
P.J. Wiseman	2	4	0	27	16	0	0	6.75	2
D.R. Tuffey	1	2	1	4	3	0	0	4.00	1
S.B. O'Connor	2	4	2	6	4*	0	0	3.00	0

Signifies not out.

BOWLING	O	M	R	W	BB	5W/i	10W/m	Avge
D.L. Vettori	83	21	218	14	7/87	2	1	15.57
S.B. O'Connor	63.5	11	224	11	5/51	1	0	20.36
C.D. McMillan	25.3	10	74	3	3/57	0	0	24.67
P.J. Wiseman	67.5	12	232	9	3/49	0	0	25.78
C.L. Cairns	93.3	13	379	10	3/80	0	0	37.90
S.B. Doull	48	12	142	1	1/78	0	0	142.00
N.J. Astle	25.1	9	69	0	–	0	0 –
D.R. Tuffey	20	1	127	0	–	0	0 –

Australia

BATTING	M	I	NO	R	HS	100s	50s	Avge	Ct/St
D.R. Martyn	3	6	2	241	89*	0	2	60.25	2
J.L. Langer	3	6	1	288	122*	1	1	57.60	3
S.R. Waugh	3	6	2	214	151*	1	0	53.50	4
M.E. Waugh	3	6	2	190	72*	0	1	47.50	4
A.C. Gilchrist	3	5	1	144	75	0	2	36.00	17/1
M.J. Slater	3	6	0	177	143	1	0	29.50	1
M.L. Hayden	1	2	0	39	37	0	0	19.50	0
G.S. Blewett	2	4	0	50	25	0	0	12.50	3
S.K. Warne	3	4	0	36	12	0	0	9.00	4
G.D. McGrath	3	4	0	30	14	0	0	7.50	0
B. Lee	3	4	1	20	8	0	0	6.67	1
C.R. Miller	3	4	0	14	8	0	0	3.50	1

*Signifies not out.

BOWLING	O	M	R	W	BB	5W/i	10W/m	Avge
B. Lee	100.4	26	315	18	5/77	1	0	17.50
G.D. McGrath	115.2	40	269	12	4/33	0	0	22.42
C.R. Miller	112	29	311	12	5/55	1	0	25.92
S.K. Warne	129.2	33	414	15	4/68	0	0	27.60
G.S. Blewett	11	1	39	1	1/24	0	0	39.00
D.R. Martyn	7	4	12	0	–	0	0	–
S.R. Waugh	7	0	20	0	–	0	0	–

Greg Blewett

Venue	How Out	Runs	(Balls)	O	M	R	W	Ct
Harare	c Campbell b Streak	1	(4)	–	–	–	–	–
	not out	4*	(3)	5.0	1	10	0	–
Brisbane	lbw b Mushtaq Ahmed	89	(208)	5.0	1	22	0	–
	not out	40*	(48)	–	–	–	–	–
Hobart	cwk Moin Khan b Azhar Mahmood	35	(84)	2.0	1	5	0	–
	cwk Moin Khan b Azhar Mahmood	29	(106)	2.0	0	5	0	1
Perth	c Inzamam-ul-Haq b Mohammad Akram	11	(19)	–	–	–	–	1
	–			–	–	–	–	–
Adelaide	c Prasad b Srinath	4	(7)	6.0	1	11	0	–
	b Agarkar	88	(262)	–	–	–	–	–
Melbourne	b Srinath	2	(8)	–	–	–	–	–
	c Ganguly b Kumble	31	(97)	3.0	1	17	1	1

Scoreboard

Venue	How Out	Runs	(Balls)	O	M	R	W	Ct
Sydney	b Venkatesh Prasad	19	(54)	3.0	2	5	1	–
		–		2.0	0	16	0	–
Auckland	c Astle b Wiseman	17	(64)	–	–	–	–	1
	c Spearman b Vettori	8	(59)	–	–	–	–	–
Wellington	c Astle b Doull	0	(9)	8.0	1	24	1	1
	b Cairns	25	(114)	3.0	0	15	0	1

Damien Fleming

Venue	How Out	Runs	(Balls)	O	M	R	W	Ct
Harare	lbw b Streak	65	(94)	15.0	6	22	2	–
		–		21.0	6	31	0	–
Brisbane	lbw b Shoaib Akhtar	0	(3)	31.0	5	65	4	–
		–		14.1	2	59	5	–
Hobart	lbw b Saqlain Mushtaq	0	(4)	24.5	7	54	2	–
		–		29.0	5	89	2	–
Perth	lbw b Saqlain Mushtaq	0	(7)	19.0	7	48	3	1
		–		19.4	3	86	2	1
Adelaide	not out	12*	(19)	24.4	7	70	3	–
		–		9.1	2	30	5	–
Melbourne	not out	31*	(59)	15.0	0	62	1	–
		–		21.3	7	46	2	–
Sydney		–		13.0	7	24	0	–
				13.0	2	47	1	–

Adam Gilchrist

Venue	How Out	Runs	(Balls)	O	M	R	W	Ct	St
Brisbane	b Shoaib Akhtar	81	(88)	–	–	–	–	3	–
		–		–	–	–	–	2	1
Hobart	st Moin Khan b Saqlain Mushtaq	6	(19)	–	–	–	–	3	–
	not out	149*	(163)	–	–	–	–	1	–
Perth	b Mohammad Akram	28	(26)	–	–	–	–	1	–
		–		–	–	–	–	2	–
Adelaide	c and b Agarkar	0	(4)	–	–	–	–	–	1
	c Laxman b Srinath	43	(46)	–	–	–	–	3	–
Melbourne	c Ganguly b Agarkar	78	(119)	–	–	–	–	1	–
	c Srinath b Kumble	55	(73)	–	–	–	–	1	–
Sydney	not out	45*	(56)	–	–	–	–	2	–
		–		–	–	–	–	2	–
Auckland	lbw b Wiseman	7	(24)	–	–	–	–	2	1
	c Fleming b Vettori	59	(99)	–	–	–	–	2	–

Wellington	cwk Parore b O'Connor	3	(21)	–	–	–	–	3	–
Hamilton	c Horne b Wiseman	75	(80)	–	–	–	–	5	–
	not out	0*	(3)	–	–	–	–	5	–

Matthew Hayden

Venue	How Out	Runs	(Balls)	O	M	R	W	Ct
Hamilton	cwk Parore b O'Connor	2	(13)	–	–	–	–	–
	c Spearman b Wiseman	37	(54)	–	–	–	–	–

Ian Healy

Venue	How Out	Runs	(Balls)	O	M	R	W	Ct	St
Harare	cwk Flower b Strang	5	(28)	–	–	–	–	1	–
		–		–	–	–	–	1	–

Michael Kasprowicz

Venue	How Out	Runs	(Balls)	O	M	R	W	Ct
Perth	not out	9*	(15)	12.0	2	53	4	–
		–		16.0	3	79	3	–
Adelaide	b Kumble	4	(7)	11.0	2	62	0	1
	not out	21*	(28)	6.0	0	23	0	–

Justin Langer

Venue	How Out	Runs	(Balls)	O	M	R	W	Ct
Harare	run out (Olonga/A Flower)	44	(73)	–	–	–	–	–
		–		–	–	–	–	1
Brisbane	c Abdur Razzaq b Mushtaq Ahmed	1	(8)	–	–	–	–	–
		–		–	–	–	–	–
Hobart	c Mohammad Wasim b Saqlain Mushtaq	59	(106)	–	–	–	–	–
	c Inzamam-ul-Haq b Saqlain Mushtaq	127	(295)	–	–	–	–	–
Perth	cwk Moin Khan b Shoaibi Akhtar	144	(286)	–	–	–	–	–
		–		–	–	–	–	–
Adelaide	lbw b Venkatesh Prasad	11	(23)	–	–	–	–	2
	c Gandhi b Kumble	38	(72)	–	–	–	–	1

Scoreboard

Melbourne	lbw b Srinath	8	(28)	–	–	–	–	1
	cwk Prasad b Agarkar	9	(26)	–	–	–	–	–
Sydney	c Venkatesh Prasad b Tendulkar	223	(355)	–	–	–	–	1
	–	–	–	–	–	–	–	1
Auckland	st Parore b Wiseman	46	(47)	–	–	–	–	–
	c Astle b Vettori	47	(64)	–	–	–	–	1
Wellington	cwk Parore b Cairns	12	(18)	–	–	–	–	1
	c Spearman b O'Connor	57	(75)	–	–	–	–	1
Hamilton	b Cairns	4	(4)	–	–	–	–	–
	not out	122*	(122)	–	–	–	–	–

Brett Lee

Venue	How Out	Runs	(Balls)	O	M	R	W	Ct
Melbourne	c and b Srinath	27	(55)	18.0	2	47	5	–
		–		19.0	6	31	2	–
Sydney		–		21.0	9	39	4	–
		–		11.0	2	67	2	–
Auckland	cwk Parore b Vettori	6	(14)	7.0	4	19	2	1
	not out	6*	(14)	12.0	4	36	2	–
Wellington	lbw b O'Connor	0	(6)	17.0	2	49	3	–
		–		23.0	6	88	3	–
Hamilton	c McMillan b Cairns	8	(15)	23.0	8	77	5	–
		–		18.4	2	46	3	–

Damien Martyn

Venue	How Out	Runs	(Balls)	O	M	R	W	Ct
Auckland	c Astle b Vettori	17	(26)	–	–	–	–	1
	b Vettori	36	(117)	–	–	–	–	–
Wellington	cwk Parore b McMillan	78	(101)	–	–	–	–	–
	not out	17*	(21)	–	–	–	–	–
Hamilton	not out	89*	(136)	7.0	4	12	0	1
	lbw b O'Connor	4	(8)	–	–	–	–	–

Glenn McGrath

Venue	How Out	Runs	(Balls)	O	M	R	W	Ct
Harare	c Johnson b Whittall	13	(20)	23.0	7	44	3	–
		–		31.0	12	46	3	1
Brisbane	c Yousuf Youhana b Wasim Akram	1	(7)	28.0	4	116	2	–
		–		21.0	9	63	2	–

Venue	How Out	Runs	(Balls)	O	M	R	W	Ct
Hobart	st Moin Khan b Saqlain Mushtaq	7	(15)	18.0	8	34	2	1
	–			27.0	8	87	1	1
Perth	c Azhar Mahmood b Mohammad Akram	0	(8)	19.0	3	44	3	–
	–			21.0	5	49	4	1
Adelaide	c Prasad b Venkatesh Prasad	4	(14)	30.0	13	49	2	–
	–			12.0	2	35	3	–
Melbourne	run out (Kanitkar)	1	(6)	18.1	3	39	3	–
	–			17.0	8	22	0	1
Sydney	–			18.5	7	48	5	–
	–			17.0	1	55	5	–
Auckland	c Spearman b Vettori	8	(32)	11.1	2	33	4	–
	lbw b Wiseman	1	(6)	23.0	8	33	1	–
Wellington	c and b Cairns	14	(26)	17.0	4	60	0	–
	–			22.2	11	35	1	–
Hamilton	b O'Connor	7	(23)	21.5	8	58	4	–
	–			20.0	7	50	2	–

Colin Miller

Venue	How Out	Runs	(Balls)	O	M	R	W	Ct
Harare	c Johnson b Streak	2	(3)	19.0	6	36	0	–
	–			34.0	10	66	3	–
Auckland	b Cairns	0	(4)	22.0	8	38	1	–
	st Parore b Vettori	8	(9)	18.0	5	55	5	–
Wellington	c and b McMillan	4	(5)	20.0	2	78	2	1
	–			21.0	5	54	2	–
Hamilton	c Tuffey b O'Connor	2	(9)	11.0	4	28	0	–
	–			20.0	5	58	2	–

Scott Muller

Venue	How Out	Runs	(Balls)	O	M	R	W	Ct
Brisbane	not out	6*	(18)	19.0	4	72	2	1
	–			10.0	1	55	1	1
Hobart	not out	0*	(0)	12.0	0	68	3	–
	–			17.0	3	63	1	–

Ricky Ponting

Venue	How Out	Runs	(Balls)	O	M	R	W	Ct
Harare	c Johnson b Streak	31	(82)	1.0	1	–	–	2
	–			1.0	1	–	–	–

Scoreboard

Venue	How Out	Runs	(Balls)	O	M	R	W	Ct
Brisbane	lbw b Shoaib Akhtar	0	(7)	5.0	1	12	0	–
		–		4.0	0	12	0	2
Hobart	b Waqar Younis	0	(3)	–	–	–	–	–
	lbw b Wasim Akram	0	(5)	2.0	1	7	0	1
Perth	c Ijaz Ahmed							
	b Azhar Mahmood	197	(288)	–	–	–	–	2
		–		–	–	–	–	–
Adelaide	run out (Agarkar/MSK Prasad)	125	(198)	–	–	–	–	–
	c Prasad b Venkatesh Prasad	21	(54)	–	–	–	–	–
Melbourne	lbw b Srinath	67	(85)	–	–	–	–	–
	not out	21*	(32)	–	–	–	–	–
Sydney	not out	141*	(183)	–	–	–	–	2
		–		1.0	0	8	0	1

Michael Slater

Venue	How Out	Runs	(Balls)	O	M	R	W	Ct
Harare	cwk Flower b Strang	4	(19)–	–	–	–	1	
	not out	0*	(0)–	–	–	–	–	
Brisbane	c Yousuf Youhana							
	b Azhar Mahmood	169	(271)–	–	–	–	1	
	not out	32*	(38)–	–	–	–	–	
Hobart	c Ijaz Ahmed							
	b Saqlain Mushtaq	97	(195)–	–	–	–	1	
	c Azhar Mahmood							
	b Shoaib Akhtar	27	(48)–	–	–	–	–	
Perth	lbw b Wasim Akram	0	(2)–	–	–	–	–	
		–		–	–	–	1	
Adelaide	c Ramesh b Ganguly	28	(47)–	–	–	–	–	
	c Ganguly b Srinath	0	(9)–	–	–	–	1	
Melbourne	c Srinath b Venkatesh Prasad	91	(179)–	–	–	–	–	
	lbw b Agarkar	3	(7)–	–	–	–	–	
Sydney	cwk Prasad b Srinath	1	(11)–	–	–	–	1	
		–		1.0	0	2	0	1
Auckland	b Cairns	5	(19)–	–	–	–	–	
	c Horne b Cairns	6	(14)–	–	–	–	–	
Wellington	cwk Parore b McMillan	143	(214)–	–	–	–	1	
	st Parore b Vettori	12	(23)–	–	–	–	–	
Hamilton	lbw b O'Connor	2	(29)–	–	–	–	–	
	lbw b O'Connor	9	(12)–	–	–	–	–	

Shane Warne

Venue	How Out	Runs	(Balls)	O	M	R	W	Ct
Harare	cwk Flower b Streak	6	(9)	23.0	2	69	3	–
		–		30.1	11	68	3	–
Brisbane	c Mushtaq Ahmed b Wasim Akram	86	(90)	28.1	11	73	1	1
		–		25.0	8	80	2	–
Hobart	b Saqlain Mushtaq	0	(1)	16.0	6	45	3	1
	not out	0*	(0)	45.5	11	110	5	–
Perth	cwk Moin Khan b Saqlain Mushtaq	13	(18)	2.0	0	6	0	1
		–		13.0	1	56	1	1
Adelaide	lbw b Kumble	86	(100)	42.0	12	92	4	–
	c Dravid b Srinath	0	(5)	10.0	6	21	2	–
Melbourne	cwk Prasad b Agarkar	2	(6)	24.0	5	77	1	–
		–		26.0	7	63	1	2
Sydney		–		12.0	4	22	0	–
		–		13.0	1	60	0	1
Auckland	c Fleming b Vettori	7	(20)	22.0	4	68	3	–
	c Wiseman b Vettori	12	(7)	20.3	5	80	2	2
Wellington	lbw b Vettori	7	(7)	14.5	1	68	4	1
		–		27.0	7	92	3	–
Hamilton	lbw b O'Connor	10	(14)	20.0	5	45	1	1
		–		25.0	11	61	2	–

Mark Waugh

Venue	How Out	Runs	(Balls)	O	M	R	W	Ct
Harare	c and b Flower	90	(154)	–	–	–	–	3
		–		–	–	–	–	2
Brisbane	c Wasim Akram b Mushtaq Ahmed	100	(148)	–	–	–	–	2
		–		–	–	–	–	1
Hobart	lbw b Waqar Younis	5	(12)	–	–	–	–	1
	lbw b Azhar Mahmood	0	(1)	2.0	0	6	0	1
Perth	c (S)Ghulam Ali b Mohammad Akram	0	(13)	–	–	–	–	1
		–		–	–	–	–	1
Adelaide	c Prasad b Venkatesh Prasad	5	(17)	–	–	–	–	–
	c Laxman b Agarkar	8	(42)	1.0	1	0	0	–
Melbourne	lbw b Agarkar	41	(110)	1.0	0	5	0	4
	not out	51*	(81)	3.0	0	12	2	–

Sydney	b Ganguly	32	(70)	–	–	–	–	2
			–	–	–	–	–	2
Auckland	not out	72*	(143)	–	–	–	–	1
	cwk Parore b Vettori	25	(62)	–	–	–	–	–
Wellington	c Sinclair b Cairns	3	(7)	–	–	–	–	1
	not out	44*	(70)	–	–	–	–	1
Hamilton	c Sinclair b Wiseman	28	(55)	–	–	–	–	–
	c Sinclair b Wiseman	18	(21)	–	–	–	–	1

Steve Waugh

Venue	How Out	Runs	(Balls)	O	M	R	W	Ct
Harare	not out	151*	(352)	4.0	1	17	0	–
			–	–	–	–	–	1
Brisbane	cwk Moin Khan b Shoaib Akhtar1		(13)	1.0	0	1	0	–
			–	–	–	–	–	–
Hobart	c Ijaz Ahmed b Wasim Akram	24	(45)	–	–	–	–	–
	c and b Saqlain Mushtaq	28	(69)	4.0	1	19	0	1
Perth	c Yousuf Youhana b Mohammad Akram	5	(8)	–	–	–	–	1
			–	–	–	–	–	1
Adelaide	c Prasad b Agarkar	150	(323)	–	–	–	–	2
	c Prasad b Agarkar	5	(23)	–	–	–	–	1
Melbourne	cwk Prasad b Venkatesh Prasad	32	(68)	–	–	–	–	–
	lbw b Agarkar	32	(41)	–	–	–	–	–
Sydney	lbw b Srinath	57	(124)	–	–	–	–	1
			–	–	–	–	–	–
Auckland	c Spearman b Vettori	17	(34)	–	–	–	–	–
	c and b Wiseman	10	(16)	–	–	–	–	2
Wellington	not out	151*	(312)	4.0	0	10	0	–
	c Fleming b O'Connor	15	(22)	–	–	–	–	2
Hamilton	c Fleming b Cairns	3	(5)	–	–	–	–	–
	retired hurt	18+	(32)	3.0	0	10	0	–

Statistics: Ross Dundas.

Index

A

Abdur Razzaq 32
Adelaide Oval (cricket ground) 59, 61, 224
Agarkar, A.B. 76
AIS Cricket Academy 118, 132, 139, 149, 169
Alcott, Errol ('Hooter') 151, 174, 190
Ambrose, Curtly 199
America's Cup 88
Angel, Jo 196
Arjuna Ranatunga 176
Armstrong, Warwick 81, 92, 95
Ashes tour 189
Astle, Nathan 107
Atkinson, Mark 150
Auckland (New Zealand) 88, 89, 90, 91, 96, 97, 228
Australia A team 132, 149, 150
Australia 2nd XI 197
Australian Cricket Board
    Academy 118, 132, 139, 149, 169
    Marsh retires 3
    players' dispute 23
    selectors 188–189
    Victor Trumper caps 84, 227
Australian Test team 1948 221
Australian Young Cricketers 143
Azhar Mahmood 43

B

Baggy Green (website) 148
Bangalore (India) 179
Basin Reserve (Wellington) 103
Basit Ali 198
bats (cricket) 224
batting averages 233–234
Bee Gees (band) 193
Bellerive Oval (Hobart) 45, 140, 148, 170
Benaud, Richie 194
Bernard, Steve 173
Blewett, Bob 134
Blewett, Greg ('Blewey')
    dropped 111
    pen portrait 132–134
    scoreboard 253–254
    v.India 58, 227
    v.Pakistan 27, 30, 220
    v.Sri Lanka 2
Bon Jovi (band) 193
Boon, David 189, 194
Border, Allan ('AB')
    Ashes tour 189
    captain 186, 194
    coach 4–7, 8–9, 17, 204
bowling
    averages 234
    beam balls 48
    depth of talent 196
    fast 54, 74, 89, 226
    seam 74
    slower balls 182
    spin 47, 94, 166, 175
    swing 74, 135, 163
Boxing Day Test 76, 150, 226
Boycott, Geoff 105
Bradman, Sir Donald 194
Brown, Bill 29, 46, 221
BSkyB (UK) 146
Buchanan, John 4–5, 56, 82, 190, 208, 217, 218
Bull Ring (Johannesburg) 198
Burdett, Les 59

C

Cairns, Chris 104, 107, 109, 114, 115, 188, 228, 229
Campbell, Alistair 16, 206
'can't bowl, can't throw' controversy 52, 168, 177
Canterbury Bulldogs 180
caps
    baggy green xii–xiii, 82, 90
    New York Yankees xiii
    Victor Trumper xiii, 82, 84, 227
Central Districts (New Zealand) 102
Channel Nine 52
Chappell, Greg 117, 134
Chee Quee, Richard 151
Chipangali (Zimbabwe) 9–10
Christmas Day 1999 64, 73
Colchester (UK) 178
Cox, Jamie 197
Crawley, John 134

cricket bats 224
Crown Casino 79
CUB Series 136
Current Affair, A (TV program) 52

D

'daktari' (dress code) 101
'dead rubber' Tests 55, 222
Dominators, The (poem) 119–120
Donald, Allan 137, 199
Doull, Simon 109
Dravid, Rahul 57, 59

E

Eden Park (Auckland) 89, 90, 91, 96, 97, 228
Elliott, Matthew 171
Emery, Phil 139
England & Wales Cricket Board 190
Essex (UK) 143–144, 178

F

Farmer, Pat 84–86, 227
fines committee 101
Fleming, Damien ('Flem')
    fast bowling 89
    man-of-the-match 137
    pen portrait 135–137, 196
    scoreboard 254
    v.India 57, 58, 63, 74, 86
    v.New Zealand 102, 103
    v.Pakistan 27, 41, 53, 54, 188
    v.Zimbabwe 11, 15, 19, 207
Fleming, Stephen 91, 114
Flower, Grant 207
Frank Worrell Trophy 147
From Outback to Outfield (Langer) 148

G

gambling 193–194
Ganguly, Sourav 57, 59, 227
Gilchrist, Adam ('Gilly')
    pen portrait 138–140
    replaces Healy 24, 218
    scoreboard 254–255
    understudy to Healy 139
    winning 83
    v.India 74, 227
    v.New Zealand 91, 93, 98, 111–112, 114, 188, 231
    v.Pakistan 27, 42–44, 48–51, 140, 148, 185, 220–222
Gillespie, Jason 2, 186, 192–193, 196, 204
Goodwin, Murray 20
Gripper, Trevor 20

H

Hadlee, Richard 95
Hamilton (New Zealand) 89
Hampshire (UK) 197
Harare Sports Ground (Zimbabwe) 14, 204
Harris, Rachel 64
Hawkes, Rechelle 64
Hayden, Matthew
    partners Slater 134
    pen portrait 141–142
    scoreboard 255
    Slater's rival 142
    v.New Zealand 111, 115
    v.Zimbabwe 16, 17
Headingley (UK) 182, 186, 199
Healy, Ian ('Heals') 21–24, 41, 138, 198, 218, 255
Hobart (Tas) 45, 140, 148, 170
Hogan, Hulk 193
Holdsworth, Wayne 143
horses 180
Howard, John xiii, 84
Hughes, Kim 64
Hughes, Merv 64, 80, 164, 189
150kmh barrier 151
Hunt, Rex 64

Index

I

ICC (International Cricket Council) 54
Ijaz Ahmed 44
illegal deliveries panel 54
India
    First Test 1999 57–63
    Second Test 1999 74–79
    Third Test 2000 80–87
    Test Series 222–228
    statistics 242–248
    winning in 117–118
'Invincibles' 218, 221
Inzamam-ul-Haq 31, 42

J

Joe (the cameraman) 52
Johannesburg (South Africa) 198
Johnston, Bill 46, 165, 221
Jones, Dean 189
Julian, Brendon 196
Julios xv, 134

K

Kasprowicz, Michael ('Kasper')
    Central Districts 102
    injured by Slater 101
    man-of-the-match 144
    pen portrait 143–145
    scoreboard 255
    v.India 58, 73
    v.Pakistan 53
Kasprowicz, Simon 145
Katich, Simon 189
Klusener, Lance ('Zulu') 137, 199
Kumble, Anil 57, 59, 62

L

Langer, Justin ('Lang')
    coached by Border 7
    pen portrait 146–148
    scoreboard 255–256
    selection of 24–26
    Test century 86
    v.India 60, 62, 80–82, 227
    v.New Zealand 91–92, 112, 189, 229, 231
    v.Pakistan 42–46, 48–51, 55–56, 140, 148, 185, 221–222
    v.Zimbabwe 14
Langer, Robbie 148
Lara, Brian 178, 199
Law, Stuart 197
Lawson, Geoff 181
Laxman, V.V.S. 227–228
Lee, Brett ('Bingers')
    150kmh barrier 151
    pen portrait 149–151, 196
    scoreboard 256
    v.India 73, 74, 77, 86, 226–227
    v.New Zealand 89, 100, 111, 113, 229
    v.Pakistan 52–53
Lee, Shane 151
Leeds (UK) 171
Lehmann, Darren 197
Leicestershire (UK) 142
Lillee, Dennis 22, 64, 76, 80, 93, 94, 117, 194, 229
Lords (UK) 182

M

McDermott, Craig 163, 170, 176
McGill, Stuart 16, 17, 206
McGrath, Glenn ('Pigeon')
    combination with Warne 95
    pen portrait 162–164, 196
    scoreboard 256–257
    v.India 57–59, 61–62, 74, 77, 80, 86, 227
    v.New Zealand 91, 100, 109, 229
    v.Pakistan 41, 54
    v.Zimbabwe 11
McMillan, Craig 98

McNamara, Brad 151
McPhee, Mark 3
March, Rod 117
Marsh, Daniel 150
Marsh, Geoff ('Swampy') 3–4, 74, 189, 190, 194, 204
Marsh, Rod 22, 169
Martyn, Damien ('Marto')
   absence 90
   pen portrait 152, 161
   scoreboard 256
      v.New Zealand 89, 92, 96, 104, 111–112, 114, 188, 231
Matthews, Greg 176
MCG (Melbourne Cricket Ground) 64, 76, 77
Mercantile Mutual Cup 174
Middlesex (UK) 148
millennium 79
Miller, Colin ('Funky')
   pen portrait 165–166
   scoreboard 257
   Test debut 166
   13th man 84
   v.New Zealand 89, 92, 96, 100, 103, 109, 229
   v.Zimbabwe 15, 20, 206–207
Miller, Keith 194
Misson, Dave ('Misso') 3–4, 190, 193
Moin Khan 30
monsoon 1, 2
Morris, Arthur 46, 221
Morrison, Danny 95
Muller, Scott
   controversy 52, 168, 177
   pen portrait 167–168
   scoreboard 257
   Test debut 28
Murgatroyd, Brian 190, 193
Mushtaq Ahmed 222
Mutthiah Muralitharan 2, 9, 26, 42, 47, 171

N

Nerds xv
net sessions 190
New Year's Eve 1999 79
New Zealand
   First Test 2000 91–100
   Second Test 2000 103, 104–110
   Test Series 188, 189, 228–231
   preparation for Tests 89
   statistics 248–253
   tour 2000 88–90, 102
Newman, Sam 64
nicknames xv
Nine network 52
1948 Test team 221
Northern Districts (Hamilton) 89
NRL 180

O

O'Connor, Shayne 111, 114
O'Donnell, Simon 182
Olonga, Henry 14, 18
one-day cricket 106, 138, 142, 161, 163, 169, 174, 177

P

Packer, James 175
Packer, Kerry 52
Pakistan
   First Test 1999 27–41
   Second Test 1999 42–51
   Third Test 1999 52–56
   Test Series 1999 185, 186–188, 208–222
   statistics 237–242
pitches 90
poetry 119–120, 193
Ponting, Ricky ('Punter')
   injury 90, 161
   joke on Steve Waugh 171
   pen portrait 169–171
   scoreboard 257–258
   successor to Mark Waugh 170
   v.India 58, 60, 74, 80–82, 86, 224, 227
   v.Pakistan 32, 41, 54, 55–56, 222
   v.Sri Lanka 2
Port Elizabeth (South Africa) 179
Postcards series (website) 148
practice facilities 197
Prasad, M.S.K. 59
Pura Milk Cup 98, 150

Index

Q

Quay West (Sydney) 79

R

Rackemann, Carl 144, 169
Rafter, Patrick 29, 46, 64
Ramesh, Sadogoppan 59, 151
Reid, Bruce 189, 194
Reid, John 138
Revesby TAB 180
Richards, Viv 64
Ring, Doug 46, 221
Robertson, Gavin 151
Romesh Kaluwitharana 176
Rowell, Greg 169
run-chase 45–46

S

Saeed Anwar 31
Saker, David 196
Saqlain Mushtaq 42, 47, 48
SCG (Sydney Cricket Ground) 84, 149, 152, 170
scoreboard 233–260
Sheffield Shield
   Fleming in 135
   Gilchrist in 139
   Hayden in 141, 142
   Kasprowicz in 143, 144
   Lee in 74
   McGrath in 162
   Martyn in 152
   Muller in 167, 168
   Ponting in 169
   Steve Waugh in 181
   Test players in 16, 17
   and Test selection 197
Shoaib Akhtar 29, 30, 44, 48, 54, 56, 77, 134, 147, 222

Sinclair, Matthew 180
Six and Out (band) 151, 174
Slater, Michael ('Slats')
   'daktari' (dress code) 101
   opening batsman 105–106
   pen portrait 172–174
   poetry by 193
   scoreboard 258
   v.India 74
   v.New Zealand 104, 108, 188, 229
   v.Pakistan 27, 30, 42, 47, 220
   v.Sri Lanka 2
'sledging' 198
snickometer 44
Sobers, Garfield 165
South Africa 198–199
speedguns 54
Sri Lanka 1–2, 8, 11, 186, 192–193, 194, 204
Srinath, Ghekko 59
Streak, Heath 18
Super Six 199
superstition 222
Sydney Cricket Ground 84, 149, 152, 170

T

Taylor, Mark 83, 112, 172, 173, 186
Tazelaar, Dirk 169
Team of the Century 22
team spirit 83, 192–196
technology 4, 190
Tendulkar, Sachin 54, 57, 58, 59, 61, 74, 78, 84, 86, 178, 222–224, 225, 227
Tests
   Australian averages 233–234
   Australian matches 233
   consecutive victories 233
Texaco Trophy 172
This is Your Life (TV program) 86
Thomson, Jeff 22
'three Ps' (motto) 218
Titan Cup (India) 138
True Blue (song) 100

U

Udayan Boys Home (Calcutta) 182
Under The Southern Cross (song) 21, 28, 41, 63, 86, 110

V

Vettori, Daniel 26, 91, 92, 95, 97, 98, 228
Victoria Falls 12-13, 205-206
video analysis 4, 190

W

WACA (cricket ground) 55, 150
Walsh, Courtney 93, 200
Walters, Doug 132
Waqar Younis 44, 47, 48, 222
warm-ups 190
Warne, Shane ('Warney')
   balls bowled 177
   captained by Border 175
   Christmas Eve 64
   controversy over Muller 177
   diet 177
   Indian bookmaker 177
   Lillee's record 76, 84, 93-95, 98, 100, 229
   pen portrait 175-177
   scoreboard 259
   v.India 57, 58, 61, 62, 63, 74, 75, 78, 80
   v.New Zealand 107, 111
   v.Pakistan 27, 32, 220
   v.Sri Lanka 176, 194
Warriors 150
Wasim Akram 30, 43, 55, 134, 140, 147, 222
Waugh, Austin 41
Waugh, Lynette 31, 41
Waugh, Mark ('Junior')
   100 Test matches 84
   'Julio' (dress style) 180
   pen portrait 178-180
   scoreboard 259-260
   selection 24-26, 170
   v.India 63, 74, 76, 179, 227
   v.New Zealand 91, 96, 102, 103, 229
   v.Pakistan 27, 31, 42-44, 220
   v.South Africa 179, 188
   v.Sri Lanka 179
   v.West Indies 200
   v.Zimbabwe 11, 14, 18, 207
Waugh, Rodger 180
Waugh, Steve ('Tugga')
   batting with Border 182
   captain 46, 56, 81-83, 186, 217-218
   chasing totals 112
   coached by Border 7
   New South Wales cricket 99
   pen portrait 181-183
   records 178
   scoreboard 260
   v.India 58, 60, 75, 224
   v.New Zealand 104, 108, 188, 229
   v.Sri Lanka 2, 186, 192-193, 204
   v.West Indies 200
   v.Zimbabwe 11, 14, 15, 18, 19, 206-207
Wellington (New Zealand) 102, 103
West Indies 117-118, 199-200
Whitney, Mike 189
Williamson, John 100
Wilson, Jeff 183
Wiseman, Paul 93
wooden spoon 99
World Cup 83, 137, 139, 182, 186, 193, 199
World Series 132, 193
World Wrestling Federation 193

Y

Young, Shaun 169
Yousuf Youhana 31

Z

Zimbabwe
   Board XI 205
   statistics 234-236
   Test 1999 14-20, 204-208
   tour 1999 1, 8-13

Photographic Credits

Justin Langer: xi, xii, 2, 12, 21, 35 bottom, 36 top and bottom, 37, 38 top left, 40 bottom, 64, 66 bottom left and right, 73, 88, 99, 101, 102, 108, 109, 110, 112, 115, 116, 157, 166,171, 176, 208, 215 top left and right, 216, 217, 232.

Allsport photographs
Jack Atley: 30, 41, 43, 44, 46, 47, 50, 51, 53, 56, 68,69, 70, 71,72 top and bottom, 77, 79, 121, 122, 123, 124 bottom, 125, 126, 127 top and lower left, 140, 143, 147, 149, 154 bottom, 155 top right, centre bottom, 184, 187, 209 top, 210 top, 211 top, 217, 221, 223, 224, 228. Hamish Blair: v, xiv, xvi, 1,3,5, 6, 10, 11, 13, 14, 15, 16, 17,18, 19, 23, 25, 28, 33, 34, 35 top, 36 centre, 38 top right, centre, bottom, 39, 40 top, 65, 66 top and centre, 67, 75, 76, 78, 81,82, 85, 87 bottom, 90, 91, 93, 95, 96, 97, 98, 100, 104, 105, 107, 130, 132, 135, 137, 138, 141, 142, 146, 150, 152, 154 top, 155 top left, 156, 158, 159 top left and right, 160 top, 161, 162, 164, 165, 167, 168, 169, 172, 174, 175, 178, 180, 181, 183, 191, 195, 203,205, 209 centre and bottom, 210 bottom, 211 bottom, 212, 213, 214, 215 bottom, 219, 226, 230. Robert Cianflone: 72 centre, 124 top. Adam Pretty: 87 top, 159 bottom, 160 bottom. Ben Radford: Andrew Shield: 92. 5.Matt Turner: 57, 58, 60, 61, 62, 63, 119, 120, 127 bottom right, 128 top and bottom, 144, 153, 225.

A Hodder Book

First published in Australia and New Zealand in 2000
by Hodder Headline Australia Pty Limited,
(A member of the Hodder Headline Group)
Level 22, 201 Kent Street, Sydney NSW 2000
Website: www.hha.com.au

Copyright © Steve Bernard, Allan Border, Justin Langer, Shane Warne, Steve Waugh
Photographic copyright © AllSport and Justin Langer

This book is copyright. Apart form any fair dealing for the purposes of
private study, research, criticism or review as permitted under the
Copyright Act 1968, no part may be stored or reproduced by any process
without prior written permission. Enquiries should be made to the publisher.

National Library of Australia Cataloguing-in-Publication Data
The Dominators: One of the greatest Test teams

ISBN 0 7336 1340 3

1.Cricket - Australia - Pictorial works. 2. Cricket - Australia. 3. Cricket
players - Australia. I. Border, Allan 1955 - 796.3580994

Book packaged by The Watermark Press
Book design by Suzy King
Printed in Australia by Griffin Press, Adelaide